SAMMY SOSA

Clearing The Vines

by
George Castle

SPORTS PUBLISHING INC.
Champaign, IL 61820

Director of Production: Susan M. McKinney
Cover design: Julie Denzer
Photo insert design: Michelle R. Dressen

ISBN:1-58261-024-x
Library of Congress Catalog Card Number: 98-89109

SPORTS PUBLISHING INC.
804 N. Neil
Champaign, IL 61820
www.SportsPublishingInc.com

CONTENTS

ACKNOWLEDGMENTS

The list of helpful folks in putting a book out on a tight deadline is too long to mention here. But I'll try.

Appreciation must go to the Chicago Cubs media relations department, whose cooperation and liberal access has always been a given, but never was more vital than in the conducting of interviews and gathering of information here. The media relations folks were under the gun due to the dual pressures of the home-run chase and the wild-card race, and they were helpful as usual. Further thanks must go to the Cubs' media-relations colleagues with the Chicago White Sox and Milwaukee Brewers for their assistance.

Once in the ballpark, the time taken by Cubs players, field personnel and front-office executives in talking about Sammy Sosa was crucial. I'm indebted to manager Jim Riggleman, team president Andy MacPhail and general manager Ed Lynch for taking blocks of time out of their heavy schedules for one-on-one interviews. And many, many thanks to hitting coach Jeff Pentland, who kept going back and forth to the visitors' dugout in Milwaukee County Stadium to try to find me. We found each other, all right, and Pentland's wisdom comprises an entire chapter here.

Another big assist goes to the numbers-crunchers at STATS, Inc. and Total Sports for providing the statistical insight about Sammy Sosa's clutch-hitting abilities, past and present. A bonus was thrown in by Total Sports' Stu Shea's constant encouragement and emergency computer assistance.

More help with the newfangled world of cyberspace was provided by the ladies of the household, Laura and Nina Castle, who clicked the mouse and keyboard when I suffered brain cramps and computer fright. They also should be praised for allowing me to mess up part of the house with notes, newspapers, magazines and whatever else I used in the production of this book.

We would not have brought you this book promptly after the 1998 season without the transcription help of Barbara

Jenkins. She typed hours of recorded interviews, freeing me to tackle the computer. I linked up with Barbara through Paul Brandt and Pete Clark, who also provided legal assistance, advice and pats on the back.

Further thanks go to Paula Blaine of *Sports Profiles* magazines and the archivists of the Skokie (Illinois) Public Library for being able to help trace the history of an amazing ballplayer and unique ballclub.

Editing and production assistance is courtesy of Dreaming Dog Publishing, which pushed the limits of time and space to give the book the necessary look-over in a punishing deadline situation.

And, finally, the biggest thanks must go to Sammy Sosa himself, who put up with me in one-on-one interviews and conversations over the past seven years—and still found time to greet me even when his world radically changed in the last two months of the 1998 season. Sorry I learned nothing from three years of high school Spanish, Sammy, so I could have made your life a little easier. You've gone far more than halfway to meet me and engage in the lively art of conversation in a language you didn't know until a little more than a decade ago. I'm sure one conversation you wish I didn't have with you was on August 1, 1998, when I told you the Houston Astros had traded for Randy Johnson just 10 hours previously.

Thanks for a season and a personality that was so well worth writing about, Sammy.

George Castle
October 1998

PREFACE

Sammy Sosa has merely gone with the flow. But he slapped some nice interest on his returns.

Growing up in Wrigley Field, a knowledgeable baseball fan does learn to appreciate the games' finer points—a pitchers' duel, moving the runner over, taking the extra base. Playing in the cozy, Friendly Confines isn't all big-bopper baseball. Sure enough, with the wind being a potential deterrent to batted balls about two-thirds of the time, you can never absolutely depend on the home run to bail you out.

And yet the home run is never far away in Wrigley. Its absence from the offensive portfolio of the home team—as evidenced by the Cubs' poor home records in 1994 and 1995—shows that any blue-pinstriped gang better have some resident musclemen on hand to duel the opponents' strongboys, or else that big white "L" flag will get hoisted atop the old scoreboard after the game.

They didn't come from far and wide to Wrigley over the decades to watch 2-1 cliffhangers. The kids stampeding down the steps from the El station, the mothers and daughters coming off the bus for Ladies Day on Thursdays or Fridays, the groups in the buses from downstate Illinois or Iowa, even the old gamblers who staked out their seats and bet on every pitch just below the centerfield concession stand in the bleachers, all loved the home-run hitter. Plain and simple.

That's what made for fun afternoons at Clark and Addison, even through all those bad years and bad decades and most of bad half-centuries. Even if the Cubs were lousy overall, they'd make a good show of it at home, often ending up with a .500 or better record in Wrigley Field despite losing 85 or 90 or 95 or more games.

My grandfather, Morrie Zutz, enjoyed Hack Wilson and Gabby Hartnett as he took precious time off from his salesman's job in days of yore. It must have been a true pleasure to watch the tobacco-spittin' gang flex its muscle only 20-odd years after Morrie, as a kid, dodged angry horse-borne Cossacks looking for Jewish kids on the streets of Kiev, Ukraine.

He lived long enough to take his first grandchild, me, to my first game around 1961. By then Morrie Zutz witnessed the prime of the effervescent Ernie Banks, the one-man, home-run gang from 1955 to 1960, and, as "Mr. Cub," the most beloved single player in Chicago baseball history. Grandpa also saw the debuts of Billy Williams, with his classic swing, and Ron Santo, who rubbed dirt all over his forearms before his first at-bat each game amid 30-homer, .300 seasons.

There were other worthy Cubs sluggers. Bill "Swish" Nicholson, the wartime bopper, who once was walked intentionally with the bases loaded by New York Giants manager Mel Ott. There was Hank Sauer, who just preceded Banks and helped "Mr. Cub" get acclimated to the big leagues as the team's first African-American player. Sauer was merely "The Mayor of Wrigley Field," and enjoyed showers of chewing tobacco packages from the bleachers whenever he belted one out of there.

Latter-day boppers included Andre Dawson, one of the classiest men of modern-day baseball, and Dave Kingman, the strong, strange, silent type, who could have held Chicago in the palm of his hand but instead pushed it away; "gone fishing" could have been his motto for his favored recreation and to where his common sense had departed. Ryne Sandberg jumped into this group, too, for his homer heroics off Bruce Sutter in 1984 and amazing emergence as the National League's best home-run hitter with 40 in 1990.

Almost always, the visitors had one more slugger than the Cubs could field. The Giants had the incomparable Willie Mays and Willie McCovey, with Jim Ray Hart the specially designated Cubs Killer. They were a particular gate attraction for Sunday double-headers in mid-summer. The entire Pirates "Lumber Company" lineup, led by Willie Stargell and Roberto Clemente, licked their chops when they arrived in Chicago. Henry Aaron and Eddie Matthews of the Braves were pretty good, to say the least. I saw Aaron's 50th, and final, career homer at Wrigley Field on a July Sunday in 1974 while the rest of the world was distracted by impeachment hearings for Richard Nixon.

And how about a veritable platoon of St. Louis Cardinals Cubs Killers, who were often denied by the faraway fences at home in Busch Stadium, but were emboldened in Chicago. They were Joe Torre, who probably to this day has happy flashbacks about Ken Holtzman hanging him curves; Ted Simmons, flowing locks and all, killing you from either side of the plate; Tim McCarver, loving those right-handed pitchers, and Mike Shannon, loving his free nights in Chicago, a true split-shift man, wrecking the Cubs during the day, napping for a few hours, enjoying the pleasures of the midnight hour and beyond, and then napping again to get ready for the Cubs.

Towering above all was the Philadelphia Phillies' Mike Schmidt. "Every time we would come into Wrigley Field, you'd figure Mike would hit at least one during the series," said Phillies broadcaster Harry Kalas. Cubs pitchers kept pumping fat pitches to Schmidt, who happily obliged them.

Left, center, right—Schmitty hit 'em everywhere. Need four consecutive homers in a game in which the Phillies trailed the Cubs 13-2 in the fourth? Call on Mike. Need a 10th-inning homer to break a 22-22 deadlock off Sutter? Bring Mike to the plate. After yet another homer, the media would approach Schmidt at his locker. He'd roll his eyes and sigh, knowing the questions forthcoming. Schmidt had no ready answers, he just was the champion Cubs Killer of all time. Schmidt and Aaron each hit 50 in Wrigley Field, but it took Schmidt just a little more than 16 seasons to amass his bounty compared to Aaron's 21. Mays had 54, but he still paled in impact compared to Schmidt.

So, out of the clear blue in 1998, Sammy Sosa outdoes all of them, home and visitors.

It figures, in baseball. A bookie type once told a fellow in the right-field bleachers to never bet on the game, that it's too unpredictable. That's the only way you could describe the events of 1998. Hollywood-style fantasy became reality, every day in your box scores, every night on the video highlights.

Who could have forecast the boom of Sosa? Here was a nice little 35-homer, 110-RBI, strikeout-prone guy who had too much pressure to carry the Cubs' power load alone. Yes, generally a media-friendly guy who gave the fans the time of day with autographs, but no Ken Griffey Jr. or Barry Bonds or Mark McGwire, and maybe not even solid as a second-echelon type of power guy. Maybe a guy who was overpaid after getting a potential $42.5 million contract in 1997.

And here's a guy who comes out of nowhere, who had 13 homers on the day McGwire had 25 in late May 1998. He goes wild, slugs 20 in the month of June alone, then catches McGwire by mid-August. They go neck-and-neck, both break the hallowed 61-homer standard established by Roger Maris in 1961 with weeks to spare, and they go into the final weekend vying for home-run supremacy at some ridiculous level nobody ever thought could be achieved by human beings. McGwire ended up with 70, Sosa with 66. How could one have thought that 61 was so special when now the record is like some kind of doppleganger?

Or maybe it should be viewed thusly: We thought the North and South poles couldn't be reached, or Mt. Everest climbed. Mission accomplished. Man on the moon? We started in 1961 and finished in 1969. Talking computers the make-belief stuff of a 23rd Century *Star Trek* in 1966? The reality of some 25 years later. Man has never put boundaries on himself as far as physical achievement or mental development. Why should limits be applied to baseball players simply because a home-run record has stood for 37 years?

Here I am, watching Sammy Sosa every home game as a baseball writer and broadcaster from the Wrigley Field press box. Add on four games at Milwaukee County Stadium. One can't help but be awed by Sosa's achievements. When was the last time he hit a first-row bleacher shot? Are all of his homers missiles, flying onto apartment roofs, bouncing down faraway alleys, breaking apartment windows, hitting the TV camera shed in center field, or, going the other way to right field, flying over the bleachers onto the street like Stargell or McCovey, left-handed pull hitters of the first order?

Almost all are. And while he won't take the place of Banks, Williams, Santo, or Dawson—yes, Sammy, you must put in more time—you find yourself endorsing his efforts. It's a wonderful human-interest story, the poor kid who didn't get an especially big head, who welcomed you into his personal space during so many sessions in the Wrigley Field locker room, who hollered a writer's name at the top of his lungs sometimes for effect.

And you're happy Sosa teamed with McGwire to single-handedly revive baseball in the manner it always should have emphasized—on-the-field achievements instead of labor talk, salary squabbles and heavy-handed, egotistical owners.

You also find yourself happy that the NFL has had to share

equal billing with baseball, finally, in September and into October. The NFL has a stage-managed, manufactured quality to it, artificially boosted further by the popularity of the office pool. Too many media managers, print and broadcast, gladly follow lock-step into turning their news columns and airtime into NFL publicity sprees long before the baseball season is over. Football encroached more and more, first into August and now into July. Now, the newsprint and airwaves gatekeepers have been forced to satisfy natural public demand for baseball.

Strangely, the NBA had been in a lockout with potential effects almost as severe as the baseball strike of 1994-95. But with the great home-run race, who cared? Who clamored for October preseason and November regular-season pro basketball action? Fans were too busy enjoying the latest long-ball spectacle. After the baseball disaster, no one wants to get near any labor tiff. Wake us at first tip-off.

What happened? Simple. The home run is sports' most glamorous play, able to change the course of pennant races, able to move mountains off the field. We love prodigious power hitters more than top-flight quarterbacks and deft left wingers. The record-breaking long-ball man might even give the bald guy in the baggy shorts and the No. 23 jersey a run for his money. Funny thing, even His Airness' first sport was baseball, and he returned for a fling in the game when he burned out on basketball.

Sammy Sosa and Mark McGwire and their brethren have called us home, to Wrigley Field and all the ballparks of our youth, to revel in what made us love baseball, and in turn all of sports, in the first place. We need a little simplicity in our lives. We're so overburdened with voice mail and computer-driven gadgets we can't operate, caught in a grossly interconnected life where a sick economy in Thailand can snowball to possibly strangle the prosperity in the whole world, bombarded by a political culture where formerly covered-up sexual indiscretions of presidents can now topple a chief executive in a society that's at the same time politically correct and scandal-mongering.

Through our big boppers and their new stratospheric records, we can at least emotionally go back to the Sunday double-headers of 30 years ago, admission unreserved and $1, hot dogs 40 cents, Cokes 15 cents, Frosty Malts 40 cents, and autographs free. Gaze out on the field and future Hall of Famers populate both teams. Turn on the TV and Jack Brickhouse is screaming "Hey Hey" for a Cubs homer. Flip on KMOX on the radio and Harry Caray is bellowing out "Holy Cow!" when a Redbird shot clears the fence.

Sammy Sosa, in particular, is a little kid let loose in the big time, enjoying every moment of it. He connects, does that little hop and skip near home plate, and he is rounding the bases with all the greats, reminding us how great the game is. There's nothing like baseball, baseball with drama, a home run breaking up a pitching duel.

After taking so many punches for four years, it's great to see baseball getting off the canvas, standing on its own, a pre-eminent sport boasting of great players breaking great records. The game needs to be saved every so often. The saviors don't volunteer for the jobs; they just do it in the course of their jobs and don't need thanks for their handiwork.

But thanks is due nonetheless. Thanks, Sammy, for helping turn back the clock and for bringing some of the best days of my youth squarely into the present. May baseball always be so enjoyable.

George Castle
October 1998

PROLOGUE

What makes Sammy run ... and hit ... and explode with record-busting power?

The answers won't quite equal all the opinions on why the Cubs can't win a pennant. But they are numerous enough to bear closer examination, because we don't have baseball players who amass 66 homers, drive in 158 runs and bat .308 every year. Or every generation.

Here is Sammy Sosa, spectacularly inconsistent for most of his career, capable of the highest highs and the lowest lows in performance. He could hit 13 homers in a month, steal a base with the best of 'em, throw like Roberto Clemente on a good day. But on other days...

Yeah, nobody let loose in the sane world would have forecast Sammy Sosa to go beyond the mid-40s homer range in 1998. A nice improvement over a downer 1997 season would have been appreciated, a little more hitting to right field, a few less strikeouts, a tightening up of his outfield defense. It was time for Sosa to step up from his constant alternating from top-of-the-line performance to fundamentally flawed efforts at bat, on the bases, and in right field.

But to zoom past a slew of baseball elite players, collaborate with Mark McGwire to break a seemingly iron-clad record, and become one of the most popular athletes in the world?

Sixty-six homers. Five more than Roger Maris' best, six more than Babe Ruth's best. Then talk about 158 RBI. That's more RBI than any player has racked up in one season since Ted Williams' and Vern Stephens each had 159 for the 1949 Boston Red Sox, one year after Joe DiMaggio had 155 for the New York Yankees.

Wait a minute. At first glance, this is nuts, linking Sammy Sosa with Maris, Ruth, Williams and DiMaggio. The spectacularly imperfect player can't walk with legends. Sacrilege?

No. Truth is stranger than fiction. Sosa outdid the best of these all-timers. Williams and DiMaggio live. They approve.

Maris died at 53, in 1985. But his six children showed up at Wrigley Field on September 20, 1998, to honor and support Sosa. They approve, too.

We won't know about Ruth's opinion, who also died too soon at 53. But knowing the history of the man, we suspect he'd nod, too, and tell Sosa—he'd probably call him "kid"—to keep it up.

Sosa linked with Ruth, that's "unbelievable," to use one of Sammy's favorite adjectives. Ruth is the one figure who absolutely towers over the game, 50 years after his death. If any one man in history was bigger than baseball, it was The Babe. He is the center of so much mythology, like an ancient god who walked the earth in the 20th Century, able to change the course of a well-established sport by his mere presence, possessed of great appetites of excess, and evoking goodwill toward the game using his name.

When I asked DiMaggio—along with Willie Mays our greatest living all-around players—in 1991 about fans putting him in a class with The Bambino, a wistful, even faraway look overcame the Yankee Clipper's dignified face. This was a holy comparison, even for DiMaggio. "I feel very, very honored that people would even mention me with The Babe," he said.

There's that billboard next to Chicago's Kennedy Expressway that once sported a mural of a semi-pensive Dennis Rodman gazing down at traffic. The Worm's image backed 'em up for miles. In the latter stages of the 1998 baseball season, Rodman was long gone, replaced by a painted image of Sosa at full extension in his home-run swing, dovetailing that with a mural of an animated Ruth.

Sosa himself appreciates the eternal impact of Ruth.

"Babe Ruth is still alive," he said after his 60th homer on September 12, 1998, at Wrigley Field. "He never dies. Everyone remembers him like it was yesterday."

As a century and millennium ebb, somebody had to walk the same path as Ruth from rough childhood to world-class status. Looks like Sammy Sosa's "The Man," using another catchword of his.

"It's a rags to riches story," said Dave Anderson, Pulitzer Prize-winning sports columnist for *The New York Times.* "People think is of Babe Ruth as having grown up in an orphanage. That wasn't quite right; it was a kind of industrial school for boys. But The Babe didn't have an easy childhood. Sammy's background wasn't that much different.

"Sammy is the Babe Ruth of the 1990s. He grew up in a big family in the Dominican Republic and had to shine shoes just to bring some money into the house. You look at both, you find comparisons."

Obviously, both Sosa and Ruth were self-made players who earned the affection of the masses through their deeds. Sosa's time came much later than Ruth, a gifted left-handed pitcher in his early 20s before he became baseball's first, and best, home-run hitter. But everything comes in its own good time. To have projected Sosa as an all-time producer three or four years ago would have been wrong. He wasn't ready, not until the precise moment when he burst on the scene this year. A well-honed athlete's emotional maturity must catch up with his physical skills, and that often doesn't happen until the late 20s.

"I'm 29, and everything is going well," Sosa said. "When I was younger, I was crazy, trying to swing at everything. Now, I have any idea of what I want to do when I go to the plate.

"I am taking charge of myself. I was trying to do too much (previously). I was trying to hit two homers in one at-bat. Years ago, if I didn't hit a home run, we didn't win. But in 1998, I've been happier with the people who came here, who want to play, who want to win. That changed my whole attitude."

To be sure, it was like a domino effect. A new, improved roster of Chicago Cubs players buoyed Sosa's spirits as 1998 began, making him forget years of losing. "It was worth the wait," a champagne-dripping, cigar-chomping Sosa said on the night of September 28, 1998, minutes after the Cubs had clinched their first post-season berth since 1989. More dominos had fallen as a happy, inspired Sosa's monster year had further improved the Cubs beyond the original projections.

Still more wait to be toppled. They're comprised of the fan and media expectations of a wealthy Tribune Co. corporate ownership to spend money on impact players, in order to make even more money, and take the Cubs to the next step. The latter, achieved at some point in the future, will finally overturn odds ranging from 99-1 to 206-1, computed by the likes of statistics services and university mathematicians, against the Cubs somehow avoiding appearing in a World Series since 1945.

But wherever the Cubs go in the next few years, Sosa will have to be the No. 1 regular player taking him there. If he has the confidence in himself, everyone in baseball finally has confidence in him. Such a feeling toward Sosa was in short supply for most of his 10-year big-league career.

Now, Sammy is the indispensable one, almost an ironman whose name you write into the lineup in the same position in the batting order without a second thought.

"I read a story years ago about Leo Durocher," Cubs manager Jim Riggleman said. "Leo said he would come to the ballpark every day and the first thing he would do is write Billy Williams' name in that third slot and then he would play around with the rest of the lineup. The one thing he didn't have to worry about was Billy Williams.

"And that's the way it is here. We know Sammy is going to come in here and hit third or fourth. Just put him out there and let him go."

Sosa's hustle, work ethic and endurance were rarely questioned. He hit the weights and took care of himself, bulking up from a sinewy 175 pounds over his 6-foot frame to possessing blacksmith's biceps and more muscle mass totaling 200 pounds in the last few years. Sosa's body is, as they say, cut.

But his patience and ability to refine his game, to slow up from his all-out pace when needed, was another matter. But maybe his development couldn't have been forced any quicker. Sosa needed to learn patience, and maybe a whole lot of folks needed to be more patient with Sosa. Look at the rewards all parties reaped in 1998.

"I think this is the way it was supposed to go for him," said first baseman Mark Grace, the only Cub to have been a continuous teammate of Sosa since his arrival in Wrigley Field in 1992. "For some people, it takes longer to adjust. Some people adjust immediately. Shawon Dunston, there's still things Shawon doesn't understand after 13 years in the big leagues. He has to be around guys like me or a coaching staff has to remind him.

"Sammy, you can tell him things and he'll understand it and he'll say, 'Yeah, you're right.' But it still takes him a little while to apply it. So you can tell him and he'll understand it and he'll know it, but sometimes it takes him a little while to apply it out there. Sammy's learning. And Sammy's trying. You're seeing the complete results now."

Teammates waited ... and waited ... for Sosa to unload his

entire potential. "When you play this game for awhile, you can see tools in players they haven't developed yet," said pitcher Steve Trachsel, a Sosa teammate since late 1993. "You know with a guy like Vladimir Guerrero, last year he was going to be better than he was. He was awesome (in 1998). You could see that with Sammy three, four years ago. There was going to be a point where he was going to be unbelievable.

"On the field, you always knew he could be a five-tool (hit, hit for power, run, field and throw) player. He wasn't real solid in right field and made a lot of baserunning mistakes, probably because he was overaggressive. He's put everything together, a complete five-tool player. He's controlled his aggressiveness."

In the eyes of one of the most complete hitters of the 1990s, Sosa has now passed all the tests of stardom. Fewer are prouder of him than former White Sox teammate Frank Thomas, who remembered Sosa as the rawest of young players in 1990-91.

"If you saw him from 1991 to 1998, it's been a 180-degree turnaround," The Big Hurt said. "He had all the tools, but early in his career he was too aggressive. He wasn't identifying pitches the way he does now.

"I've never run across a player with the power, speed, with the arm. The things he could do on the basepaths. The process for him has been developing over the past four years. He's been getting more solid. It's great to see a guy like that reach his potential. But that's not staying that anyone's home-run potential is to reach and pass the home-run record."

Sosa will never stop learning—and the Cubs' field staff will never stop teaching him. But he basically has his post-graduate studies nearly wrapped up. He is what he is, having celebrated his 30th birthday.

"At this point he's been coached and continues to be coached," Jim Riggleman said. "Every now and then he needs a little fine-tuning. But, basically, if the fine-tuning involves harnessing him, most of the time at this point we would rather live with the consequences of him being unharnessed than to try to harness him."

The word is around baseball now: Be careful when you pitch to Sammy Sosa. The scouts have taken note of his advancement. They have cut down on the negatives that they report back to their front offices.

"He is just so much more disciplined than in the past," said Al Hargesheimer, special assistant to Detroit Tigers general manager Randy Smith. "His concentration is better now. It shows up both at bat and defensively. He's not so reckless. In the past, he could be somewhat scatterbrained. And he probably felt he had to do too much as far as driving in runs."

Sosa's persona wants to please all the people, all the time. In real life, that's just not possible. In baseball, it would be fool-hardy.

So when the crowd cheers, Sosa had to learn to keep his emotions under control. He made a lot of progress in 1998.

"Here at beautiful Wrigley Field, the place is full, people get excited and you get excited with them with runners on base," said Jim Lefebvre, his first manager with the Cubs. "Now he has more control over his emotions, he's got more patience. He's a good hitter. Before, he had great talent, a tremendous amount of skills and just needed to refine it."

Not only did Sosa become a .300-plus hitter with runners in scoring position in 1998, he also began waiting out pitchers. He still would strike out an enormous number of times—only three fewer, in fact, than his alarming 1997 total of 174 that paced the National League. But Sosa often worked pitchers to full counts before they'd nail him. And he cut down his overanxiousness with men on base. A survey by the internet service Total Sports showed that the "old" Sosa often had a much higher percentage of swings on first pitches with runners on first and third or second and third. That often put him in a hole while pitchers worked to strike him out on bad pitches.

But in 1998, Sosa developed a "short game," slapping singles to left field or doubles in the gap with men on base. "You don't have to hit a home run to win a game," he said minutes after starting a two-run, ninth-inning rally with a single against San Francisco Giants ace stopper Robb Nen on August 21, 1998, at Wrigley Field. Three more singles and a walk resulted in a 6-5 victory. Trying to go "downtown" against the flame-throwing Nen would have been near-suicidal.

And he finally bottled his ability to hit to right field con-sistently. Sosa always had talked about going the other way, but could never put it into practice for more than a few weeks at a time. He hit 19 of his homers to right, while 17 were boomed out to center field. He fell into his old pull-or-nothing habits for a couple of weeks when the pressures of both the home-run race and the wild-card chase got intense in mid-September. Yet Sosa had gone past the point of no-return; he was a changed hitter for good.

Sosa may have lost the home-run race to Mark McGwire 70 to 66, but he won the lion's share of the votes for National League Most Valuable Player simply because he could do more overall at bat-and do it when it counted the most.

Sosa collected 108 RBI on his 66 homers, for a total of 68 percent of his season RBI production. That meant he drove in 50 additional runs by other means. In contrast, McGwire had 118 RBI on his 70 homers, around the same proportion. But he drove in only 29 additional runs by other means, for an 80 percent figure of RBI via homers.

In 1927, Babe Ruth had 100 of his 164 RBI on his 60 homers (61 percent). In 1961, Roger Maris had 102 of his 142 RBI via his 61 homers (72 percent). So Sosa stacks up well historically among the all-time big boppers.

The all-around offensive game—featuring great power, clutch RBI production and high average—is a rare feat in itself. Yet that is melded to defensive prowess in right field and the ability to steal bases. That narrows down the field of comparison. Sosa has to be more athletic than Babe Ruth. Could a comparison to Henry Aaron in his prime be in order?

Bud Selig doesn't see why not.

The best years of the baseball commissioner's baseball lifetime obviously took place in 1957 when his beloved Milwaukee Braves won two consecutive pennants and a World Series title. Sparking the Braves offensively and defensively was eventual all-time home-run king Aaron, whose defensive abilities and speed on the basepaths sometimes took a back seat to his overall offensive excellence. Aaron never came close to 61 homers, never even sniffed 50 in one season. But at his best, his offensive portfolio and value to the Braves was every bit as good as Sosa's.

"Henry Aaron was an extraordinary all-around ballplayer," Selig said. "He could run, throw brilliantly, was a great fielder and never made a baserunning mistake. An extraordinary hitter, of course. A superstar in the true sense of the word.

"Sammy has all the tools to be the same way. The more you watch Sammy, the more you're impressed with him as a complete player. The jewel for Henry Aaron was his consistency. Sammy will have to do that over a period of years. But there's no doubt about it, Sammy's at that level."

Others in the game do want to see the consistent performance over a few yeas. Sammy's knocking at the door of the very elite, and could easily let himself in for permanent residence.

"I'm very hard-pressed to say Sammy's at the (Barry) Bonds and Ken Griffey Jr. level yet, because of the number of strikeouts," Cubs closer Rod Beck said. "And because he goes out of his (hitting) zone a little bit.

"But considering the age (14) Sammy started playing, he's on a pace to be as good, if not better, than these other players. If the opportunity comes up to take a few more walks and steal a few more bases, like he did a few years ago, ultimately that's the player we'd like to see and Sammy would like to see out of himself."

Off the field, Sosa is far unlike the quiet, dignified Hank Aaron or the oft-standoffish Barry Bonds. Although he developed a penchant for one-liners and sideways looks that would have entertained a hearty life-lover like The Babe, Sosa was very disciplined in his public comments. He always deferred to Mark McGwire as the seemingly superior home-run hitter and tried to shy away from talking about his own efforts to surpass 61 homers. It might have become monotonous, but Sosa kept emphasizing the Cubs' playoff push and his own desire to play in the post-season.

That stance alone set well with Cubs teammates, some of whom were critical in the past over Sosa's fundamental flaws and alleged emphasis on personal goals.

"I don't know if anyone's the perfect team player," Steve Trachsel said. "But Sammy said all the right things, about the focus on getting his team to the playoffs. Absolutely, it wins points from the players all the way to the front office. They don't want a player who's talking about 'me, me, me.' You talk about that when you're doing your contract."

Media skeptics, through whom some of the past criticism of Sosa was funneled, also were won over.

"Going to the opposite field also has meant more hits, more RBI, more runs scored and a batting average 50 points above his career mark. That, in and of itself, is an incredible achievement," wrote columnist Barry Rozner on September 17, 1998, in the *Daily Herald*, circulating in Chicago's north, northwest and west suburbs.

Rozner continued: "He understands now that you can always get better and that learning in baseball never ends, no matter what you accomplish. ...There's no ceiling on how good Sosa can be, and he's shown that he'll continue to make adjustments. He says that he wants to be a winner. He has shown us that 35 homers and $10 million a year isn't satisfaction enough.

"That's why I'm proud of him."

The word "proud" wasn't limited to won-over eyebrow-lifters in the Fourth Estate. Even crusty baseball warhorses, brought up in an age when you didn't fraternize with opponents, were so struck with the class and dignity with which Sosa carried himself down the stretch.

Cincinnati Reds manager Jack McKeon, oldest on the job in the game, please step to the plate on behalf of Sosa.

"We were in Cincinnati (August 22-26, 1998) and I called him over during batting practice," McKeon said. "I told him, 'I'm so proud of you.'"

Why would McKeon praise the one Cubs player who could most inflict further indignities on the Reds during a lousy season?

"He doesn't try to win games just with homers," he said. "He had gone out and really improved himself over past years' performances. And I loved the fact Sammy was trying to give something back to his country. A lot of guys won't do that."

McKeon asked Sosa for three signed baseballs, one each for grandsons Kellan McKeon and Avery and Zachary Booker. Sosa sent back six, plus Dominican cigars from his own "Sammy Sosa special reserve" collection.

"You see Sammy Sosa smiling 99 times out of 100. What more can you ask for?" McKeon said.

He wasn't the only baseball management-type giving thanks for Sosa's emergence. At mid-season, the lords of the game had an aloof, standoffish fellow, Mark McGwire, chasing the home-run record. McGwire simply did not want glory in achievement, and usually limited media access to himself. Suddenly, the affable Sosa jumped into the race, ran neck-and-neck with McGwire through the final weekend, and smoked out whatever good personality was submerged in McGwire's hulking frame.

Both players verbally ended up enjoying the race to pass Roger Maris. From such disparate backgrounds as McGwire's Southern California and Sosa's Dominican Republic, products of the solid middle class and the San Pedro de Macoris barrio, they developed instant rapport when they had dual press conferences with each other. They always publicly pulled for each other to reach and surpass the record, and even wished they could end in a tie for the home-run crown.

Generating their own aura of good feelings, Sosa and McGwire teamed to lift baseball out of doldrums that threatened to take up permanent residence and hold baseball back in the hole it had dug after the 1994-95 strike.

"It was great, the way they had friendly competition between the two," said Wendy Selig-Prieb, president of the Milwaukee Brewers. "They were pulling for each other. ... I've never seen anything like this.

"This has been the lead news story and, by its contrast, provided a nice relief from what's going on in Washington, D.C. Talk about role models; I can't imagine any better personalities than these guys. We should seize upon this, and we should try to do fan-friendly things at our ballparks. The Brewers had five sellouts to end our season—all games with McGwire and Sosa. Fans may not have come to any other games. This can only help build interest in baseball."

Sosa became a baseball marketer's dream. Promoters of the game have been trying to add a lot of circuses to the basic bread that had gone stale — or rancid, in the case of the strike. And yet nothing substitutes for near-superhuman accomplishments on the field.

Especially thankful was John McDonough, the Cubs' vice president of marketing and broadcasting, who pioneered both the Beanie Baby giveaways and the off-season fan conventions that are now so popular in baseball and even other sports.

"There is no marketing program, no promotion that can ever come close to on-field achievements," McDonough said. "All the national acclaim that Sammy and McGwire achieved has nothing to do with marketing. No promotional strategy would be in the same class as that. You accept it as good fortune."

McDonough said a marketer couldn't have scripted a more natural, more fan-appealing personality than Sosa.

"He blends talent with charisma, a certain kind of innocent charm," he said. "He's not a manufactured product. He give something to baseball that it's needed for a long time-humility. He's a very humble guy."

And here's someone else linking Sosa with a great athlete who basically competed in a higher league.

"This was the only time in this decade in Chicago sports that an athlete reached Jordan-esque proportions," McDonough said. "Michael Jordan, to be sure, is in a category by himself. You can't beat what he accomplished—six championships in less than a decade. But for two months, in August and September, Sammy Sosa came very, very close to doing the kinds of things Michael Jordan always does."

Now comes the acid test. Will success spoil Sammy Sosa? Will he be able to carry himself so well two, three, four more years in a row?

Those who knew Sosa on his way up certainly have reveled in the present. They can't say enough about how they admire what he's accomplished—and where they feel he'll go from here.

"I have nothing but love for him," said Frank Thomas. "It's really his time to make everyone not doubt him, because he had a lot of doubters in his career."

Former minor-league teammate Dean Palmer, in 1998 the Kansas City Royals' third baseman, expects Sosa to earn back the affection, plus interest, he doled out in 1998.

"I think he has a chance to become one of the most popular players who ever played the game," Palmer said. "McGwire as well, with the way he hits the ball, and with the way Sammy plays. If you like baseball, you're going to play to see them play. Sammy's got a chance to be one of the best players ever."

If that happens, it will prove the old adage, "It's not how you start, it's how you finish." On planet Earth, Sammy Sosa from about as far away as you can, from about as humble as you can, to look down benignly on his impossible dream come true.

1998 NATIONAL LEAGUE UMPIRES

4 Mark Hirschbeck	13 Larry Poncino	22 Joe West	31 Bob Davidson
5 Angel Hernandez*	14 Frank Pulli*	23 Ed Rapuano	32 Dana DeMuth
6 Bruce Froemming*	15 Jim Quick*	24 Jerry Layne	33 Mike Winters
7 Eric Gregg	16 Rich Rieker	25 Charlie Williams	34 Greg Bonin
8 Jeff Kellogg	18 Charlie Reliford	27 Steve Rippley*	35 Gary Darling
9 Brian Gorman	19 Terry Tata*	28 Larry Vanover	36 Wally Bell
11 Ed Montague*	20 Tom Hallion	29 Bill Hohn	40 Jerry Crawford*
12 Gerry Davis	21 Harry Wendelstedt*	30 Randy Marsh*	

*Crew Chief

Houston

3 Carl Everett, OF
5 Jeff Bagwell, IF
7 Craig Biggio, IF
8 Matt Galante, Coach
10 Mike Hampton, LHP
11 Brad Ausmus, C
12 Ricky Gutierrez, IF
13 Billy Wagner, LHP
14 Derek Bell, OF
15 Richard Hidalgo, OF
16 Tom McCraw, Coach
17 Sean Berry, IF
18 Moises Alou, OF
19 Doug Henry, RHP
20 Tony Eusebio, C
21 Dave Engle, Coach
24 Mike Cubbage, Coach
25 Jose Cruz, Coach
27 Tim Bogar, IF
28 Bill Spiers, IF
35 Dave Clark, OF
36 Jack Howell, IF
37 Shane Reynolds, RHP
38 Sean Bergman, RHP
42 Jose Lima, RHP
43 Bob Scanlan, RHP
45 Chris Holt, RHP
46 Trever Miller, LHP
47 C.J. Nitkowski, LHP
48 Vern Ruhle, Coach
49 Larry Dierker, MGR
51 Jose Cabrera, RHP
52 Mike Magnante, RHP
54 John Halama, LHP
59 Ramon Garcia, RHP

No.	Player	Pos.	1	2	3	4	5	6	7	8	9	10	AB	R	H	RBI
7	Biggio	2b	K	3A4 GO			HBP		GO 4-3						
14	De. Bell	rf	K	Flo 9		Flo 3									
5	Bagwell	1b	K		K										
36	Howell	3b		K											
18	M. Alou	cf		K		K									
35	Da. Clark	lf	Flo		K		K								
12	Gutierrez	ss		Sing.		K									
11	Ausmus	c			K	GO 4-3		K							
37	S. Reynolds	p		S 3-4			K		K						
28	Spiers ph/9th														

Pitchers	IP	H	R	ER	BB	SO	Notes
Reynolds (L, 2-3)	8	8	2	1	2	10	116 p's, 72 k's

CUBS

1 Lance Johnson, OF
2 Jeff Pentland, Coach
3 Dan Radison, Coach
4 Jeff Blauser, IF
5 Jim Riggleman, MGR
7 Tyler Houston, C-IF
8 Sandy Martinez, C
9 Scott Servais, C
12 Mickey Morandini, IF
15 Kevin Orie, IF
17 Mark Grace, IF
18 Jose Hernandez, IF-OF
20 Matt Mieske, OF
21 Sammy Sosa, OF
24 Manny Alexander, IF
26 Billy Williams, Coach
27 Phil Regan, Coach
29 Robin Jennings, OF
30 Jeremi Gonzalez, RHP
31 Kevin Foster, RHP
34 Kerry Wood, RHP
35 Bob Patterson, LHP
36 Kevin Tapani, RHP
37 Brant Brown, IF-OF
39 Tom Gamboa, Coach
40 Henry Rodriguez, OF
41 Marc Pisciotta, RHP
43 Dave Bialas, Coach
44 Amaury Telemaco, RHP
45 Terry Mulholland, LHP
46 Steve Trachsel, RHP
47 Rod Beck, RHP
51 Terry Adams, RHP
54 Mark Clark, RHP
58 Ben VanRyn, LHP
63 Rick Kranitz, Instructor

No.	Player	Pos.	1	2	3	4	5	6	7	8	9	10	AB	R	H	RBI
37	B. Brown	cf	K	Sing.	Sing		K								
12	Morandini	2b	K		K	DP 1-6-3		Sing.							
21	Sosa	rf	K	Sing		K		Flo 9							
17	Grace	1b	3b E-3	BB		GO 3	Sing.								
40 H. Rodriguez lf / 18 Je. Hernandez lf			SF	K		K	PB 5-4?							
4	Blauser	ss	GO 6-3	2b	8 RBI	Sing	R&B 8-4-?								
8	S. Martinez	c	BB	Flo 9	Flo 5										
15	Orie	3b	K		GO 5-3										
34	Wood	p		K	GO 3-1		Flo 8								

Pitchers	IP	H	R	ER	BB	SO	Notes
Wood (W, 3-2)	9	1	0	0	0	20	A-15,758 / T-2:17

Kerry Wood

5/5/98-5/6/98

1

Pride of a Nation

S ammy Sosa was many things to many people in 1998.

But to the eight million citizens of the Dominican Republic, Sosa's homeland, he was everything. He was a hero during the great home-run chase. He was a stereotype-buster; helping to put to rest the long-held, but false, image of Latins as hot dogs and stats-hungry wild swingers at the plate. He was a spokesman who showed that his people loved a laugh as much as anyone else. And he was a model family man; showing his love for his wife, children, mother, brothers and sisters almost daily.

In the end, though, he was a benefactor in a time of need. The Dominican Republic is located in the eternally poor eastern two-thirds of the Caribbean island of Hispaniola; an island shared by the even more impoverished country of Haiti. Sosa's native people had precious few possessions to lose in time of disaster. Disaster struck, though, in late September 1998.

Hurricane Georges hit the Dominican head on, killing hundreds of people, leaving thousands of others homeless, and destroying 90 percent of the main cash crops upon which the fragile economy depends.

Authorities in the capital of Santo Domingo did not open shelters until strong winds and cloudbursts of rain had already inundated the city. WGN-TV reporter Bob Jordan said that citizens used machetes to cut down trees in the wake of the storm; he never heard a power saw.

Sosa had given so much to his family and people from the time he signed his first pro baseball contract and dispatched his precious dollars back home to his mother, Lucrecia. He put much of his own money back into the Dominican economy, building a shopping plaza, opening a baseball school where the players were also housed and fed, and founded a Christmas-present donation fund for kids. "All he wants to do is give and provide for people," Chicago sportscaster Steve Grad, a friend of Sosa's from the early 1990s, said.

Sosa's celebrity and ability to marshal resources to help his afflicted people were never more needed than when the hurricane ripped through the island, especially battering his hometown of San Pedro de Macoris. He quickly established a Sammy Sosa Foundation with the Cubs to funnel donations of money and supplies to the Dominican. Sosa and teammates Henry Rodriguez and Manny Alexander went to the Dominican consulate in Houston after the September 26 game to help load supplies for shipment. United Parcel Service even donated a plane to ferry about $35,000 in supplies per trip to Santo Domingo.

"I've been working hard to raise money and do what I can for my country," Sosa said. "It's not about home runs. It's about human beings back in my country. They have nothing. A lot of people are dying and have no homes and no food. It's a tough situation."

You could say the same thing about the Dominican Republic that has often been said about Mexico: So far from God, so close to the United States. Just 600 miles from Miami exists Third World poverty, whose people could not afford such a disaster. And yet, benefiting from the great riches of the country in which he works, Sosa has drawn attention to the Dominican Republic like no other baseball player or other kind of celebrity could.

"As far as I'm concerned, he's the real Dominican ambassador. I just shuffle papers," said Bernardo Vega, Dominican ambassador to the United States.

What Sosa has done—by supporting his family; showing his everlasting love for his mother who kept the family together through abject poverty; and by helping his countryman—is display the sharing nature of the Dominicans. They have so little, yet divide up meager possessions and finances among themselves as best they can.

"It's unbelievable," said Cubs outfielder Rodriguez, a native of Santo Domingo. "I grew up in a really poor area. My family was poor and we shared. Shared everything. Even with other (poor) people, they come and ask for something, a piece of bread or whatever, and we share."

"Family is the key," said Bill Chase, Sosa's business advisor who met him when he was a child. "If you give them a chicken, they put it in a pot and split it. Once they get to know you, no matter how poor, they open their hearts and homes to you."

"When you're from the States, the people are really, really nice and they want you to feel like you are really home," Rodriguez said. "The poor people are the ones who really treat you well."

Rodriguez described Dominican working conditions that could be a time capsule of America in the 1930s.

"If they work, they work six days a week," he said. "People live with whatever they can. They make 2,000, 3,000 pesos a month and they live with that. They know they have to live with that and that's how it is."

What's the dollar equivalent of 3,000 pesos?

"It's about $200," Rodriguez said. "And they survive."

Wealthier Dominicans like Rodriguez own guns. Sosa has machine gun-toting guards at his home. But Rodriguez said the specter of violent crime is no worse than in the United States.

"Not even close," he said. "Sure, you carry guns. You have security with shotguns in your house because you want security for your family and your kids. It's not really because we feel we are going to get robbed or we are going to get killed or whatever. But we use security like everyone else."

The Catholic church has provided a backbone for Dominicans through the grinding poverty that produces a per capita annual income of less than $1,500.

"We're religious people," said Omar Minaya, the Rangers scout who signed Sosa in 1985, who now is the highest-ranking

Hispanic baseball executive in the game as assistant general manager of the New York Mets.

"The church provides a lot of discipline," Minaya said. "The humbleness of the people comes from the church. It teaches humbleness, goodness and sharing."

Such an environment can't kill dreams. The fondest of dreams are turned into reality by hundreds of Dominican teenagers who have signed pro baseball contracts in recent decades. If baseball is America's pastime, it is the Dominican Republic's passion, a way off the island for the boys playing on hardscrabble, rock-strewn fields, using milk cartons for gloves, broomsticks for bats, and rolled-up paper for baseballs. Bottle caps make great ball substitutes; they dive and dip and simulate tricky breaking pitches for the aspiring hitters.

More than 40 Dominicans play Major League Baseball, including 10 from San Pedro de Macoris, a modest-sized city of 90,000, a 90-minute drive east of Santo Domingo. George Bell, Julio Franco and Alfredo Griffin hail from San Pedro, all playing on a rough field nicknamed "Mexico" by the locals. Sammy Sosa got his start there, too.

It is in this culture of alternating hope and despair that Sammy Sosa grew up. He was one of six children of Bautista and Lucrecia Montero. His siblings include Luis, 36; Sonia, 35; Juan, 34; Raquel, 32, and kid brother Jose, 24. The family was left to fend for itself when Bautista Moreno died when Sammy was 7.

"She deserves all the credit," Rodriguez said of Lucrecia Sosa. "To raise six kids in the whole family, I think it takes a lot of hard work, a lot of energy, a lot of crying and seeing that you could not afford to buy a pair of shoes for each of your kids. She deserves everything. Whatever, I don't think there's enough words to describe what she did. She did everything. It's unbelievable."

Although Lucrecia would remarry, change the family name to Sosa and add stepsons Carlos and Nani to the brood, the kids had to go out and scrounge for a few pesos here and there to add to the meager household treasury. The young Sosa followed in the path of so many San Pedro de Macoris boys, administering shoeshines in a centrally located plaza area called the Parque Duarte.

It was there that Sammy Sosa got his first break that started him on the path toward 66 homers, 158 RBI and dual status as baseball spokesman and Dominican national hero.

Massachusetts native Chase had arrived in San Pedro de Macoris in 1979 to start a shoe factory in a tax-free enterprise zone started by the Dominican government to lure foreign investment. The government had no other choice; part of the sugar-based industry had declined. Beggars populated almost every street corner.

"Dominicans are excellent workers with excellent hands," Chase said. "Having a job meant something to them. They didn't mind repetitive work, and were orderly. At one point I had 1,500 workers, and I can't ever remember where we had a fight."

Chase scouted out San Pedro de Macoris upon his arrival. His life—and that of the boy he would meet—was about to change.

"The first night in town, I didn't know the area well, I go down to the town square, and there are 200 kids shining shoes," Chase recalled. One local resident knew two of the kids: Sammy and Juan Sosa. He pointed them out to Chase, telling him they were nice kids.

"They shined my shoes," he said. "Every night, I'd go to the square and just watch everybody, and the kids shined my shoes. Sammy had that big smile; a lot of the kids do."

Chase continued to go to Parque Duarte for his shoe shines. Then he began patronizing an eatery called Restaurant 29 that was popular with scores of Americans attending a local medical school. The cagey Sosa kids figured out Chase's habits and began waiting for him at the restaurant, earning a peso a shine.

But Sammy and his brother didn't stop there. They found out where Chase and wife Debbie lived. By now Sammy was joined by little brother Jose, who was too young to shine shoes.

"They were likable kids," Chase said. "They knew how to get to your heart. Jose wasn't shining shoes. He would entertain me, do handstands. I'd give him some pesos for that."

One day Debbie Chase took a bite of a locally grown apple, not the Washington state Delicious quality. "She didn't like it, and the boys asked if they could give it to their mama," Chase said. Debbie Chase began to buy the Sosa boys clothes and other necessities, while her husband let them hang around the shoe factory when they weren't attending school. Chase's customers were administered shoe shines from the Sosas, and so Lucrecia Sosa sometimes found her sons bringing home $5 bills—a king's ransom in the Dominican. With indoor plumbing a luxury in the San Pedro barrio, the Sosa boys took weekend showers at the factory.

"They have trenches and outhouses," Chase said. "They'd take empty cement drums and let rain water collect in them. That was their shower."

Sosa was so busy hustling pesos that he didn't play baseball regularly. Luis Sosa, who had played, got his brother started in the game in an organized fashion at 14. Chase bought him his first real glove.

Sosa did not at first impress as a player. "I never thought he'd turn out like this. He was a mediocre player," David de la Cruz, now manager of Sosa's baseball school team, said to Lester Holt and a crew documenting Sosa's San Pedro roots for Chicago's WBBM-TV.

But the raw, gangling Sosa knew what to do to impress Rangers scouts in his 1985 tryout. His mother was overjoyed when he signed.

"It was the greatest thing that happened to me in my whole life," Lucrecia Sosa told the WBBM-TV crew. "I thought he could get there. I did think he could be someone in baseball."

Sosa brought his first Rangers contract to Chase for his analysis. "He was a lot smarter than people give him credit for," he said. By then, Chase was a surrogate father for Sosa, who called him "Papa." So Chase gave him some fatherly advice as the kid embarked on his first trip to America: Be careful with women, and work hard."

With Sammy away in the Texas minor-league system, the Chases virtually adopted Jose Sosa, the baby of the family, as their pride and joy. But Bill Chase's business advice would now be a permanent part of the Sosa portfolio. Sosa had sent an estimated 90 percent of his pittance pay as a new minor-leaguer back to his mother. McDonald's was his gourmet meal in America.

"When the paychecks ran out after the season, he had the winter to get through," Chase said of the off-seasons of the late 1980s. He loaned Sosa money to get him through the cash crunch. After Sosa finally made it to the White Sox, he was so overjoyed he wanted to buy Lucrecia Sosa a house. Sosa now made decent bucks as a big leaguer, but the home still cost $50,000. Again, Chase came through. "I loaned him the money for that," he said. "No problem. He was family and I was doing well."

Any Dominican boy would be happy to be able to place his mother in a better home once he garnered any kind of baseball affluence. Any gesture of payback for all the hard work is cherished.

"I think when you buy a present for your mom, it doesn't have to be a house," the Cubs' Rodriguez said. "It doesn't have to be a car. They appreciate anything because it comes from one of the kids. I bought a house for my mom. My mom is crazy about that. And not because of the house itself, but because I bought it. It's really amazing how mothers react when their kids bring to the house a piece of bread or whatever. They feel so proud because you're her kid."

Sosa's salary eventually escalated into the seven-figure range with the Cubs in the mid-1990s. He took care of his family and bought himself a nice four-bedroom home in a swanky Santo Domingo neighborhood. More importantly, he began investing in his home country.

In 1996, he and Chase began building 30-30 Plaza, financing the $1.2-million project named for Sosa's 30-homer, 30-stolen base feats with his own money. The three-story combination of offices and shops near Parque Duarte surrounds a statue of Sosa in the courtyard. Sosa has helped sisters Sonia and Raquel become proprietors of boutiques in the complex. The building of the complex generated an estimated 60 construction jobs per week.

"A lot of people, when they get a lot of money, they throw it away," Sosa told Carrie Muskat, who wrote articles on his business investments and life in the Dominican for the Cubs' team newspaper, *Vine Line*, and *USA Today Baseball Weekly* in the winter of 1996-97. "They forget about tomorrow. I'm not trying to do this. I know I'm not going to play forever. Someday I'll have to pack up and come home.

Sosa was loyal to his country long before his celebrity was used to organize hurricane relief.

"I'll never forget where I came from," he told Muskat. "I'm proud of the United States. They've given me everything that I have. They gave me the opportunity to be Sammy Sosa today. But I have to remember that these are my people, people I have to take care of, people I have to give jobs to when I opened the plaza. This is my life."

Sosa did not stop with 30-30 Plaza, though. He established a Sammy Sosa baseball school in San Pedro. The players take the field with the name "Sosa" emblazoned on their jerseys. Sosa feeds and houses the players, buys their equipment and pays the salaries of the employees. Best of all, he gives hope where none might have existed.

"I have the opportunity and faith in God that I'll make it," one player told the WBBM-TV crew.

"I have to help my family," said player Bautista Mateo.

The "next" Sosa, according to the Lester Holt report, is a 16-year-old slugger named Raphael Salano. He had a role model to follow through the 1998 season.

By 1998, Sosa was giving away about $500,000 a year out of his own pocket. He bought 250 computers for Dominican schools. Chase told Sosa that he should start structuring a foundation in which to handle fundraising to get tax breaks.

"You're paying a lot out and getting no credit," Chase suggested.

Chase originated the charitable foundation that swung into action with hurricane relief. He also advised Sosa on the endorsement deals that began to head his way as his home-run total mounted.

But Sosa didn't have to attain any higher profiles. He already had won the everlasting affection of his people. And he was able to unite the fractious political factions back in Santo Domingo, at least for a day.

"One of our bishops said that Sosa and Mark McGwire gave a great example of how competition should be held, that we should be more like Sosa and not fight with each other," ambassador Bernardo Vega said. "Politicians should imitate them. The Dominican Congress is controlled by the opposition (to President Leoneo Fernandez, a Sosa pal). It was not passing legislation. There was a stalemate in discussing a new budget and taxes. But there was a unanimous vote in declaring Sammy a son of the nation."

In the wake of stiff competition from other Caribbean resort areas, the Dominican Republic is trying to build its tourist industry. Sosa can't do anything but help, while also improving the image of Dominicans in the United States.

"He's doing more for our country than our tourist board to show it's worth visiting," Vega said. "Among certain people there was a notion that Dominicans were people of violence, that they were into drugs and illegal migrants. The proportion of Dominicans into drugs is less than in the U.S. What Sammy is showing is who the average Dominican is."

Vega can also drop Sosa's name in an attempt to drum up foreign investment.

"I was giving a speech to a group of American investors and I wasn't getting much applause," he said. "But the moment I mentioned Sammy Sosa, everybody applauded. I took the opportunity to explain about his hometown. It just transformed from an old backwater to an expanding city with a lot of free trade zones. Now we are the fourth-biggest supplier to the United States of clothes and apparel. The No. 1 supplier of sugar and cigars, the sixth biggest supplier of shoes.

"Essentially we live from tourism and all these assembly plants for exporting."

If Sosa has done well for the Dominican image aboard, he has become a passion at home. Even in the wake of the hurricane, without electricity and access to TV and radios, Dominicans went to great lengths to find out news of Sosa's feats as the 1998 regular-season wound down. They queried visiting Americans, who possessed the ultimate prize—satellite trucks that could down-link the latest news about Sosa.

Prior to the disaster, the country practically shut down during Cubs telecasts, while gambling parlors were jammed with locals, betting like old-fashioned Wrigley Field bleacherites, on every pitch, high, low, ball, strike.

Sosa's games were tape-delayed for late broadcast in the Dominican for four seasons. But on September 1, 1998, just after Sosa slugged his 55th homer, a complete Dominican TV crew took over a spare Wrigley Field press box booth to beam the games live back home. Regular programming on Television Dominicana, the government-run channel, was postponed during the games.

"People in offices had problems because their employees watched the game," said broadcaster Jose Ravel of Deportes En La Cumbre, the Dominican Sports Broadcasting Co. "They don't work. But most of the offices ended up bringing in a TV."

Most Dominican fans knew Mark McGwire would break the homer record before Sosa, but that didn't cool their ardor for their hero. And through his homer chase, he gained popularity over an old Dominican mainstay.

"Two years ago, Felipe Alou (Montreal Expos manager) was the most popular man in the Dominican," Ravel said. "Right now, it's Sosa. Sosa has brought happiness. Everyone was thinking about Sosa."

Ravel and Co. further whipped up enthusiasm with a lot of home-run call. A typical Sosa homer was described back to the Dominican thusly: *Batazo largo, grande la bola se va y la saco. Sammy Sosa. Bay Bay Charley*. Translated: "Long drive, big, the ball is going, and it's out. Sammy Sosa. Bye, Bye Charley." Charley? A famous Dominican softball player, Ravel said.

Even as the media demands became nearly suffocating, Sosa ensured he'd spend time with the visiting Dominican media. The old-country, welcome-you-to-my-house feeling had taken over.

"He wanted to make them feel good because they came here to see him, see the team," Henry Rodriguez said. "He really wants to make sure that they feel fine and they feel like they're Dominicans. That's the way he's been reacting since the first day."

A world away in San Pedro, Lucrecia Sosa's life changed, too. Reporters clamored for her attention every day, filling her home with all the other family members and friends who were over to help celebrate the once-in-a-lifetime feat. But the Sosas, mother and son, are people persons. Few were turned away.

Not even a hurricane can sweep away the good feeling of Sammy Sosa, pride of a little country. The faith and hope of a proud people toward their favorite son was best summed up by Julia Sosa, Sammy's 80-year-old grandmother, in an interview with the *Chicago Tribune*'s Phil Hersh.

"The things God does are big," Julia Sosa said.

2

Sammy Starts Down the Long Baseball Road

S ammy Sosa advanced rapidly once he began playing organized baseball at 14. Helped by his older
brother, Luis, he learned the nuances of the
game just in time to be signed by a local Dominican
professional baseball club run by Francisco Acevedo.
By agreeing to play for Acevedo, Sosa would be
brought to the attention of scouts for teams in the
United States.

Acevedo fulfilled the agreement by contacting
Omar Minaya of the Texas Rangers. Minaya was a
coach in the rookie-level Gulf Coast League in Florida.
Dominican baseball officials had a select group on
which to call. Minaya said that in 1985, only four
teams—the Rangers, Los Angeles Dodgers, Toronto
Blue Jays and Pittsburgh Pirates—were putting in a
lot of time scouting the talent-rich country.

Minaya had part-time scout Amado Dinzey check
out Sosa. Dinzey reported that the kid was available
to be signed, and Sosa was brought to a team tryout.

Other Rangers officials noticed Sosa at the tryout, simply because Sosa intended it to be that way.
His street smarts enabled him to stand out from the
crowd.

"The first thing that got your attention was his aggressiveness, vibrancy and enthusiasm," then-Rangers scouting director Sandy Johnson said. "It was if he was saying, 'I can get these guys' attention.' He would not be denied about getting your attention. His mission was going to the tryout camp and getting signed that day. His body language was such that everything was at full speed.

"At this stage, he was 5-foot-10, 150 pounds, all arms and legs. He was like a young colt. He was not one of the faster ones; he didn't run a good time (in the 60-yard dash). He was very crude and kind of out of control, although in a good way. But he had some things going for him.

"He got in the batting cage, and even though he didn't smoke the ball or crush it, you saw he had tremendous aggressiveness and bat speed. He showed enough where you wanted to give him an opportunity. He had the flair."

Minaya knew exactly what Sosa had in mind.

"He knew he had to throw and run hard. He basically was going to show you, 'I will get this done, just give me the opportunity.' He showed his passion for the game. I saw the desire to succeed, to be the best. He had confidence along with his aggressiveness.

"The only way Sammy Sosa knew how to get out of the Dominican was by swinging the bat. If he doesn't swing the bat, he's not going to get signed. He's not going to get a visa, he's not going to play in America."

Sosa, still just 16, signed for $3,500 on July 30, 1985, with the Rangers projecting him as a hopeful. "Scouts project certain players will get faster with proper diet and a structured program," Johnson said.

To prepare the Dominican signees for the culture shock of playing in the U.S., the Rangers sent the kids to a baseball academy on the grounds of the University of Santo Domingo. Sosa commuted 30 miles each way every day from San Pedro de Macoris. The trip via a local bus took 90 minutes.

"We gave him and the other young players meal money," Minaya said. "Whatever he'd get, he'd split with his family."

Sosa continued his attention-grabbing style when he made his pro debut in 1986 at Sarasota (Florida) of the Gulf Coast League. He teamed with two other top Rangers prospects who would go on to make something of themselves: outfielder Juan

Gonzalez and third baseman Dean Palmer. As an utterly unpolished 17-year-old, Sosa batted a respectable .275, led the Gulf Coast League in doubles with 19, hit safely in 17 of 18 games from July 30 to August 18, 1986, and tied for second in the league in games played.

"The key was that first season," Johnson said. "He played well."

Minaya filed a postseason scouting report on Sosa that finally was published in *Baseball America* on August 17, 1998. Rating his tools on a 1-to-5 scale, with 5 being the major-league average, Sosa graded a 5 only on speed. But in future projections, Minaya would show prescience in giving Sosa a 6.5 in power and 6 in arm strength. Sosa drew 5s in speed, hitting and defense.

Summing up Sosa's strong points, Minaya praised him for playing "very hard and aggressively. ... Samuel is a kid that possesses a lot of potential. He is very aggressive and wishes to play in the major leagues very badly. ... He is very confident but needs to be disciplined and taught American customs." And, as a preview of the crowd- and media-pleasing Sosa of 1998: "Most people love his personality, and he is a pleasure to watch playing."

At the same time, the flaws that would hold Sosa back and draw criticism for another decade were candidly appraised in the report by Minaya, who wrote that the kid "swings at anything and flies open." The coach also was concerned that Sosa didn't "have a strike zone" and possessed a "very long swing at times."

That was accurate, Sosa would say later.

"I had a quick bat, but I didn't have the power and the discipline that I have right now," Sosa said. "I was over there, aggressive guy, aggressive player, that was going to go out there and swing at everything. Boom, boom, boom."

"Once he's in America, how's he going to get out of the minor leagues?" Minaya later said. "By taking walks? They don't pay you to take walks. They pay you to put up numbers. And the only way you put up numbers is by swinging the bat."

Sosa's fielding was raw, too.

"A base hit to the outfield, Sammy would sprint in and the next thing you knew, the ball was by him," Minaya said. "He would attack the ball like he was a third baseman coming in on a bunt, sweep the ball, pick it up, throw the ball and who knows where it was going to go. Most of the time he would sweep, look for the ball in his glove, and it wasn't there. So he'd go running back."

Even with his fundamental flaws, Sosa's outgoing personality quickly won over his employers. He proclaimed himself a "people person" throughout his dream season of 1998. Johnson knew that more than a decade previously, not only from the tryout, but also from his first season at Sarasota.

"My wife, Linda, and I can remember how Sammy and a pitcher, Felipe Castillo, came to our apartment with helpings of beans and rice," Johnson said. "Felipe was the cook in that group, a pretty good one. Of course, Sammy was the bullshit artist, getting Felipe to do the cooking. But that was a really friendly gesture from a couple of kids. Felipe was still pitching (in 1998) in Taiwan."

Third-base prospect Palmer, who went on to a good career with the Rangers and Kansas City Royals, also was impressed by Sosa's personality at the time.

"He definitely was outgoing," he said. "When I was first with him, he didn't know a whole lot of English at all. But he learned quickly because he was so outgoing. He tried to talk to everybody, get along with everybody, fit in anywhere. Within a couple of years, you pretty much could have a normal conversation with Sammy. He was always having fun and a joy to be around.

"Juan Gonzalez was the opposite. He was more quiet and I think that's why he didn't pick up English as quickly as Sammy did."

In 1987, Sosa began attracting attention throughout the game at Gastonia (South Carolina) of the South Atlantic League. He led the team in batting (.279), games played (129), runs (73), hits (145) and doubles (27). He also began showing flashes of power with 11 homers and 59 RBI. His 11-out-of-10 scale of aggressiveness at the plate also came into full bloom there with 123 strikeouts in 519 at-bats.

"I feel that was a turning point for Sosa, Gonzalez and Palmer," Johnson said. "They were a little over their heads, but all three got to play every day. All each of them had to do was to get 500 at-bats in a season. And as Sammy moved up, what really improved dramatically was his running speed. By the time he was 19, he really was a flyer."

"The organization looked at Sammy Sosa as a player of unquestioned talent who had a chance to be a star player," said Tom Grieve, the Rangers' general manager in the late 1980s, who now is a team broadcaster. "He was a 'five-tool player,' someone who could run, throw, field, hit and hit with power.

"When you got to know him, he had an unusual enthusiasm for the game and for life. This was a kid with great pride. He had shined shoes and peeled oranges in the Dominican to survive. We felt he had solid character with unusual enthusiasm that you don't see in many minor leaguers. You want to see that aggressiveness, wanting to stretch a single into a double. If he's going to make mistakes, you want him to do it when he's young."

Sosa seemed in a hurry to reach the majors.

"He knew he was going to be something special," Palmer said. "He played as hard as I've ever seen anyone play the game. This guy hustled, he never dogged it, always gave 100 percent. He knew he wanted to be a big-league baseball player and nothing was going to get in his way."

Carefully moving him up the minor-league chain, the Rangers advanced Sosa to a higher Class-A league in 1988. At Port Charlotte (Florida) of the Florida State League, manager Bobby Jones assumed responsibility for the kid's development. Now manager of the Tulsa Drillers of the Texas League, Jones will never forget the attempt to harness Sosa's immense natural skills.

"You knew he was going to play in the big leagues," Jones said. "His work ethic was outstanding; his hustle was outstanding. He was a hungry ballplayer and wanted it more than anyone else.

Managing Sosa was like hopping a roller coaster.

"He'd hit a one-hopper back to the pitcher and it would be a bang-bang play at first base," Jones said. "He'd look bad on a curveball in the dirt, then take those pitches later on. You'd hang a curve to him, he'd hit it nine miles. The prettiest thing was to watch him hit a ball to right-center field and running the ball out for a triple.

"One time, I had the bunt sign on. He swung away and fouled a pitch off. Then I put the indicator on (still a bunt). He swung away and hit into a double play. I reamed him out in the dugout in front of the other players, fined him $25 and benched him the next three days. But the next day, he came and apologized to me."

Sosa's final Port Charlotte numbers would show the schizophrenic nature of his earlier career. He batted just .229 with 106 strikeouts in 507 at-bats. But he also led the Florida State League with 12 triples, matching the second highest total in the minor leagues and ranking as the most ever for a Rangers Class-A player. He also amassed his highest pro stolen base total, 42, and was caught stealing 24 times. Despite Jones' disciplinary benching, Sosa led the league outfielders with 131 games played.

Sosa's days in the Rangers organization would come to a close in 1989 after he had played 66 games at Class AA Tulsa, got called up by the parent club, then was optioned to Triple-A Oklahoma City for 10 games prior to the July 29, 1989, trade to the Chicago White Sox.

But Sosa hasn't forgotten his Rangers connections.

Minaya is now a competitor of Sosa's as No. 2 man in the New York Mets' front office.

"I want Sammy to hit a home run every game, but the Cubs to lose those games," he said. "I'm rooting for Sammy individually. Whenever I sign a player, it's not only finding the talent, but also molding the person. I have a responsibility to stay with him, care about him, even after he goes to another team."

Johnson also has a rooting interest against Sosa's teammates as assistant general manager of the Arizona Diamondbacks.

"He makes it a point to seek me out," Johnson said. "He calls me 'Papa.' He kept gesturing at me when I was sitting in the dugout with Buck Showalter when we came through Wrigley Field during the season. We gave each other a big hug. His vibrancy is the same it has been since Day One at that tryout camp.

"You never want to see him beat your butt. But, deep in your heart, you never root against him. You never stop rooting for him."

Poor Johnson. He had to endure the sharpest of split emotions when Sosa slugged his first career grand-slam homer against the host Diamondbacks at Bank One Ballpark on July 27, then repeat the feat the following night in front of another huge Phoenix crowd.

Sosa and fellow former Rangers minor-leaguer Jose Hernandez also remembered Jones' daughter, Jill, when she attended a Cubs-Rockies game in Denver in 1998. The pair greeted her enthusiastically.

And Grieve appreciates the chance to meet Sosa these days.

"Over the years, when I'd bump into Sammy, you'd see him as the kind of guy who you could go up to and get a good feeling about him," Grieve said. "He always would take the time to talk to you."

Jones said Sosa never forgot some of his old minor-league teammates.

"At Port Charlotte, we had a utility player named Freddie Samson, who was married with a little kid," he said. "Sometimes after a game, Sammy didn't have enough money to eat. Freddie would have him over to eat. Years later, when Sammy was in the big leagues, he'd come to Port Charlotte. He took the whole Samson family out to get shoes and then took them to dinner."

Ever the scout who took a bit of a chance on Sammy Sosa, Minaya never stops evaluating his prize find.

"Sammy, Juan Gonzalez, other great hitters have their best years from age 28 to about 33 to 34," he said. "I still feel Sammy has a lot more to show. This has got to be a once-in-a-lifetime kind of year, but he can still be around 50 homers for a number of seasons."

Cubs fans forever damned the day in 1964 when Lou Brock was dealt away. Sammy Sosa was the Rangers' Lou Brock.

Monday, June 15, 1998

1998 NATIONAL LEAGUE UMPIRES

4 Mark Hirschbeck	13 Larry Poncino	Wendelstedt*	30 Randy Marsh*	38 Sam Holbrook
5 Angel Hernandez	14 Frank Pulli*	22 Joe West	31 Bob Davidson	40 Jerry Crawford*
6 Bruce Froemming	15 Jim Quick*	23 Ed Rapuano	32 Dana DeMuth	41 Jerry Meals
7 Eric Gregg	16 Rich Rieker	24 Jerry Layne	33 Mike Winters	43 Paul Schrieber
8 Jeff Kellogg	18 Charlie Reliford	25 Charlie Williams	34 Greg Bonin	44 Kerwin Danley
9 Brian Gorman	19 Terry Tata*	27 Steve Rippey*	35 Gary Darling	
11 Ed Montague*	20 Tom Hallion	28 Larry Vanover	36 Wally Bell	
12 Gerry Davis	21 Harry	29 Bill Hohn	37 Bruce Dreckman	

Crew Chief

Milwaukee

1 Fernando Vina, IF
2 Jose Valentin, IF
3 Phil Garner, MGR
5 Geoff Jenkins, OF
7 Dave Nilsson, IF
8 Mark Loretta, IF
9 Marquis Grissom, OF
10 Marc Newfield, OF
12 Chris Bando, Coach
13 Jeff D'Amico, RHP
14 Jeff Juden, RHP
16 Jesse Levis, C
20 Jeromy Burnitz, OF
21 Cal Eldred, RHP
22 Mike Matheny, C
23 Lamar Johnson, Coach
24 Darrin Jackson, OF
26 Jeff Cirillo, IF
27 Bob Wickman, RHP
28 Mike Myers, LHP
30 Bob Hamelin, IF
31 Bronswell Patrick, RHP
32 John Jaha, IF
33 Bobby Hughes, C
35 Bill Castro, Coach
36 Joel Youngblood, Coach
37 Steve Woodard, RHP
38 Doug Mansolino, Coach
40 Chad Fox, RHP
41 Jose Mercedes, RHP
42 Scott Karl, LHP
43 Doug Jones, RHP
45 Don Rowe, Coach
46 Paul Wagner, RHP
47 Al Reyes, RHP
48 Brad Woodall, LHP

No.	Player	Pos.	1	2	3	4	5	6	7	8	9	10	AB	R	H	RBI
1	F. Vina	2b	F10	HBP	F10		K									
26	Cirilb	3b	BB	Fl0	6-3		sing									
20	Burnitz	rf	K	F10	F10	BB RBI	K									
32 Jaha / 24 D. Jackson pr/9th		11	K	F10 8	K	BB										
7	Nilsson	1f	BB	BB	F10 BB											
9	Grissom	cf	F10	sing.	F10 6-3											
2	Valentin	ss	HR 2RBI	K	K	K										
33	Hughes	c	K	K	6-3 6-3											
21	Eldred	p		GO 6-3	K	BB 4-3										
30	Hamelin ph		7am 4-6													
43	D. Jones p/8th															
			0	2	0	0	0	0	0	3						

Pitchers	IP	H	R	ER	BB	SO	Notes
Eldred	7	10	5	5	0	6	
D. Jones /8th							

CUBS

1 Lance Johnson, OF
2 Jeff Pentland, Coach
3 Dan Radison, Coach
4 Jeff Blauser, IF
5 Jim Riggleman, MGR
7 Tyler Houston, C-IF
8 Sandy Martinez, C
9 Scott Servais, C
10 Terrell Lowery, OF
12 Mickey Morandini, IF
17 Mark Grace, IF
18 Jose Hernandez, IF-OF
19 Jason Hardtke, IF
20 Matt Mieske, OF
21 Sammy Sosa, OF
24 Manny Alexander, IF
25 Derrick White, OF
26 Billy Williams, Coach
27 Phil Regan, Coach
30 Jeremi Gonzalez, RHP
31 Kevin Foster, RHP
34 Kerry Wood, RHP
35 Bob Patterson, LHP
36 Kevin Tapani, RHP
37 Brant Brown, IF-OF
39 Tom Gamboa, Coach
40 Henry Rodriguez, OF
41 Marc Pisciotta, RHP
43 Dave Bialas, Coach
45 Terry Mulholland, LHP
46 Steve Trachsel, RHP
47 Rod Beck, RHP
51 Terry Adams, RHP
54 Mark Clark, RHP
63 Rick Krantz, Instructor

No.	Player	Pos.	1	2	3	4	5	6	7	8	9	10	AB	R	H	RBI
27 B. Brown cf / lf			GO 4-3	F10 8	GO 4-3		GO 3									
12	Morandini	2b	GO 6-3	K	K	F10 9										
21	Sosa	rf	HR	HR	K	HR										
17	Grace	1b	GO 3	sing	sing	GO 4-3										
40 H. Rodriguez lf / 47 Beck p/9th			F10 8	F10	K	F10 8										
18	J. Hernandez	3b	K	F10 8	3b	sing										
8 S. Martinez c / 9 Servais c / 24 M. Alexander ss			sing.	2b	F10 4	sing FC 2-3-5	SF7 RBI									
34 Wood p / 54 T. Adams p/8th / 10 Lowery ph/8th cf/9th			RBI R sing	GO 4-3	F10 8	K	RBI 4th									
			1	3	0	0	0	0	1	2						

Pitchers	IP	H	R	ER	BB	SO	Notes
Wood	7⅓	3	5	5	6	9	A-37,903
T. Adams /8th							
Beck							121, 65 K's

Track Kerry Wood's Strikeouts K K K K K K K K K K K K K K K K K K K K K K K K K K K K K K

3

Larry Himes' Two Best Trades—For Sammy Sosa

The classic days of players coming up and thriving with the organizations that signed them have been consigned to history. Trades, minor-league releases and free agency have promoted dizzying movement in such a fashion that fans hardly know most players' roots in the game.

A common trade, especially in the free-agent, high-salary era, is the dealing of a young prospect for a veteran who can immediately help a pennant-seeking club. Rarely, though, does that young player get traded twice without becoming a baseball vagabond.

In keeping with his 1998 accomplishments, Sammy Sosa was that rare individual, being cast aside twice and ending up on top of all of baseball. The men who dealt him away—Tom Grieve of the Rangers and Ron Schueler of the White Sox—have not conducted their lives haunted by the deals amid Sosa's monster 1998 campaign, although Grieve possesses the proverbial second thoughts from the cold analysis of history.

And, at the same time, Cubs scout Larry Himes, who served tenures as general manager of both the

Cubs and White Sox, can be as proud as a father for trading for Sosa not once, but twice. The satisfaction he derives is not from getting some kind of upper hand in dealing with both Grieve and Schueler, but in Sosa's maturation into an impact player in the major leagues. And Himes, who took a lot of grief for not playing the front-office and media political game more adeptly, displayed once and for all how his scouting talents enabled him to find a raw talent with an unlimited upside in Sosa.

Grieve was the first executive to expose Sosa to the majors in 1989. Just 20, Sosa was called up to the Rangers on June 15 of that season after batting .297 with Tulsa of the Texas League.

Sosa barely had much Double-A experience, let alone any time in Triple-A. He was only playing in his fourth pro season, a raw kid just starting to learn Baseball 101.

"I think one of the things we fell victim to is promoting players at a young age before their experience in the minors warranted it," Grieve, now a Rangers announcer, said. "We didn't have a lot of money (for veterans) at the big-league level, and this was what we could afford to do. We had a large group of very talented players in the minors."

Sosa's first game was on June 16, 1989, against the New York Yankees. Sosa collected a single and double in four at-bats. Five days later, he slugged his first big-league homer off the Boston Red Sox's Roger Clemens, of all people, at Fenway Park in Boston.

"I thought he had the right attitude," then-Rangers manager Bobby Valentine, now piloting the New York Mets, said. "I thought he'd have decent long-ball potential. Not big power, but maybe around 15 to 20 homers."

But the Rangers' needs soon changed. Always playing a distant second to the NFL's Cowboys in the Dallas-Ft. Worth market, the Rangers began challenging the American League champion Oakland Athletics for the AL West division lead in July. The management philosophy changed.

"We felt we had an opportunity to win if we could add a potent bat to the lineup," Grieve said. Lo and behold, the White Sox had a bat to spare. Himes continued dismantling the last remnants of Chicago's early 1980s contender in favor of younger players filtering their way up through the farm system or from other organizations. The Sox had slumped to a 32-56 record at the All-Star break in '89, and obviously had nothing to lose by dumping another veteran.

"We knew Harold Baines was going to be a '10-5' guy for us in 1990," Himes said of the rule that gives veteran players the right to refuse a trade if they've logged 10 years of big-league service and five with their present club.

"We didn't want to get in that situation," Himes said. "The only thing we could do was trade Harold. So we went out looking for clubs who were in the race and needed help down the stretch. But we hadn't focused in on Sammy or any of the other Rangers prospects. That only happened after we started talking trade. Tom said they'd have interest in Harold.

"When we did our research, we realized the kids had done well at Port Charlotte." Himes' first choice, though, was to go for Juan Gonzalez. "Gonzalez was our No. 1 guy, further along than Sammy, and bigger and stronger," he recalled. "We were looking at a guy who was more mature physically. Sammy had more in the way of projections. I didn't feel they'd give us Gonzalez. But you ask for the moon in your first conversation, then go down later on."

Grieve wasn't surprised when he heard of Himes' personnel demands.

"He said he wanted Sammy Sosa or Juan Gonzalez and Wilson Alvarez," he said. "I said, 'Absolutely not, we will not trade those players.' Himes said he didn't see a trade (for Baines), that those were the guys he wanted.

"Obviously, I changed my mind. The more we analyzed it, the more we fooled ourselves into believing this trade was good for the Rangers. The Rangers always had been an organization whose creed was not to take a short-term gain at a long-term loss. Our crown jewels were our young players. Unfortunately, we went against our philosophy."

Grieve took Gonzalez off the table, and Himes began focusing on Sosa.

"We loved both players," Grieve said. "We signed both at the same time. Both came up through the minor-league system on the same teams. They were our youngest and best players. It wasn't as if one was head-and-shoulders above the other. But we thought Juan would be more of an impact player, more of a home-run hitter. Of course, that's very difficult to determine at that age. We were going to lose a player that hurt us in the long run either way."

Himes, accompanied by scouts Danny Monzon and Lou Snipp, traveled to Oklahoma City after Sosa had been optioned down to the Triple-A club on July 20, 1989. The trio watched the kid for four days.

"Sammy didn't do anything tremendous," Himes said. "We watched infield practice and saw he had a great arm. We knew he ran well. The thing that impressed us most about him was not just his physical ability, but his work ethic. It was really hot and muggy in the late afternoon when the team took batting practice all four days. After BP finished, Sammy stayed out there by himself, set up a portable net with a batting tee, and took a lot of swings on his own before finally going back into the clubhouse."

Suddenly the Sox scouting contingent was joined by team vice chairman Eddie Einhorn, who happened to be in the area on other business.

"Eddie said to me, 'This better be a good deal, or there will be some consequences,'" Himes said.

On July 29, 1989, Grieve and Himes pulled the trigger. Sosa, Alvarez and infielder Scott Fletcher went to Chicago in exchange for Baines and infielder Fred Manrique. The Baines angle got most of the publicity in the trade, and from the Chicago end, Fletcher was the focus as a former White Sox. Sosa was described in media accounts as the Rangers' "top-rated" minor leaguer. At the time, Himes gave the first public hint of the baseball insiders' view of Sosa.

"We like Sosa for his attitude, his hustle and certainly his talent," he said. "He is a five-tool player: hit, hit for power, catch, run and throw."

White Sox chairman Jerry Reinsdorf paid almost immediate tribute to Baines, retiring his No. 3 within a month of the deal. Baines eventually would return to the Sox and was still going strong with the Baltimore Orioles in 1998.

But Baines provided little benefit for Grieve's grand scenario. He slugged just three homers and drove in 16 runs the rest of the 1989 season as Texas fell back to a final 83-79 record, 16 games behind Oakland. Sosa became a regular with the Sox. Alvarez threw a no-hitter in 1991, and he established himself as a rotation mainstay at Comiskey Park all the way through his trade to the Giants in 1997.

"We weren't good enough to catch Oakland," Grieve said in hindsight. "People asked me when I left as GM what was my biggest mistake. Easy. That was my biggest mistake. What was not wrong about it was that it got our fans excited. It gave hope and provided enthusiasm, that we would be willing to trade young players for a higher-paid veteran. Obviously, if we had won our division with Harold Baines, I would not be saying the same things."

Sosa already had a big-league reputation—not all of it good —when he was traded from the Sox to the Cubs more than 2 1/ 2 years later. He had shown flashes of his enormous potential in his 1990 rookie season with the White Sox, but had regressed badly in 1991, earning a mid-season demotion to the minors.

Two factors came into play there. The Sox's other younger players like Frank Thomas, Robin Ventura and Jack McDowell had quickly come into their own. A couple of productive veterans were needed to round out the developing pennant contender. Meanwhile, Schueler had taken over from the fired Himes as Sox general manager after the 1990 season. He had no particular attachment to Sosa, who soon began hearing his name connected to trade rumors. In November 1991, Sosa said he was offered to the Houston Astros.

Nothing was completed over the off-season of 1991-92. Sosa went to Sox spring training camp at Sarasota, Florida, without a lot of expectations under new manager Gene Lamont. He went through more than a month of drills and games, performing poorly, while trade talks began to heat up again. Schueler and his staff believed the Sox were "a hitter away" from winning the American League Western Division.

While the Sox sought an out for Sosa, Himes—then in his first spring as Cubs general manager—began investigating trades for left fielder George Bell, who was quickly wearing out his welcome on the Cubs after just one season on the North Side. Himes had watched Bell play for the Cubs during the 1991 season while working as a part-time scout for several teams. He thought the slugger was out of place.

"George, to me, was always a designated hitter," he said. "I watched him play defense in Wrigley Field and I didn't think he was a National League player. He didn't like using the leather."

One report had Himes talking with the Boston Red Sox

for outfielder Mike Greenwell. But Himes claimed at the time the market wasn't very good for Bell.

"There wasn't a lot of interest," he said. "Not because they weren't interested in George, but because all these teams already had DHs."

While taking one last look at Bell in Cubs camp at Mesa, Arizona, Himes contacted White Sox advance scout Bart Johnson, who had worked for the GM on the South Side, while Johnson was monitoring Cactus League games.

"I mentioned to Bart that we may have George Bell available," Himes said. "When Bart relayed that on to Schu, it was a matter of exchanging names. I knew Sammy wasn't fitting into their picture. He was an extra outfielder to them. But he was more than an extra outfielder. If he played every day, he would have an opportunity to realize his full potential."

Schueler had called up "four or five clubs where we thought we were close" to a deal. Eventually, he began talking with Himes. Schueler consulted with Reinsdorf, then finally cut the deal on March 30, 1992, adding left-handed reliever Ken Patterson in the package to the Cubs, as spring training was coming to a close. In addition to Bell, the Sox received $400,000 from the Cubs.

The initial media reaction was that the Sox got the immediate benefit in a proven hitter, while the Cubs could draw dividends years in the future if Sosa developed the way many projected. Under a March 31, 1992, headline calling the deal a "draw," *Chicago Sun-Times* baseball writer Dave Van Dyck called it "good for both teams." In analyzing how the Sox got an immediate pennant-contending boost, Van Dyck wrote the next day: "Bell had become a big buzzard in the clubhouse. Other players wondered whether Bell really missed the last week with a bum ankle or bad attitude. ... If Ron Schueler sent any signals, it was that he wants to win this season, problems be damned."

Sun-Times sports columnist Jay Mariotti wasn't as kind to Himes. Mariotti wrote that Himes had dispatched Bell in exchange for "a head case and a middle reliever. In one swoop, Himes seems to have assured the South Side of mid-October baseball this season while completely stripping the North Side of the same opportunity. ... Sammy Sosa, whom the Cubs get in the deal, is kindly described as an enigma. He runs well and catches the ball, but does anyone trust him? You accept Sosa as a throw-in for George Bell. But the central figure? ... Himes has been rooked."

Freed from the bench and possibly another trip to the minors, Sosa was ecstatic. "He knows what I can do," Sosa said of Himes, just before he packed his bags to leave Sox camp. "He got me from Texas and now he gets me again. I don't know nothing about their team. All I know is I'm going to play every day."

Himes believed Sosa just needed a change of scenery. "He needed to get out," he said. "I always looked at Sammy as being like Minnie Minoso with his energy and enthusiasm. All he needed was a chance to play."

"Once we decided this was the way we were going to go, I don't look back," Schueler said. "I look ahead. The best trade in the world is one that works out for both clubs. If it does, that club will always come back and talk to you (about more trades)."

The Sox got their immediate boost from Bell, who led the team with 25 homers and drove in 112 runs in 1992. Slumping the next year, he contributed much less to the AL West title drive in 1993. Bell's attitude went to pieces during the American League Championship Series with the Toronto Blue Jays when he verbally—and nearly physically—tussled over playing time with Lamont. By the time the Sox revved it up for their aborted World Series quest in the strike-shortened 1994 season, Bell was gone, and so was his career.

Sosa suffered a broken right hand and broken left ankle, limiting his playing time to 67 games in 1992. But when healthy, he racked up his first 30-30 season in 1993, with 33 homers and 36 steals. And, starting in 1993, Schueler began importing a right fielder-of-the-year: Ellis Burks, Darrin Jackson, Mike Devereaux.

Like many GMs before and after him, Schueler took a gamble, trading away tremendous future upside to plug a hole in the present. He didn't necessarily lose the gamble; maybe Sosa wouldn't have developed at Comiskey Park in the same manner he has at Wrigley Field.

From the Cubs fans' perspective, though, Himes made a great trade that will long outlast his troubled tenure in the front office. On June 15, 1964, the Cubs traded away a young Lou Brock for Ernie Broglio, a pitcher who ended up with a bum elbow. Now the Cubs got Sammy Sosa, player on the come who kept getting better as time progressed—all the way to the base-ball record book in 1998. A few more years of Sosa's peak pro-duction, and he can be mentioned in the same breath as Brock and similar greats.

The sting of being rejected by the White Sox was felt by Sosa in 1992. But it has faded through the years.

"After they got rid of me I became a much better player. It seems like a long time ago," he said.

Sosa was all but done being grist for trades. Briefly, around the All-Star break in 1995, his name was connected with the Baltimore Orioles in a possible deal involving young reliever Armando Benitez. But the "deal" was only Orioles general man-ager Roland Hemond collecting names of "impact" players who could help his club. Sosa was taken aside in the dugout to be assured that he was staying at Wrigley Field, that the Baltimore report was wildly exaggerated.

"You would be crazy to want to get rid of a player like that," Cubs president Andy MacPhail said late in 1995. "The quick-est exit (from the Cubs) is to not play with 100 percent of your energy and enthusiasm. And there's no question in my mind Sammy gives 100 percent. He plays every day, and he gives you everything he's got."

The very last word on Himes' trades for Sosa was said by the slugger himself only an hour after he belted his 62nd homer on September 13, 1998. Sosa was busy dedicating the moment to everyone under the sun. One reporter brought up a glaring omission, and Sosa quickly made amends.

"Thank you for reminding me," he said. "I have to thank you. Larry, you were a part of my life. You took the chance to trade for me, twice. I love you."

Finally, Cubs fans got to root for one of the game's pre-mier players who had been let go by someone else. Things do even up if you wait long enough in baseball.

4

Ups and Downs on the White Sox

A 20-year-old player receives the break of his life. He gets called up and is inserted as a regular in a rebuilding team's lineup. He gets off to a good start in his first few games. He has a nice rookie season.

You'd think you'd have the whole world at your fingertips. And maybe Sammy Sosa believed that for the first year of his tenure with the Chicago White Sox. Maybe he thought he'd enjoy the bulk of his career on the South Side.

But after another season, Sosa was mentally buried. He had lost the confidence of new team management. He couldn't adapt to his hitting coach's unique style of instruction. When all was said and done at the start of the 1992 season, Sammy Sosa said he was glad to "get out of jail."

He shouldn't have felt singled out. What happened to him has happened to scores of big leaguers before and after his aborted career with the White Sox. A young player comes up, perhaps needing more minor-league experience. He has success, then failure. Management, shifting its priorities, pulls the plug on him. He goes on to success elsewhere. The Sammy Sosa Story is baseball at its most classic, first depressing, then uplifting.

"He had a lot of doubters early in his career, and now no one's doubting Sammy," said Sox slugger Frank Thomas, Sosa's friend since the White Sox days.

Sosa's arrival at old Comiskey Park in 1989 was greatly anticipated after his trade from the Texas Rangers along with Wilson Alvarez for Harold Baines on July 29. He continued to impress White Sox general manager Larry Himes with his hitting at Triple-A Vancouver, finally receiving the call-up to the 52-72 White Sox on Monday, August 21, 1989.

"I'm an aggressive player," Sosa said then. "I can throw. I can hit. I can do everything in baseball." About his earlier one-month stint with the Rangers: "I was ready. I've been ready all my life."

Then-Vancouver manager Marv Foley cautioned that Sosa was, well, just 20.

"You're going to see a young one," he said. "He's a little rough around the edges, that's all. He can run, he can throw, he can hit, hit with power and catch the ball.

"Now, there's no telling what he could do."

Displaying his trademark confidence, Sosa in his first game as a White Sox went for 3-for-3, including a two-run homer in the ninth inning, in a 10-2 victory over the Minnesota Twins in Minneapolis. Sosa also walked twice and stole a base, batting sixth and playing right field. His lineup protection? Russ Morman, a first baseman, batting seventh.

"That'll happen to a kid ... can't handle the pressure," laughed Sox manager Jeff Torborg at the time.

"Pressure?" Sosa said. "For what?"

Chicago Tribune beat writer Alan Solomon described Sosa as a "20-year-old locked in a Rickey Henderson body." The sky seemed the limit for Sosa when he went 2-for-5 the next night in an 8-7 loss to the Twins. He'd go on to collect three homers and drive in 10 runs in 33 games total finishing out the 1989 season.

Nine years later, Torborg recalled how taken he was by Sosa's sheer physical tools.

"I took one look at him, and I said there's our answer in right field," Torborg, now a baseball announcer for Fox Sports, said. "He had that burning speed and a terrific arm. And, as a person, he showed respect and genuine sincerity. He was polite."

Sosa soon became a Torborg favorite. The manager "tried to treat him like he was a son." But when Sosa strayed from sound fundamentals, Torborg had to apply what he called "tough love."

"One time he was really overaggressive, and tried to score on a wild pitch that just got a few feet away from the catcher and was tagged out at the plate," he said. "You just tried to point things out to him."

Sosa could take the good-cop/bad-cop approach from Torborg. His relationship with hitting coach Walt Hriniak would not fare as well.

"I'm here to learn," was Sosa's first public comments about Hriniak in 1989. "Everything he tells me, I'll do." But the basis for trouble was beginning.

At that point, Sosa only had 66 games' worth of Double-A experience. He had played just 35 games at the Triple-A level. But Himes believed even a raw Sosa was better than anyone else Torborg could have put out in right field, despite Sosa's need to master fundamentals.

"One of the things you do is look at what you have," Himes said. "We didn't have much."

Sosa went on to get a boost from the Sox's almost unexpected upsurge in the standings in 1990. After the sad-sack finish of 1989, the Sox zoomed to a 20-10 start in the farewell season to old Comiskey Park. By early July, they had moved up to 47-26 first place in the American League West. The powerful Oakland Athletics overhauled them in the West in the second half of the season. But the young, enthusiastic Sox, breaking in rookies like Sosa, Frank Thomas, Robin Ventura, and Alex Fernandez, and with Bobby Thigpen setting the all-time saves record of 57, enjoyed one of baseball's best overall seasons with a 94-68 record. The height of emotion came on September 30, when a crowd of 42,849 witnessed the farewell game of the old ballpark in a 2-1 victory against the Seattle Mariners.

Sosa picked up the nickname "The Panther" with his quick, lithe and powerful movements in right field. He hit just .233, had an alarming 150 strikeouts in just 532 at-bats, and made 13 errors in the outfield. But he also collected 15 homers, 26 doubles, 10 triples and 70 RBI while stealing 32 bases. He ranked second in the American League in outfield assists with 14.

"We had the best defensive outfield in the American League in 1990," Himes recalled. "Many other outfielders in the majors didn't have the season he did."

Along with center fielder Lance Johnson and left fielder Ivan Calderon, the Sox outfield was one of the speediest in the majors. Johnson, who became fast friends with Sosa, stole 36 bases while Calderon swiped 32.

"I remember when he watched me for two years and I didn't take a big swing and he was taking a big swing and he was striking out," Lance Johnson said. "Ivan Calderon was teasing him. He used to call him Zorro. And Sammy, he didn't want to come in the dugout because he knew Ivan was going to be all over him. But Ivan loved him. That little experience helped Sammy mentally."

Sosa felt comfortable with his teammates, particularly the tight-knit group of Latin players.

"Ivan Calderon, Ozzie Guillen, Melido Perez, Carlos Martinez ... they helped me out," he said. "Somebody who can talk Spanish, you can be around."

But amid the upbeat Sox finish, storm clouds gathered. Himes, Sosa's sponsor, summarily was dismissed in September by Sox chairman Jerry Reinsdorf, no doubt because of Himes' militancy over control of baseball operations and his one-on-one style in dealing with the powerful team mogul. More importantly, hitting coach Hriniak, a Reinsdorf favorite, and Sosa did not exactly see eye to eye over Hriniak's "head-down" mechanics of hitting. An old-school type, Hriniak taught players to keep their head focused on the ball all the way through their swing. That hardly suited the young Sosa's aggressive, all-or-nothing style.

"Walter's style was a variation of Charlie Lau's," Torborg said of an equally prominent hitting coach who had worked for the White Sox a decade earlier. "You keep your head down and finish high with your swing. You release (the bat) with your top hand. If you're a right-handed hitter, your right thumb finishes (on the swing) in your right ear. Some people sarcastically describe this approach as the 'helicopter swing.'

"Sammy was so strong, he had an uppercut swing. He was such a gung-ho kid and wanted to do everything to please everyone. He tried to adopt to Walter's style, but it didn't fit him."

Hriniak's handling of Sosa rankles Sox slugger Thomas to this day.

"At times in his career, Walt Hriniak was very unfair to him, very critical of him, a little too much, and Sammy took it the wrong way," Thomas said. "Walt was an old-school guy. At that point, he said Sammy was uncoachable. That was not true. Sammy never had someone come across the way Walt did. And Walt could give you a little pressure at times. He was pushing Sammy a little too much, a little too early in his career."

Himes agreed. "I don't think Sammy could adopt to that style," said the ex-GM, no Hriniak fan himself, said. "The best thing that happened to Sammy was not doing it."

Hriniak will not comment these days on his time with Sosa. But in 1992, after Sosa's trade to the Cubs, the often-salty coach had nothing but good things to say publicly about him.

"He listened to me," Hriniak said at the time. "I worked with him one-on-one, every day. It will help him that he'll play every day. Repetition works; it works in baseball and everything else in life."

Surprisingly, one former Hriniak pupil believed Sosa actually was helped in small way by the coach.

"I thought Walt did a lot of things to help hitters, including me," Johnson, now reunited with Sosa as his Cubs center fielder, said. "Walt taught me to survive, and I'm sure Sammy learned to survive, too, from him."

Away from Hriniak, Sosa continued to work hard before games as a White Sox player. Sox coaches of the day did not have complaints about his desire to improve himself.

"Sammy was a good worker," coach Joe Nossek said. "He wanted to be better. That (work ethic) was never a problem with him."

But the downward trend accelerated into 1991. Ron Schueler had become general manager. In baseball parlance, Sosa wasn't Schueler's player. He hadn't traded for him. The Sox were on the move upward in the standings, but Sosa's performance did not follow suit.

Schueler, also a veteran scout, had a different analysis of Sosa than Himes at the time.

"All kinds of tools, things you're looking for in the perfect player, as a scout," Schueler recalled. "But at that point in his career, he couldn't do anything to help you win a game. He'd throw to the wrong base, run you out of an inning. You needed a walk, he'd swing at three pitches in the dirt. Unbelievable tools, but no discipline whatsoever.

"He got a little overmatched, and wanted to swing like everything was going to be a home run. He did not try to hit the ball the other way or try to get guys over."

Sosa started 1991 with a big bang, slugging two homers and driving in five runs in the season opener at Baltimore. He went on to have a decent two-week (20-for-60) spell in early May. But he slumped badly as the weather warmed. By late July, he was down to an even .200. Out of the lineup, he sank lower in the Sox's plans. Management had begun their flirtation with the surgery-rehabbing Bo Jackson by this point.

On July 19, 1991, Schueler optioned Sosa to Vancouver. Old White Sox hero Ron Kittle took his place on the roster.

"That just ripped his heart out," Himes said of the demotion. Center fielder Johnson, though, believed Sosa was tough enough to handle the setback.

"I thought it was better for his future if he went out and played (in Triple-A)," Schueler said. "I was trying to send a lesson that you haven't arrived yet. You still have things to work on. Three weeks later I went to Phoenix and saw him play. He was making better contact. But we felt as an organization we were getting closer to winning, and Sammy wasn't the guy who was going to go out, play every day, and do the things to help us win.

"Gosh, as far as ability, there wasn't anybody here who doubted this guy was going to hit a bunch of home runs if he got a chance to play."

But Torborg earned Sosa's trust for life. The manager promised he would get Sosa recalled from the minors. With the team slumping and falling out of the pennant race, Sosa was summoned back from Vancouver on August 27, 1991. Torborg and Sosa hugged as the promise was fulfilled. Their meetings on the baseball trail today are just as warm.

But not long afterward, Sosa would lose his last important ally in management when Torborg left the Sox for the high-profile New York Mets manager's job. In truth, Torborg was forced out. But the change of managers to the low-key, but tough-minded Gene Lamont didn't improve Sosa's situation. Upper management's collective opinion of him seemed to be cast in stone.

Even today, Schueler's standards are still pretty high in rating Sosa's ability to truly help a team win. A collection of 30- and 40-homer seasons from 1993 to 1997 did not dissuade the Sox GM from his original evaluation of Sosa.

"I don't think he arrived until this year (1998). I really don't," he said. "This is the first year where he's doing things from a team standpoint in winning games. I see him not swinging at bad pitches, taking walks, trying to hit the ball the other way with two strikes. I don't think he's trying to hit home runs. And I think he's hitting the cutoff man better than before, running the bases better than before. You could put up numbers. But, remember, those are individual numbers. That doesn't win games."

Schueler also had questions about Sosa's handling of his personal life in 1991. Sosa may have made mistakes of immaturity at the time in handling his first taste of success and affluence at the big-league level. He was more flamboyant in his personal behavior than he is today. Like most young players, he went out after hours. Sosa, always a generous fellow, also caused the Sox worry with his spending habits. So, just as important in Schueler's mind is Sosa's growth off the field.

"We had questions about his makeup off the field," Schueler said. "I think he's grown up more, I think, off the field than on the field. He's really grown up as a person. I see a lot of people who never grow up. Jose Canseco's never grown up. He's still has the same wild side with fast cars and all that stuff. I give Sammy a lot of credit, because I didn't know if he could handle his life making $8 million or $9 million."

Mention Ron Schueler today to Sammy Sosa, and a look of puzzlement envelopes his face. He still cannot understand what happened with the White Sox. At the same time, his past on the South Side is not something upon which he dwells except to offer some respectful comments about former teammates. Long before Sosa called Mark McGwire "The Man," he bestowed the same title—at least for Chicago—on Frank Thomas.

Sosa never desired to be another "Big Hurt". He just wanted to play regularly somewhere, anywhere, without a rigid philosophy. So Sosa got what he wanted when he was traded to the Cubs on March 29, 1992. Johnson still can remember Sosa's sense of utter relief when he was told of the deal. Like many others predicting Sosa's future at the time, Johnson proved to have great intuition.

"When he was traded, I told Sammy he would never play for another team (besides the Cubs)," he recalled. "He was just made for Wrigley Field and the fans."

Johnson and others could have made a mint in the Sosa's futures business. The White Sox had bowed out early, though. That was a gamble they simply did not want to take. Six years later, Sosa's career is thriving in a way Frank Thomas said couldn't have happened on the South Side.

"I have a big sense of regret," Thomas said of Sosa's departure. "It was a good move for him to get away from the organization, since we figure Walt Hriniak was going to be here a long time. Things work out in mysterious ways. I'm happy things have worked out for him."

5

Sammy Finds a Baseball Home

Wrigley Field, 1992-1994

Adjusting quickly to his new digs at Wrigley Field, Sammy Sosa could breathe fresh air emotionally. He had a starting job in center field, the support of a general manager who had traded for him twice, and the always-appreciative Wrigley Field fans ready to cheer his feats.

"It makes it better for me," he said upon his arrival on the North Side. "I'm playing every day. I feel good here. It's like I've been here all my life.

"It doesn't matter how you start, it's how you finish. If I go 0-for-4, 0-for-3, I've got to forget about it. I've got to come tomorrow with a new attitude.

"I know I'm going to hit. You keep working and everything's going be good."

Years would pass before Sosa would truly appreciate the significance of his hopeful words. In 1992, he still had a lot of growing up to do on the job in the majors. He'd face almost a lifetime's worth of challenges—continuing to learn the game in fits and spurts while dodging a lot of verbal brickbats from fellow players, baseball executives and media—all between Opening Days 1992 and 1998.

Sosa's effort to learn on the job in the majors was tough enough. He also had to mentally strengthen himself against the losing seasons, a cauldron of dissension almost every year in the clubhouse, and sideshows that included hex-busting goats coming onto the field. He had to try to grow as a player and a person during one of the wackiest periods in Cubs history, one that was not quite conducive to baseball at its best.

Greeting Sosa after he arrived at Cubs' spring training camp in Mesa, Arizona on March 30, 1992, was general manager Larry Himes and manager Jim Lefebvre, starting his first season with the Cubs. Lefebvre was eager to help straighten Sosa out after he finally got away from White Sox hitting coach Walt Hriniak. A longtime hitting coach at different levels, Lefebvre teamed with Cubs Hall of Famer Billy Williams to start working with the promising but unpolished slugger. Both Lebevbre and Williams shared the same instructional philosophy for hitters.

"One of the coaching principles that I have is you never coach style out of a player," Lefebvre, now hitting coach of the Milwaukee Brewers, said. "Every player who gets to the big leagues has a little bit different swing. How they get that he did not want to accept. It would have never worked for him. He was getting criticized for a style that he just did not want to do.

"When I got him, he was confused. He was somewhat down. The first thing I did when I got him in my office is tell him, "From now in, we're going to do it your way.' He jumped up and got into his stance. You could see he was very proud of it. We took him out to batting practice in Mesa and he was hitting bombs all over the ballpark.

"The most important thing I had to do with him is give him the confidence that if he went 0-for-two on some days, we're going to stay with him and keep working with him."

Lefebvre and Williams had ensured that Sosa no longer would feel he was being second-guessed as he batted.

"When Sammy made an out or took a swing, he'd look back at the bench," Williams said. "That's what they did over there (White Sox)—analyze his swing while he's up there. I said look at the pitcher, that's the guy trying to get you out.

"Mechanically, I saw a player who dives into the ball. If you commit too soon, the pitcher will throw the running fastball and run it in on your hands. He was breaking bats."

Lefebvre and Himes would part acrimoniously after the 1993 season. But, starting out, they agreed on an important principle—to show patience with Sosa.

"One of the biggest things about the big leagues is when you see great talent like that, we expect it to immediately happen," Lefebvre said. "In some players it does happen. Junior (Ken Griffey, Jr.) was one. But other players, it does not. Look at how many players come into the league who couldn't hit certain pitches, or weren't good defensive players, whatever. Suddenly, they become very disciplined. When Sammy first came to Chicago, he was searching for his identity."

Sosa couldn't find his identity for years. Lefebvre offers a specific timetable for players reaching their comfort zone.

"When I worked with him in the cages, I could see it coming," he said. "But when the game started, his emotions and his youth and his excitement, sometimes it didn't happen in the game. It usually takes about 1,500 at-bats, I feel, before a guy can say 'I belong in the big leagues, I know what I need to do to become a big-league hitter.'

"I wasn't going to take his aggressiveness away from him. We'd talk, but sometimes it isn't what you said but what you didn't say. Patience is so important at this level working with young players."

As hitting coach, Williams had to develop a one-on-one rapport with Sosa. His approach was far more sugar than vinegar, based on experience. Williams always can recall how an irascible Rogers Hornsby, then Cubs hitting instructor, took him under his wing in spring training, 1959, when Williams was trying to advance to Double A in the Cubs farm system.

Hornsby, who once batted .424 and was possibly the greatest right-handed hitter in history, got along with practically nobody. While a big-league manager with the Reds in the early 1950s, he was accused of urinating on one of his players while both were in the shower. Cubs players staged a mutiny against Hornsby while he was manager in 1932. Bill Veeck, Sr., Cubs president and father of the baseball Barnum, then fired Hornsby and appointed Charlie Grimm as manager. The Cubs surged and won the pennant.

Yet Hornsby's knowledge of hitting was akin to Ted Williams. He'd always get second and third chances to work in the game. The Cubs rehired him in 1958, and somehow Hornsby—

bad persona and all—took a liking to Williams, a young, soft-spoken African-American player possessing a natural, fluid swing. Hornsby reported to the Cubs front office that Williams and a 19-year-old kid named Ron Santo were the only minor leaguers with big-league potential; the rest might as well be ashcanned.

Williams derived confidence from Hornsby's endorsement and instruction. So, in a strange form of baseball linkage, some of the wisdom from a .400 hitter was being passed down through the decades to Sammy Sosa through Williams.

Remembering his experiences, Williams realized how the power of positive reinforcement goes a long way.

"You have to put your arm around him," he said of gaining Sosa's confidence. "With the Sox, there was a guy telling him to do it this way, do it that way. Sammy was like he was in a bubble. He didn't know how to do it and what to do with it. It took him until about mid-season when we could start really trying to do some things with him. The kid had to have some confidence in you, and then you could tell him some things.

"You want to keep his aggressive attitude. I saw a kid who wanted to work hard, every day."

All along, Williams wanted Sosa to adjust his stroke to the situation, but not change it altogether. That meant Williams, who combined a devastating mixture of power and contact, never having struck out more than 84 times a season, had to accept Sosa frequently air conditioning the ballpark with his big swing.

"When you go talk to Sammy in the batting cage, you know he'll hit some balls out of the ballpark," he said. "But he'll also strike out a lot."

Williams always cited the example of Reggie Jackson. "Mr. October" was modern-day baseball's whiff king at the plate, but few were better with the game on the line. Near the end of his great 1998 season, Sosa would get to hear that from Jackson himself during a visit to the Cubs' clubhouse in San Diego.

"Reggie said, 'I might strike out three times in a row, but on the fourth time I might hit a three-run homer,'" Williams said. "When you talk about Reggie Jackson, it's a great player who struck out a lot. Willie Stargell struck out a lot. It's just a question of being able to adjust when there's a man on second and nobody out."

With the support of his general manager, manager and hitting coach, Sosa started out slowly in 1992, mirroring the performance of the Cubs as a team. On May 11, the team was 12-19 and had fallen to the cellar. Few players were hitting. That increased the pressure on a young player like Sosa to produce. Sosa collected just one RBI, on Opening Day, and batted just .211 in his first 24 games. He finally collected his first Cubs homer, a solo shot off the Houston Astros' Ryan Bowen, on May 7.

The young slugger had to struggle to get on his feet amid the first torrent of clubhouse dissension that would always rear its ugly head over the next five seasons.

Jerome Walton, the Cubs' 1989 National League rookie of the year, had seen his career backslide over the next two seasons. By 1992, he was a part-time left fielder, often injured and unhappy. On June 19, Walton would be optioned to Triple-A Iowa, his once-promising Chicago tenure winding down. "Lefebvre blackballed me," Walton later said, blaming the manager for his difficulties in latching on to another job. Somehow Walton managed to salvage his career as a backup through most of the 1980s with the Atlanta Braves, Cincinnati Reds and Baltimore Orioles.

Another clubhouse sourpuss was left-handed starter Danny Jackson. Often injured himself, Jackson wasn't pitching all that well when healthy, his record dropping to 4-9 at mid-season before Himes, amid several desperate moves to add hitting, traded him to the Pittsburgh Pirates for third baseman Steve Buechele.

Overall, grumbling was widespread due to the deteriorating hopes for retaining young ace pitcher Greg Maddux. The right-hander, just emerging as the game's best hurler in 1992, had made concessions in his contract dealings with a Tribune Co. attorney the previous autumn, prior to Himes' appointment as GM. But the team had pulled its contract offer off the table, angering Maddux and Scott Boras, his tough agent. Himes, who admitted that "politics is not my strong suit," did not have the ability to schmooze Maddux and Boras back into the fold. Further negotiations in mid-season broke down, leading to Maddux's disastrous departure as a free agent the following November, one of the single worst moves in Cubs history.

And all-time great outfielder Andre Dawson realized Himes wasn't in a hurry to re-sign him, the general manager being concerned about Dawson's often surgery-repaired knees and lack of range in right field. Dawson was further angered when he claimed Himes did not have the respect to talk to him as he passed by.

So many Cubs players began to unite in their anger at Himes. All the while Sosa, struggling to get established, was seen as the general manager's prize acquisition, a majority of one in the clubhouse. His status, though, did not affect his eagerness to get his North Side career started.

Overall, the Cubs' lineup was chockfull of holes after Dawson, Ryne Sandberg and Mark Grace were penciled in. Shortstop Shawon Dunston was lost for the season, and more, due to back surgery early in the campaign. Spring-phenom Gary Scott, who earned the third-base job starting in both the 1991 and 1992 seasons, flamed out and was demoted to Triple-A, never to contend for a Cubs job again. Beset by a farm system that had declined after the 1987 departure of former GM Dallas Green, Himes had to cull the waiver wire for journeymen such as Doug Strange and Jeff Kunkel, along with sore-kneed, washed-up slugger Kal Daniels. Maddux and the newly signed Mike Morgan pitched superbly, but often lacked run support.

Without much speed in his lineup, Lefebvre placed Sosa in the leadoff spot despite his propensity for strikeouts. The manager stuck with him through his cold start until he finally got started. Lefebvre made one important adjustment, moving Sosa down to the sixth slot in the order, removing pressure from the struggling player. As a result, he began enjoying his first hot spell as a Cub when frigid spring weather of '92 began to break. Sosa slugged four homers in a 10-game span from May 31 to June 10, including his first two-homer Cubs game in St. Louis on the latter date.

Sosa homered in the second inning off Cardinals rookie Mark Clark, who five years later would become a Cubs teammate. Clark served up another Sosa blast in the sixth, providing Maddux with a 4-0 lead. Maddux eventually won 4-2.

Obviously, then-Cardinals manager Joe Torre's strategy for pitching the young, undisciplined Sosa didn't work out that night. But Torre, now manager of the New York Yankees, tried to have his pitchers stick with a game plan to take advantage of Sosa's strikeout propensities.

"You could throw Sammy one way, you could overpower him high, if you had that kind of fastball, and we didn't have a pitcher with one," he recalled. "What you tried to do is get ahead of him and not throw him a strike. It was basically pitch around the strike zone to him. I don't think he was disciplined as a hitter. If you're in that type of mode, a pitcher has to take advantage of that."

Other pitchers who would end up as Sosa's Cub teammates later in the 1990s zeroed in on the numerous holes in Sosa's undisciplined swing.

"He was very much a free swinger like Shawon Dunston," remembered Terry Mulholland, at the time a top southpaw starter for the Philadelphia Phillies. "If you got ahead of him, you could get him to chase quite a few different pitches out of the strike zone, whether they were breaking balls or high fastballs. Sammy's natural hitting style was as a lowball hitter.

"You could pitch around the guy's power and still get him out. He was a guy in the lineup who, when you needed an out, as long as you were smart and didn't give him his pitch, you had a good chance of picking up an out.

"Being a primarily fastball-oriented power pitcher, I enjoyed challenging guys inside. Sammy was no different. I tried to get the ball in above his hands inside the strike zone, then work out from there. Basically, if you got ahead of him 0-and-2, 1-and-2, you'd try to get him to swing at a pitch up the ladder, something that wasn't a strike. The last thing you wanted to do was work toward his power."

Cubs closer Rod Beck, just breaking into the San Francisco Giants' bullpen in 1992, recalled his team's pattern of feeding Sosa one particular pitch until he cried "uncle."

"Once you got him to two strikes, however that was, you gave him nothing but sliders until he swung and missed," he said. "Throw the sliders outside, in the dirt. No strikes. You could throw him fastballs, but they had to be up and in. You could get him out without throwing strikes.

"Without a doubt, it was (overanxiousness), especially facing a closer in his last at-bat. He wanted to deliver for his club, compete and win so badly that he'd tried to hit a pitch five feet outside. Aggressiveness is a good thing, but you have to be smart with it."

Sosa couldn't learn about closing up the holes in his swing from the bench. Disaster struck in the next game after his two-homer performance against the Cardinals, on June 12 at Wrigley Field. In the fifth inning of a 5-2 Cubs victory over the Montreal

Expos, Sosa suffered a fracture of the fifth metacarpal bone in his right hand after being hit by a pitch from the Montreal Expos' Dennis Martinez. He was disabled until July 27.

"We're not that deep as it is, and we lose another key guy," Lefebvre said after the June 12 game.

Somehow, the Cubs muddled around just below the .500 mark until Sosa's return. And the budding slugger was certainly eager to get back in the swing of things. Returned to the leadoff spot against the first-place Pittsburgh Pirates on Monday night, July 27, at Wrigley Field, Sosa homered on the first pitch against Doug Drabek. As a preview of things to come, the ballhawks on Waveland Avenue collected the long-gone souvenir. Sosa wasn't done, though. He went on to go 3-for-4 with two RBI and two runs scored.

"I wanted to come back quick," Sosa said afterward. "I was excited about being back, and I wanted to show what I could do. But I wanted to be patient.

"I know they (the Cubs) were looking for me to come back. I'm healthy and can do everything now, and it'll get better the more I play. I want to give it everything I've got."

In a poignant kind of way, Sosa's big day helped Maddux again. The ace, by now determined to test the free-agent market after the season after more contract talks broke down, struck out 10 Pirates to equal a career high at that point. This would prove to be the last time the present and future stars' best efforts confluence as Cubs. What might have been had Maddux stayed in Chicago while Sosa matured...

On Tuesday, July 28, Sosa continued his sizzling ways at the plate with a 3-for-5 performance, including an RBI double, in the Cubs' 11-1 victory over the Pirates. Fans and media began to get a bit excited as the Cubs, despite their holes, were now in hailing distance of the Buccos.

Twenty-four hours later, Sosa would really get the town buzzing about his potential, saving his best for last in the three-game series with the Pirates. Before the largest Wrigley Field crowd of the season (36,554), Sosa fanned three times earlier in the game. "I never let a strikeout get me down," he said. Proving he was as good as his word, Sosa blasted a booming two-run homer in the bottom of the 11th to give the Cubs a three-game sweep of the National League East leaders. The Cubs were just 49-51, but had crept to within four games of Pittsburgh.

"It's not every day you get to be a hero," Sosa said. "Baseball's not like that."

"Just think: He hit the first pitch of this series for a homer and the last pitch for a homer," Lefebvre said. "This is quite a time in the young man's life. You can tell by his face how much he's enjoying it."

Sosa's teammates saw him for the raw talent that he was. They also raised their eyebrows slightly at his overaggressiveness.

"The thing that would rub some veteran guys is like when Andre (Dawson) is playing right field and Sammy's playing center," first baseman Mark Grace recalled of one 1992 game. "Andre would call for a ball and run him right over. And he did it twice in one game. So finally Andre sat him down in the clubhouse and said, 'Look, I'm getting too old for that shit. When I say I got it, I got it!'"

Grace feared for Sosa's—and his teammates'—well-being.

"No, you can't (go in fast gear all the time)," he said. "It was funny, but you were afraid he was going to hurt somebody."

Grace knew all along Sosa had to learn basic baseball fundamentals on the job in the majors in 1992.

"He was very, very talented," he said. "But he didn't really know anything about baseball other than see ball, hit ball. I catch it, you throw it. He was very erratic in the outfield. He didn't know anything about hitting the cutoff man and keeping the guy off second base to keep the double play in order. He didn't know anything about the guy on second base, nobody out, hitting the ball to right field.

"It took him a long time to understand that little things win games. Not just balls hit in the street every day."

Despite the wildly fluctuating quality of Sosa's game, visions of the town's next superstar abounded. Sosa was 15-for-39 in his first nine games off the disabled list with three homers and nine RBI. But his 1992 season ended in his 10th game when he fouled a pitch off his right ankle, fracturing it. Sosa finished 1992 with eight homers, 25 RBI and a what-might-have-been feeling from his manager from the hindsight of six years later.

"If it wasn't for those injuries, he might have been there sooner," Lefebvre said of Sosa's emergence as a productive power hitter.

The Cubs' dalliance with pennant contention ended soon after Sosa's disablement. Although the team enjoyed an 18-12 August, they fell seven games behind the Pirates by month's end, then nosedived in patented Cubs style in September. Chicago was 68-64 after Morgan's complete-game victory over the Dodgers at Wrigley Field on September 2. The Cubs were still over .500 at 75-74 on September 19, but finished the season 78-84 in fourth place, 18 games out. Maddux's 20-11 season and 2.18 ERA—second-lowest by a Cubs starter since the 1945 pennant season—thoroughly wasted.

The downer ending was a perfect stage-setter for Maddux's final departure for the Atlanta Braves after some frantic last-second negotiating late in November. The undercurrent of bad feelings burst to the surface and now enveloped fans and media. Viewed as the team's savior a decade earlier, Tribune Co. now had the image of a penny-pinching, quarterly profits-being-maintained-at-all-costs corporate monolith that had no emotional ties to doing whatever possible to bring the Cubs a winner.

Dawson, one of the most popular Cubs of modern times, followed Maddux out the door, signing with the Atlanta Braves. The sole advantage from the end of The Hawk's memorable Cubs career was the ability of Lefebvre to move Sosa to his natural position in right field. But now Himes had to scramble to fill even more gaping holes. He signed right-hander Jose Guzman from the Texas Rangers. Fans and media bellowed that the GM signed the "wrong Guzman." They wanted hard-throwing Juan Guzman of the Toronto Blue Jays. A Toronto player Himes did acquire was free-agent outfielder Candy Maldonado. Himes also signed free-agent relievers Randy Myers and Dan Plesac, and center fielder Willie Wilson.

At least when spring training 1993 began, the one rock of stability seemed to be Sosa in right field. Relaxed, he went on to lead the Cactus League in homers. But Ryne Sandberg suffered a fractured fifth metacarpal bone in his left hand after being hit by a pitch by the San Francisco Giants' Mike Jackson in the spring opener on March 5. Sandberg came back on time, but the lingering effects of the injury robbed the second baseman of his trademark 25- to 30-homer power in 1993. With Sandberg weakened, Sosa now became the Cubs' No. 1 power source.

Meanwhile, additional pressure was placed on Morgan, never a staff leader or even a winning pitcher prior to 1992, to be the No. 1 starter in place of his departed buddy. Maddux came back to immediately haunt the Cubs, beating Morgan 1-0 on Opening Day, April 5, 1993, at Wrigley Field. Jose Guzman salvaged some measure of revenge the next day by taking a no-hitter against the Braves all the way to two out in the ninth inning. Otis Nixon spoiled the no-no by slapping a single to the opposite field in the hole between shortstop and third base. Guzman's Cubs career would go steadily downhill from that point on.

The Cubs muddled along around .500 in the early going. But Sosa picked up where he had left off the previous August with a two-homer, five-RBI day on April 23 as Guzman beat the Cincinnati Reds 7-4 at Wrigley Field. Two weeks later, Sosa would give yet another preview of his greatness in a slugfest against the Colorado Rockies at Clark and Addison.

The Cubs trailed 10-5 after 8 1/2 innings. But they began staging a desperate rally in the bottom of the ninth inning. With two out, two on and an 0-and-2 count, Sosa muscled a pitch from reliever Darren Holmes into the left-field bleachers to tie the game 10-10. He later would slug a two-run homer in the bottom of the 11th to make it close after the Rockies pushed across four runs. The Cubs went on to lose the free-for-all 14-13 as Sosa went 5-for-6 overall.

"The last couple of games I struggled," Sosa said afterward. "So today I came early and went to the video room and watched to see what I was doing wrong. I went back to spring training (style). Then I wasn't trying to hit home runs, but just trying to make good, solid contact."

Sosa began to display his enormous power potential. He recorded two-homer games on June 17 and August 6 against St. Louis, and June 30 against San Diego.

In the latter game, Sosa recorded hits in his last three at-bats. After a day off, the Cubs played the Colorado Rockies at Denver's Mile High Stadium on July 2. He went 6-for-6 while setting a Cubs team record with nine consecutive hits in an 11-8 victory before 62,037. Such luminaries as Billy Williams, Andre Dawson and Ryne Sandberg had collected eight straight hits. The night's feat was the first 6-for-6 outing by a Cub since Jose Cardenal in a 14-inning game on May 2, 1976 at San Francisco.

"Right now I'm just being patient, more patient than I used to be," Sosa said after the hitting spree, repeating a mantra he'd often use—and finally seriously follow five years later.

"He's using the whole field and pulling the ball when he needs to," a hopeful Lefebvre said after the game. "He's been more disciplined at the plate and that's something we've been stressing."

But Sosa's outbursts of power couldn't lift the Cubs above a break-even pace. Mediocre starting pitching kept the team wallowing around .500 all the way through mid-season in spite of general manager Himes' professed goal of a record of 10 games over .500 at the All-Star break. Tension gradually built, especially when the future status of Lefebvre, popular with his players but in the second year of a two-year contract, was in question.

Even the quiet Sandberg began to speak out.

"Suddenly you're playing as if you're under a timetable and what's going to happen if you don't," he told reporters at the time. "Where are we headed? And if there are questions about the manager, what's next?

"I'd like to see a little more stability and continuity in what we're trying to accomplish."

Continuity wasn't the byword when several of Himes' off-season acquisitions were concerned. Candy Maldonado was a bust in left field; Derrick May took over the lion's share of the playing time. Willie Wilson never really got untracked in center; he yielded to Dwight Smith, a mediocre fielder, at that crucial outfield position next to Sosa. Wilson spent much of his time in a reclining chair in front of his Wrigley Field locker; he wasn't often in a good mood. One afternoon, he engaged in a shouting match in the shower area with May and Smith. Lefebvre had to sprint from his office to break up the row.

With players gradually forming one side and Himes another, Sosa found himself almost an island unto himself as the GM's prize acquisition.

"Sammy was Larry's boy," Grace said. "So as long as Larry was here, Sammy was the kind. And he knew that." But Grace said that's not to Sosa's detriment. Why would he turn down a GM as a sponsor?

"Having Larry here was probably the best thing for Sammy," he said.

But did that association cause the resulting internal criticism of Sosa?

"No," said Grace. "We never held it against Sammy. Ever. It had nothing to do with his personality or the kind of guy he is or the type of player he is. There was never any resentment for that at all. That's silly."

"It wasn't his fault," Sosa's friend Glenallen Hill, who joined the Cubs in September of 1993, said of his association with Hims. "Larry recognized Sammy's talent. A lot of the problems could have been alleviated if the lines of communication could have been open. It just wasn't open, and it snowballed."

Even so, despite the fact Sosa was the most productive power hitter, he began to draw more player and media barbs for his fundamental lapses. Talk-show host Mike Murphy of all-sports WSCR-Radio ("The Score"), like his fellow on-air personalities working under orders from program director Ron Gleason to provide "entertainment," branded Sosa "Roberto Clemente without a brain." Player criticism was funneled through several writers, including scoop-chasing Barry Rozner of the suburban *Daily Herald*. Rozner, who grew up a Cubs fan in Chicago's northern suburbs, hung with some of the players on the road, and thus was able to get their "A," off-the-record material about Sosa's seeming drive for individual statistics.

The criticism intensified in September when Sosa came closer to being the first Cub in history to achieve the 30-homer, 30-stolen base plateau. At the same time, a different agenda was being followed by many of his teammates. Out of the money at 64-68 going into September, they went into overdrive to try to save Lefebvre's job.

Five years later, Lefebvre calls a lot of the snickering about Sosa "jealousy."

"People wanted more out of him," he said. "When he was hot, he was extremely exciting. When he was cold, he struck out a lot. Sammy was the kind of guy who'd swing at anything that was breaking up there. It wasn't that he couldn't hit a curveball; he wasn't swinging at the right kind of curveball. He was swinging at balls in the dirt, balls that were breaking below the knee."

Hill said some teammates never could comprehend the mindset of somebody as talented as Sosa.

"The perception of his energy by his teammates was misunderstood," he said. "It's because they didn't have anyone like that on their team, although there were other players in the league like that. Those players stand out.

"It was a new fire that they just didn't understand. Sammy brings a lot of energy and desire. A lot of players don't want to or can't handle that. Everyone can't be president. Sammy has the desire to be front-row, center-stage."

Years later, present-day Cubs manager Jim Riggleman was asked about the backbiting. His answer: It's human nature.

"The nature of people is generally to try to bring other people down," Riggleman said. "You know, it's a shame that we watch people become successful and then there's a certain segment of the population that wants to try to bring people down. It's a sense of raising your own self-esteem if you can bring other people down. So if there is a sore to be picked at, people will pick at that sore. In Sammy's case, he had a catchy name, he was flashy on the field."

Sosa was undeterred by the criticism. "I don't think Sammy gave a shit about the off-the-field stuff," Grace said. "He'd just come out and play his game."

Sosa finally completed his 30-30 goal with a steal of second in the sixth inning of the Cubs' 3-1 victory over the San Francisco Giants at 3Com Park on September 15, 1993. For a moment, Sosa even thought of removing the base as a souvenir.

"I was thinking about taking it," he said after the game. But it wasn't my place to do it. If I was at home it would have been different."

Lefebvre believed the feat would give Sosa "pride, responsibility and build his stature...It sets a standard not only for him for years to come, but young Cub players who will follow."

He hasn't changed his opinion today.

"Sammy really wanted to be a 30-30 guy," Lefebvre said. "That was important to them. About most superstars, there's the feeling they're just concerned about their numbers. That's what you pay them for. I want guys to reach their numbers, their goals. Sammy was determined to do that. He was still a developing player, still trying to get his feet on the ground, and wanted to do something special.

"A lot of people thought he was putting himself above the team, trying to think of his personal goals instead of team goals. It didn't bother me. I did talk to him about it. He never ran on a red light. He wanted to probably run more than we wanted. We would give him a sign to steal, and then he did."

Cubs pitcher Steve Trachsel had just been recalled from the minors for the final month in September 1993. Seeing Sosa's drive for individual goals, "I just assumed that was what his normal game was," he said.

"I did hear a couple of other players saying that they felt the 30-30 was more important to him than helping the Cubs win," Trachsel said. "I remember Ryno (Sandberg) said one day, 'If knew 30-30 was such a big deal, I would have stolen five more bases (back in 1990, when Sandberg slugged 40 homers and swiped 25 bases) to become the first Cub to do it.' He didn't think it was that big of a deal. For me, I always took the view that if it's not helping the team win, you should be doing something else."

Said the *Tribune*'s Joseph A. Reaves: "Players were pissed off at Sammy swinging at pitches in the dirt and stealing bases at what they considered selfish times. That was enough for them to be mad at him. But I don't believe any of the criticism was because he was Himes' boy."

Once he passed the 30-stolen base mark, Sosa did not stop. He tied a Cubs record by swiping four bases in a September 29, 1993 game in which the Cubs won big at Los Angeles. Angered by Sosa violating baseball etiquette by stealing with his team ahead 6-1, Dodgers pitcher Roger McDowell threw behind the Cubs' Rick Wilkins when he batted.

In hindsight, Grace said Sosa's drive for 30-30 was within the framework of team play.

"It was for the most part, legitimate," he said. "You know, it was only a couple of times that he stole bases at bad times. But it was pretty legitimate. It was a pretty legitimate 30-30."

Proud of his achievement of 33 homers and 36 steals in 1993, Sosa showed up at spring training in 1994 adorned with a necklace with the lettering "30-30" attached. He was basking in his first string of individual success, and teammates once again furrowed their brows.

"He had a little bit of that 'Look at me' syndrome, 'Look at what I'm capable of doing,'" Trachsel said. "He had the jewelry, the little crazy haircuts."

With Himes in charge, many Cubs personnel were skittish about trying to harness Sosa's talents in the manner that the likes of hitting coach Jeff Pentland did in 1997-98. But the hesitancy probably went beyond nervousness about offending any one executive.

Do you dare risk your job in any situation, working for any honcho, tinkering with five-tool talent?

In 1998, Riggleman offered up a good enough theory.

"I think from the time that he left Texas," he said, "where he signed and got the minor-league instruction, the tendency is a lot of times for people to leave these extremely talented people alone and just let them play. And if they make mistakes, the tendency is to question their mistakes but not to re-teach them."

One coach who acted fearless in the increasingly paranoid Cubs atmosphere in 1993 was the newly hired bullpen coach Tony Muser, a former White Sox first baseman. An intense and dedicated man who appreciated what the game had done for him, Muser, in 1998 the Kansas City Royals manager, was old-school, but not so much that he couldn't communicate with the modern player.

Never afraid to risk his job when he wanted to right a wrong on his team, Muser confronted Sosa before a '93 game at Mile High Stadium in Denver.

"After the first round of batting practice, players normally run the bases," he said. "They practice their leads and get their legs in shape. Sammy didn't run on this day, though.

"I put my arm around him and asked him, 'Do you have the flu?' Sammy said, 'I'm not running today. I'm on my own program.' I told him there's only one program—that of the Chicago Cubs. We started verbally going at it by the batting cage and people started to notice. Sammy walked away in disgust and sat in the dugout.

"For three days we didn't talk to each other. It was like a husband and wife fighting. Then Sammy came up to me in the outfield before a game and said he was sorry. I told him I was sorry, too. I believe some trust came out of it. Confrontation can be healthy if there's respect implemented from that."

Muser told Sosa he would always meet him half way. Five years later, after Muser became Royals manager, Sosa came up to him when the Cubs came through Kansas City to remind him of that halfway vow.

With that philosophy, Muser was able to approach Sosa on his stolen-base techniques. The coach noticed that teams were pitching out on Sosa because he always ran on the first or second pitch.

"I advised him to shut it down early in the count," Muser

said. "Sammy ran again early and was thrown out. I think he learned from that situation."

Muser kept his head about him as 1994 dawned. He was in a minority in the Cubs organization. The other shoe had dropped when Himes, citing the fact Lefebvre had failed to produce a running team, among other foibles, cashiered the manager two days after the end of the 1993 season. The Cubs had gone 20-10 since September—a rare season-ending surge among all the collapses in franchise history—and finished 84-78. That was only the third time the Cubs had finished above .500 since 1972. But to no avail—Lefebvre was given the gate.

"He didn't deserve to be fired," Grace said.

Muser and fellow coach Tom Trebelhorn competed for the managerial opening, each being administered psychological tests, certainly an unusual part of the interview process for a big-league manager. Trebelhorn, a former Milwaukee Brewers manager, won out. But the feeling quickly grew that neither he nor Himes were long-term employees.

Over the winter of 1993-94, Himes was told by Tribune Co. to cut his player payroll. He dumped left-handed pitchers like Greg Hibbard—the leading winner in 1993 with 15 victories—and Chuck McElroy, both of whom were making mid-range salaries. Also being shown the door were pitchers Mike Harkey, Bob Scanlan and Dwight Smith, who, despite his shaky fielding, had carved out a niche as a pinch-hitter and part-timer player.

Himes himself feared for his job security at the time. His contract ran out after the 1994 season, and no extension was forthcoming from Tribune Co. But he dutifully followed orders, cut the payroll, and set up disaster for 1994.

Sosa and Grace, normally rocks of stability in the lineup, slumped as the Cubs started out 6-15 in 1994. After enjoying a good spring in Arizona, Sosa hit just .225 in April. That contributed to a record 12-game Wrigley Field losing streak. But mere numbers could not truly describe the mondo bizzaro atmosphere.

In an effort to mollify the increasingly restive fans, the intellectually bent Trebelhorn held an infamous "firehouse chat" with the loyalists at Chicago Fire Dept. Engine Co. No. 78, just beyond the left-field wall, after the April 29, 6-5 loss to the Colorado Rockies. The fans pressed forward and mobbed him. "When are you going to win?" he was asked. "Tomorrow," he bellowed back. "Now go get yourself a beer."

When things calmed down, Trebelhorn said he hurt more than the fans. "But all their frustration don't equal the frustration I feel," he said. "I'm trying to look beyond the frustration of the record and look for a game to be played perfectly to get us going again."

Trebelhorn finally got that game five days later, on May 4 at Wrigley Field—with the help of a four-legged friend. Two talk-show hosts from Chicago's WMAQ-Radio had obtained a billy goat from some Wisconsin pre-ministry students to lift a 1945-vintage hex off the team. Billy Goat Tavern owner Sam Sianis was in tow with the goat. His uncle, William, had supposedly put an everlasting hex on the Cubs when the team refused to admit his mascot goat to the 1945 World Series despite the elder Sianis possessing a ticket for the beast. The goat and entourage were still refused admittance to the ballpark until Ernie Banks, "Mr. Cub," agreed to use his pull to gain admittance. The goat paraded from right to left field along the warning track, then walked amid a battery of cameras toward home plate, angering Steve Trachsel as he warmed up.

"It was a distraction," Trachsel said. "The goat was kind of in my way. If they believe that's the way it is, they should have him sit in the front row."

Hex lifted, at least for a day. Trebelhorn tried for instant offense by placing Sosa in the leadoff slot and center field. Sosa homered off the Cincinnati Reds' Tom Browning to help spark a 5-2 win, with Trachsel recovering from the goat's visit to throw a four-hitter over seven innings.

Sosa would go on to enjoy his first of a number of hot months in the majors in the seasons preceding 1998. He had 11 homers and 23 RBI for May, 1994, hitting .317. He would not hit below .300 in any succeeding month, batting .339 in his final 53 contests and finishing the strike-shortened season on August 10 at an even .300. Sosa also had 25 homers and 70 RBI, winning the Cubs' Triple Crown.

But whatever positive momentum he had established in his career was buried by the Cubs' lousy season (49-64), the oncoming strike, and continued clubhouse dissension. Derrick May had a verbal tussle with Trebelhorn, while Willie Wilson stalked out of the clubhouse after being put on waivers while a radio reporter hollered "good riddance" as Wilson went through the door.

Ryne Sandberg pulled off the shocker of the year by retiring on June 12, his wife Cindy at his side, adorned in a short corncob pattern sundress that brought snickers from the media mob in the Wrigley Field Stadium Club. The Sandbergs' marriage had been the subject of rumors for years, but on this day the future Hall of Famer publicly said he had just lost his desire to play at the top of his game, inferring there was anger at the atmosphere that Himes created. A week later, out of the public eye, Cindy Sandberg filed for divorce in Phoenix. Her husband had quit the game apparently to help maintain split custody of his two children, an arrangement that would not have been possible if he was still a traveling ballplayer.

To this day, Himes is angry that Sandberg used him as a scapegoat when personal problems were the real motivation behind his retirement. He also has enmity toward Grace; the feeling is mutual. Grace has minced no words in talking about Himes, even calling him "Satan" at one point.

Grace has put the '94 season under his bad-memories file.

"It was really a farce," Grace said. "We were a bad team with a bad general manager and a manager, Tom Trebelhorn, a really nice guy, but I just don't think the right man for the job here.

"It was just a weird year. It was absolutely no fun at all to come to the ballpark. And then there was the strike. It was an awful year for the Cubs and baseball. Whether Sammy did well or not, or whether I did well or not, or whether anybody did well or not, it was just no fun."

But until the lords of baseball—management and union—decided to call off the '94 season, Sosa continued to do what he does best—play baseball, and stay out of the game's politics.

"That does not affect how Sammy plays," Glenallen Hill said of negative events away from the field. "Sammy gives 110 percent no matter what the situation is. At that particular time, there was a power struggle, within the team and in baseball. There was a lot of stress. But he got through it."

By the time the severely wounded game of baseball resumed in late April 1995, Sosa would have a new team corporate overseer, team president, general manager, manager, and half a supporting cast. The seeds for his greater days were being planted. But he would still have a lot to overcome before the whole world knew about him.

6

Two Steps Forward, One Step Back

When a friendly New York judge did something legions of negotiators and Bill Clinton could not do—end the disastrous strike of the winter of 1994-95—Sammy Sosa and his teammates arrived at their delayed spring training at HoHo Kam Park in Mesa, Arizona, to see a whole bunch of new faces on and off the field.

Cubs officials ensured the Chicago media would have a series of free lunches with frequent press conferences at the Wrigley Field Stadium Club starting September 9, 1994, one month into the strike. Golden-boy appointee Andy MacPhail was unveiled as the new team president—a position that had been unfilled since 1991.

Earlier in 1994, Tribune Co. bigwig Jim Dowdle, most noted for hiring Harry Caray back in 1981, was put in charge of cleaning up the mess at the Friendly Confines. Expectations rose because Dowdle wasn't from the bean-counter part of the mega-company; he had built up the TV operations from a nice little signal passively picked up via satellite to a vigorous superstation coupled with an active production arm that churned out syndicated shows like *Geraldo Rivera*.The hope among frustrated fans and media was that Dowdle would unlock the considerable Tribune Co. treasury that had been bolted shut for 1994 and only sporadically had been opened since Dallas Green was fired in 1987. "Please, oh great corporate pooh-bahs, spend money you already have to make money." A higher payroll of talented veterans would earn its money back through the sale of otherwise empty seats in April, May and September and higher WGN-TV and radio broadcast revenues.

"A team in Chicago, just like New York and Los Angeles, should always be in contention because of the size of the town and the money that's available there," former Cubs star Andre Dawson said, speaking for the masses.

Unfortunately, no Bleacher Bum or product of Ladies Day in the grandstand had ever risen to power in Tribune Co. or the top of the Cubs' front office. Thus, the emotional push to take radical action to enable the Cubs to win was not emanating from the 24th floor of Tribune Tower. A further twist came in 1998, when the *Chicago Sun-Times* found that a number of Cubs executives grew up as White Sox fans in the Chicago area.

Dowdle did not look far to find his hand-picked choice to run the Cubs' day-to-day operations. MacPhail already had two World Series teams under his belt in 1987 and 1991 as Minnesota Twins general manager, although the talent nucleus led by Kirby Puckett had been in the organization prior to MacPhail's arrival.

If you talked about respect in the game, MacPhail possessed it in droves, ranking as a third-generation baseball executive. His father, Lee MacPhail, inducted into the Hall of Fame in 1998, had run the New York Yankees and Baltimore Orioles before being named American League president. His grandfather, Larry MacPhail, a mercurial type who liked his liquid refreshments, was an innovator in the 1930s, introducing night baseball to the majors in Cincinnati and later to Brooklyn, bringing a pennant to Ebbets Field in 1941 after a long dry spell, and later co-owning the New York Yankees.

Andy MacPhail was far more like his father than grandfather in temperament. He was low-key and thoughtful, purposely taking the straight-and-narrow approach in his management style to distance himself from the wild fluctuations of his grandfather. "Slow, steady and unspectacular" became his byword for the way in which he and his management team would improve the Cubs. Unfortunately, MacPhail also had grown up on the East Coast, far out of emotional range of the decades of woes at Wrigley Field. He experienced only a relative touch of Cubdom starting out his management career in the Chicago front office in the mid-1970s. Several seasons and torrents of criticism would pass before MacPhail would move off his snail's pace plan to improve the Cubs.

Rather than also appointing himself general manager to replace the reassigned Larry Himes, MacPhail opted to stay in the background and hired a neophyte general manager, Ed Lynch, only 37 and with just four years' front-office experience with the San Diego Padres and his old team, the New York Mets. Conventional wisdom had MacPhail calling the shots while Lynch was trained in the often-thankless GM's tasks, and after four years no one has ever been sure just where MacPhail's hands-on authority ends and Lynch's latitude begins. The feeling was that in his early 40s, MacPhail wasn't about to retire from the backstage wheeling-and-dealing of players.

But, early on, Lynch was given the power to hire his own manager and front-office staff. He lured away Jim Riggleman from the talent-stripped Padres. Riggleman had a job offer to manage the Pods in 1995, but was leery about his job security due to a pending ownership change. Despite the uneven talent level and newly-reborn losing tradition at Wrigley Field, Riggleman jumped to take the job.

Trying to get adjusted to the Cubs' unusual tradition, MacPhail and Lynch tried to break a cycle that had doomed the franchise to disasters like 1994.

"It was probably brought on by not winning for so many years," Lynch said. "A new general manager would come in, feel the pressure to win now, take whatever prospects he had at the upper (minor-league) levels, tried to move them for players to win right away, and those players you bring in don't work out.

"You lose the players you bring in, and the prospects you traded. The cycle starts all over again. We wanted to have to have patience with some of our young players—patience enough to understand it was foolhardy to go out and try to win everything when you're not even in a position to compete."

That is the position MacPhail and Lynch decided the Cubs were in during the spring of 1995. But the honchos were caught in a bind. The Cubs' farm system had sharply declined in the early 1990s from its productive peak prompted by Dallas Green's appointees in the 1980s. They couldn't strip the team down and stock it with kids, a la the 1998 Florida Marlins.

Lynch and MacPhail opted to try to make the Cubs respectable and competitive. But the often-halfway measures they would take over the next few seasons would keep the team spinning its wheels around .500, frustrate and anger fans, cause more dissension by players, and put more pressure than necessary on Sosa as the team's only consistent power source until the 1998 season.

Lynch made some good moves off the bat as 1995 spring training began. He snared a fiery center fielder in Brian McRae for a wobbly minor-league pitching prospect. And he signed a bargain-basement free-agent pitcher, Jaime Navarro, who had worn out his welcome with the Milwaukee Brewers. Navarro, always leaning toward extra weight, had dieted and was hungry for a starting job instead. He pitched his way into the rotation before the Cubs broke camp.

But Lynch made another couple of moves that would backfire and cause problems for Sosa and the Cubs for several years. Trimming the payroll of some mid-range salaries as Himes had done more than a year previously, he let outfielders Glenallen Hill and Derrick May go. A Sosa friend who really enjoyed playing in Wrigley Field, Hill had batted .297 in 1994 with 10 homers. Combined with the 10 homers he amassed with his first month with the Cubs in September, 1993, the strongman left fielder had enjoyed a successful run in Chicago and was decent lineup protection for Sosa. Quickly hunting for work, Hill hooked on with the San Francisco Giants.

"What happened?" he asked me as I saw him in the Giants' clubhouse in Phoenix that spring. Hill hugged me—the first and last time a major-leaguer had ever greeted me in that manner. I had no explanation other than salary-cutting. If management had believed some reports that Hill was a clubhouse disruption in 1994, they were way off-base. Lynch and MacPhail now opted to go with a platoon of rookies in left field—the home-grown Ozzie Timmons and speedy Scott Bullett, a Himes' acquisition from the Pirates organization.

The promise of power in left field was shaky. McRae believed anything more than 10 homers was gravy. Mark Grace,

Shawon Dunston and Steve Buechele were mid double-digit home-run threats, at best, in the infield. Ray Sanchez, who had taken over for Sandberg at second, sometimes had trouble hitting the ball out of the infield. And catcher Rick Wilkins, fighting a sore back, had dropped off severely from his surprise 30-homer season in 1993.

That left Sosa as the sole 20-homer-plus power man in the Cubs' lineup, an unwelcome tag he would possess for three seasons. Management was taking a strange path to improve a team that had gone an historic-worst 20-39 at home in 1994 at Wrigley Field and was often out-homered by visiting teams.

At least the management continued to show patience with Sosa, even though he was prematurely placed in the role as franchise player and may not have been ready at this point for cleanup-hitter duties. The Sosa of 1995 would have made a dandy No. 5 hitter, but he was going to be thrown to the sharks to sink or swim without a life preserver. There was going to be no "slow, steady and unspectacular" process by which Sosa could grow into the role as the big tuna of the Cubs.

Lynch remembered the earlier scouting analyses of Sosa.

"What we saw was a young player who was rushed to the major leagues, and was just in the process of learning to play the game," he said. "He had started playing at an older age (14 in the Dominican Republic). He never really picked up a bat until he was a teenager. He really was forced to learn the intricacies of major-league baseball at the major-league level instead of in the minor leagues.

"We saw a guy who had 30-homer and 100-RBI potential, a 'plus' runner with a 'plus' arm, who was like a bull in a china shop. With refinement and maturity, he'd really become a good player."

Riggleman was eager to manage a physical specimen of Sosa's build, remembering his raw talent as an opposing manager in San Diego.

"You know, it's pretty obvious the things that you saw back then as the opposing manager," he said. "Those were things that worried you when you played him because he could beat you in a lot of ways. He could run the ball down pretty good in the outfield. He could throw you out. When you came in to play him, he's right in the middle of the lineup and you knew that he was gonna be one of the threats here at Wrigley Field you had to deal with."

Riggleman also had noted that coaches were hesitant to deal with Sosa because of his raw ability. Sosa himself brought up the subject early in the 1995 campaign.

"One of the things I sense after being around Sammy for a few weeks was that at sometime or another—it came up in conversation with him—that he knew that some people did not instruct him because there was a little bit of fear of him. He was a physically imposing person."

Huh? Sosa's got blacksmith's arms, but he's barely 6 feet tall.

"Yeah, but he's a very strong guy and he had quickly gotten pretty good money as soon as his first three years in the big leagues were up," Riggleman said. "He's quickly establishing himself as a potential all-star, superstar guy. So, what he had mentioned to me one time, and I saw examples of this where he felt that people would talk about him, about his game, he should have done this, why doesn't he do this, he needs to do this differently—but nobody would ever say it to him. Coaches, instructors, teammates, this type of thing.

"People just didn't want to instruct him because they felt he's a tremendously talented guy and I think that the feeling was that he may take it wrong."

Sosa told Riggleman to call him in at any time if his game went awry.

"He came to me one time and said, 'Hey, anything you want me to do, just tell me. Just talk to me man to man,'" the manager said.

The new manager's dictum for Sosa in spring training 1995 was "refinement of some of the little things—baserunning and throwing—and (for Sosa to) get credit as a good defensive player. I told Sammy he was a 'five-tool player' (hitting, hitting for power, running, throwing and fielding)."

Sosa himself did not like the superstar projection. As a preview of his self-effacing style of the home-run chase of 1998, he waved that rating away.

"I don't like the term 'superstar,'" Sosa said as 1995 got underway. "It can happen. But I don't want to say it (about himself). Let other people say it."

Sosa's '95 start mirrored that of his team. By the end of May in the strike-shortened campaign, he had 41 hits, including 10 homers, in 130 at-bats. And without a lot of talent, the team began 20-11 before enduring a series of ups and downs just below and above the .500 mark that would last the rest of the season. Jim Riggleman received some surprisingly good starting pitching from Jaime Navarro, Frank Castillo and unheralded Jim Bullinger, who got off to a 10-2 start.

But the hitting sagged, and the left-field platoon wasn't working out, as many could have figured. The aging Steve Buechele did not get untracked at third base. So on June 16, 1995, Lynch traded Mike Morgan, by then an excess starting pitcher, to the St. Louis Cardinals for third baseman Todd Zeile. Twelve days later, Lynch dispatched Rick Wilkins to the Houston Astros for outfielder Luis Gonzalez and catcher Scott Servais. Gonzalez had been a certified Cubs Killer with 10 homers and a .351 lifetime average against Chicago.

Gonzalez and Servais performed well as complementary players in the second half of 1995. Zeile, bothered by a bad thumb, turned out to be a bust as a Cub.

Sosa was headed for his first All-Star berth. A brief rumor cropped up about a possible trade to the Baltimore Orioles, but that was quickly refuted. And when Sosa slumped during one mid-season spell, Riggleman took him and infielder Jose Hernandez aside for some one-on-one talks and a refresher course in basic fundamentals. Coaches Tony Muser and Max Oliveras also were present for reinforcement.

"What we did," Riggleman said, "was I talked to Sammy and I said, 'Look, you should be recognized around baseball as a superstar, all-star, potential superstar, one of the elite players in the game. That's the way you should be recognized in the game among the people we play against, opposing managers and everybody. The thing that people want to focus on with you is that the one or two times that you missed the cutoff man or that you throw to the wrong base or you get thrown out stealing.'"

Muser, in 1998 the Kansas City Royals manager, recalls encouraging Sosa to go more to right field and center field, to "slow himself down a little, sacrifice something, to execute finer points of the game instead of relying on brute strength and power."

By now, Sosa's perceived flaws were being magnified by a few critical sportswriters and shoot-first, ask-questions-later sports-talk show hosts. To read and listen to the accounts, he was a wild man, swinging at everything, throwing the ball eight rows into the box seats (that did happen once in 1995) while missing the cutoff man, and running recklessly on the bases until he made an out.

Riggleman heard all of the knocks against Sosa.

"Here's this tremendously talented guy but a lot of things were said that were not true," he said. "Such as, he misses the cutoff man. I don't know how many times I heard that. From the time I got here I never saw him miss the cutoff man. Throws to the wrong base. Or he runs with his head down. Doesn't know where the ball is. This type of thing.

"These things were said but they very rarely actually happened. That is the nature of being the central star of the club. People are going to, if you do make a mistake they are going to highlight it more, and have a tendency to try to bring you down."

Ed Lynch also was irritated by the media emphasis on Sosa's foibles.

"Here's a guy who would throw out eight consecutive runners coming from second and trying to score," he said. "Then maybe he'd slip in the outfield and throw the ball eight rows back in Wrigley Field, and you'd see that over and over again on SportsCenter and all the shows."

Still, his teammates desired to see more consistency in the outfield.

"There were times when Brian McRae and I would just say he's gotta get better out there if we're gonna succeed," Mark Grace said.

Sosa could settle down with Riggleman's low-key support. The mid-season talking-to apparently had some immediate results. Sosa suddenly broke out into his hottest streak to date in the majors as August got under way.

As the Cubs struggled to stay in the National League wild-card race, Sosa began pumping out homers at an unprecedented rate in modern Cubs history. He had seven homers in seven games from August 17 to 24, and a total of 13 homers and 30 RBI in an 18-game stretch through September 4. Sosa's total of 10 homers in 13 games from August 17 to 30 represented the fastest power pace by any Cub since Hack Wilson in 1928—and a feat not surpassed until Sosa himself did it in June, 1998. Although several homers came late in blowout Cubs victories at Coors Field, the majority were belted at crucial junctures of tight games. Sosa had a pair of two-homer performances in victories over the Braves, 7-5 at Wrigley Field on August 28 in Chicago and 6-4 on September 2 in Atlanta.

"I just want to win, especially since we have a chance for the playoffs," Sosa said after the latter game. "The numbers will take care of themselves."

But he could never do enough. One teammate took note of Sosa popping up with runners on first and third and one out in the first inning of a 2-0 loss to the Braves in Atlanta on September 3. "Sammy's not a clutch hitter," he said, requesting anonymity.

The player was wrong, at least when most clutch-hitting numbers for 1995 were considered. STATS, Inc., one of the two top statistical services used by Major League Baseball, reported that Sosa hit .341 with runners in scoring position that season with 14 homers and 84 RBI. With runners in scoring position and two out, he hit .338 with 7 homers and 34 RBI. The only category in which he failed was with the bases loaded. Sosa was just 1 for 7 with two RBI. The psychological burdens of his repeated blankings with the bags drunk would not be lifted until mid-season 1998.

Sosa's power pace slowed considerably as September, 1995 continued. His two-run homer on September 4 against the Rockies at Wrigley Field was his 33rd of the season, good for his 101st RBI. But he would belt only three more homers while driving in just 18 more runs the rest of the season.

Oddly enough, the Cubs staged a last-ditch drive for the wild-card berth in the season's final week without much help from Sosa. After winning three in a row against the Pittsburgh Pirates, pitcher Frank Castillo came within one strike of a no-hitter against the St. Louis Cardinals at Wrigley Field on September 25. Bernard Gilkey spoiled the gem by tripling just out of reach of Sosa in right center with two outs in the ninth.

The Cubs would go on to win their next four games, two in dramatic fashion against the Houston Astros at home, to get within a game of the wild-card lead. But the Astros won the final two games of the season to knock the Cubs out of playoff contention, a little bit too late with the Rockies ending up as the wild-card team in only their third year of existence.

Sosa ended up with his second "30-30" Cubs season, finishing with 36 homers and 34 stolen bases. More importantly, his 119 RBI was an impressive total in just 144 games of the truncated season. Through 1995, that was the third-highest RBI total by a Cub since Hall of Famer Billy Williams drove in 129 in 1970. Andre Dawson had knocked in 137 in 1987 in winning the National League's Most Valuable Player Award. Williams batted in 122 in 1972, when he captured the batting title with .333.

Working the numbers even more, Sosa's RBI count was the fifth highest since Ernie Banks drove in 143 in 1959 (factoring in Ron Santo's 123 in 1969). Nobody amasses that high of an RBI total in 144 games without coming through when it counted sometimes.

Second-leading home-run producer on the '95 Cubs? Mark Grace, with 16. Shawon Dunston had 14.

Not deemed a serious issue at that point was Sosa's strikeout total of 134. That was the most since Byron Browne fanned a team-record 143 times in 1966. Sosa would soon hold the team record, yet that, too, would not be his distinguishing mark.

After the 1995 season, Sosa drew praise from Dawson, by then finishing his career with the Florida Marlins. He projected a better future given more maturity on Sosa's part.

"He still has some things to learn out there," The Hawk said. "You have to avoid prolonged slumps and bad habits. In Montreal, I used to try to carry the load and do too many things. Doing it is one thing, but going beyond that is another, so you run into a brick wall."

A frequent Gold Glove outfielder, Dawson put himself into Sosa's shoes in right field in the Friendly Confines.

"Sure, he overthrows," he said. "You have to learn to control that. I never liked throwing the ball all the way on the fly because of the chance of an overthrow. I threw to either hit the cutoff man at head-level or one-hop the ball to the catcher. I feel I worked that to perfection.

"Wrigley Field isn't the easiest right field to play in the league. It all boils down to confidence. Once Sammy gets settled down there, he'll have a tendency to relax a little more."

The critics barked that Sosa was not a winning player. Dawson took issue with that view.

"I disagree with the assumption that they can't win with Sammy, when he showed he can carry a team all by himself," he said. "I remember that two-week span (in August 1995) when he was phenomenal."

Sosa would have to do more carrying of the Cubs by himself in 1996. MacPhail and Lynch decided to go with a pat hand of a 73-71 team in the off-season. The payroll did not increase.

Biggest news was the return of Ryne Sandberg, announced on Halloween eve in 1995. Sandberg had re-married two months previously and was a recharged fellow; his new wife, Margaret, was a tremendously outgoing type who often acted as a spokesman for her quiet husband. Whether management really desired Sandberg's return will never be known.

But the team's hand was somewhat forced by Ryno's icon status in Cubs history. At the same time, an attractive free-agent named Craig Biggio briefly became available. Although Biggio was loyal to his Houston Astros, all bets would have been off if the Cubs had swooped in with a megabucks offer to the leadoff man who combined speed and power. Then and now, Tribune Co. could far outspend Astros owner Drayton MacLane despite the latter's activist bent toward his franchise. Biggio said at the end of the 1995 season that he liked playing in Wrigley Field. He also shared an agent with Mark Grace—Barry Axelrod, who always has had a good rapport with the Cubs.

Shortstop Shawon Dunston was let go during the off-season of 1995-96. No significant pickups to the lineup were made. Lynch plucked singles-hitting Dave Magadan off the castoff club to play third base. When he got hurt, another waiver-type, Leo Gomez, took over the starting job and helped for awhile. With the departure of stopper Randy Myers, who had shown wear and tear in the second half of 1995, the Cubs could only come up with slowballer Doug Jones as a replacement in the bullpen.

Just as significant as the lack of important additions to the lineup and bullpen was the decision to keep the same starting rotation intact. MacPhail, Lynch and Riggleman thought they had a good starting five with Jaime Navarro, Frank Castillo, Steve Trachsel, Kevin Foster and Jim Bullinger. A gifted free-agent pitcher, Kevin Brown, had come onto the market in the off-season of 1995-96 after a down year with the Baltimore Orioles. Throwing the hardest sinker in baseball with master control, Brown would have been perfect for Wrigley Field. A season later, MacPhail said that "in retrospect," the Cubs should have pursued Brown. But they didn't, and they would suffer as a result in 1996.

Perhaps Sosa was mentally ready for another leap forward in spite of the Cubs' failings. A lot of the sideshow flashiness, such as his trademark jewelry, was disappearing at this point. He was 27, a family man, established as a middle-of-the-lineup regular with five years on the job with the same team.

"I think as you get older you realize you don't need the necklace," Riggleman said. "The thing that I've tried to say to players through the years is let your style of play be your signature on the game. Not how many different ways you can wear your uniform. How much jewelry you can wear during the game. How flashy the pair of shoes you have on in the game. How many sweatbands you can wear. Or how many gloves out of the back pockets. There are actually players who are meticulous about the way they have gloves hanging out of their back pockets.

"It has nothing to add to the game except a visual difference from everybody else. There is a particular player that I managed at one point. I told him, 'You may as well have a neon sign on your forehead that says, Please notice me. Because every day you're doing something different, you're wearing something different, you're taking the field at a different time than everybody else.'"

Riggleman feels fortunate he never had to engage in such a conversation with Sosa.

"Somewhere along the line Sammy recognized that. On the (team) flights he dresses conservatively and stylishly. He's somebody that people would look at and it was like watching Johnny Carson when he was on. You kind of look at what he was wearing. He's a conservatively stylish dresser."

The more middle-of-the-road Sosa entered 1996 with 15-homer man Luis Gonzalez as his lineup protection in the No. 5 slot. Sosa started off relatively slowly. But he would soon give a sneak preview of his 1998 pace as he smashed out of an 0-for-18 slump against the New York Mets May 3, 1996 at Wrigley Field.

Much-ballyhooed Mets lefty Paul Wilson cruised into the ninth leading the Cubs 2-1 on two hits, both good for the only run in the first. The tying run had reached second base with two outs in the ninth and Mark Grace up. Dallas Green, in his latest incarnation as Mets manager, ordered Grace walked intentionally in order to face Sosa, who had fanned three times previously in the game.

"There's certainly nothing to question.There were a lot of reasons to do what he did," Riggleman said of the strategy after the game.

Maybe the right strategy, but it is the wrong result when Sosa's getting untracked. He blasted Wilson's first pitch, a slider, into the left-field bleachers for a three-run, game-winning homer, allowing Harry Caray a classic "Holy Cow" broadcast call.

"I was just trying to be ready for a strike," Sosa said after the game. "They know Grace is a better hitter than I am now, the way I've been struggling."

Sosa received some inspiration from familiar faces.

"My family is all here again now and I feel more happy," he said. "My family, my brothers, everyone. I can't live without them."

He then fulfilled a vow for much of the rest of the year.

"I'm not saying I'll be 20-for-20 now, but I'll be different tomorrow and the next day now because I'm comfortable," Sosa said.

Sure enough, two days later on May 5, 1996, Sosa provided more thrills for Caray and Cubs fans—and extra work for window contractors.

With nobody out in a 4-4 tie in the ninth inning, Sosa smashed a game-winning homer against Mets reliever Jerry DiPoto. The bomb broke a second-story window on the fly in the apartment building on the southwest corner of Waveland and Sheffield avenues. Two years later, fans would hang out of this building's second-story windows with fishnets trying to get some of Sosa's historic homers. But on this day, people just plain gawked.

"The Happy Homewrecker" headlined the next day's *Chicago Sun-Times*. "Sammy's got what we call stupid power. It's just so much power, it's stupid," Grace said after the game.

"There are only a few guys with power like that—Gary Sheffield, Mike Piazza, Barry Bonds and Sammy. People were saying Sammy should have a day off (when he was struggling), but you never know when he'll have a day like today."

Sports trivia expert Eddie Gold claimed the blast was among the four longest in Wrigley Field history. A No. 5 could have been added on June 20, 1998, when Sosa hit an ICBM atop the roof of the two-story building at 1038 W. Waveland, the first structure west of the apartment building he assaulted against DiPoto. But no one could look into the future, and they simply enjoyed the awe of the moment.

Gold cited Dave Kingman's April 14, 1976 bomb that hit the porch of the fourth house down the street from Waveland on the east side of Kenmore Avenue. An "X" had been placed on the sidewalk in front of the house for several years afterward.

Then there was the bomb hit by Roberto Clemente, Sosa's idol, in the ninth inning of the second game of a doubleheader on May 17, 1959. The missile left the ballpark to the left of the Wrigley Field scoreboard, landing in a gas station across the street.

And Gold's favorite old-time Cub, Bill "Swish" Nicholson, departed the premises to the right of the scoreboard on April 24, 1948, ricocheting off a building and hitting the hood of a northbound-car on Sheffield Avenue.

Obviously, Sosa was in a good mood after the game. He joked when asked if he or the Cubs would pay for the broken window. The team, of course, would end up picking up the tab.

"I didn't think I hit it that hard," Sosa said. "I've just trying to look for base hits, just making good contact."

Almost forgotten amid the talk of all-time tape-measure jobs was another Sosa homer, a two-run blast, in the first inning off Mets starter Pete Harnisch. And in the fourth, he threw out Jeff Kent trying to score on Rey Ordonez's single—his fifth outfield assist of the '96 season up to this point.

Sosa would amass more memorable power feats in his merry month of May 1996. On May 16, he became the first Cub in history to homer twice in one inning in a 13-1 victory over the Houston Astros at Wrigley Field. In an eight-run seventh, he led off with a blast against Jeff Tabaka, and then later tagged Jim Dougherty with a two-run shot.

"Everyone knows when I struggle I swing at everything," Sosa said after the game. "When I'm comfortable, I swing at my pitch."

Oddly enough, Sosa had to play second fiddle in this game to fellow Dominican Amaury Telemaco. Considered the Cubs' best starting pitching prospect in 1995-96, Telemaco had just been recalled to make his first big-league start in this game. He pitched 5 2/3 no-hit innings, eventually settling for a one-hitter over seven innings. All the lead stories focused on the rookie, who would start off well, slump later in '96 and never again flash his early promise before being let go by the Cubs to the Arizona Diamondbacks early in the 1998 season.

Sosa completed a 10-homer May, but the Cubs dipped despite his long-ball prowess. They fell to 21-31 at the end of the month and spent much of the next two months struggling to get back to the .500 mark. The Cubs fell to last in the league in hitting.

But while other Cubs sagged, Sosa picked up his own pace. On June 5, he amassed his first three-homer game at the pro baseball level, drawing a shower of head adornments in honor of the "hat trick" of power at Wrigley Field in a 9-6 victory over the Philadelphia Phillies.

"(Luis) Gonzalez had to explain to me what was happening, about hockey and everything," Sosa said after the game.

Sosa homered in the fourth and sixth against Terry Mulholland, and then completed the hat trick in the seventh against Toby Borland, against whom he would blast the rooftop homer across Waveland two years later.

Mulholland recalls the situation.

"I made the mistake of trying to throw a fastball down and away, and I left it up over the plate," the left-hander said of the first homer. "He was covering the plate rather well by that point in his career."

The trio of long balls gave Sosa 20 homers at the early juncture of the season. So what was to come in 1998 was actually starting to develop two years earlier. He'd finish June with a total of 26 homers for the season, and looked forward to his second straight All-Star appearance. He also was making more consistent contact than at any point of his career with a pair of 10-game hitting streaks between June 11 and July 3.

But Braves manager Bobby Cox, the National League All-Star manager, inexplicably left Sosa off the roster of backup players. To be sure, the NL was always loaded with good outfielders, too many to accommodate each year in the Midsummer Classic. Yet the Sosa snub was glaring, and it seemed to fire the right fielder up even more in July, as if to prove Cox was wrong.

For the month, Sosa batted .358 in 26 games with 10 homers, 29 RBI and 22 runs scored. Included was his third 10-game hitting streak of the 1996 season. His week of July 22 to 28 alone, in which he batted 12-for-30 with four doubles, four homers, 10 RBI and nine runs scored, earned him National League Player of the Week honors. A few days later, with his month completed, the league honored him with its Player of the Month award, the first Cub to be so honored since Andre Dawson in May, 1990.

Even more important, Sosa began adopting the style that would serve him so well two years later. He began slugging a decent portion of his homers to right field, slowly evolving away from his pull-or-bust style.

But even amid the positives, the clubhouse grumbling of 1992-94 had returned. The Cubs needed help both in the lineup and on the mound. Steve Trachsel had earned an All-Star berth with a cool 2.00 ERA at mid-season, lowest by a Cubs starter at that point of the season since Dick Ellsworth in 1963. Jaime Navarro was having another solid season. But Kevin Foster had slumped and had been demoted to the minors, while Frank Castillo and Jim Bullinger experienced sharp dropoffs from their 1995 performances. Ryne Sandberg had revived his power game somewhat, but nobody in the lineup could win a game consistently with home runs other than Sosa.

Always candid and outspoken, Brian McRae began to question why MacPhail and Lynch were slow on the trigger to make a trade to improve the club. The dissent spread to Mark Grace, by now a close friend of McRae, and then all corners of the locker room. Hearing of the nay-saying, I quickly called Arlene Gill, the personable and efficient assistant to MacPhail and Lynch, asking to talk to the two honchos ASAP. A few minutes later, I was admitted to MacPhail's office, where he was discussing minor-league callups or something similar with Lynch. I told him of the clubhouse unrest. Their answer was of mild concern, something to their effect of "We're upset that they're upset."

Sosa, though, was not one of the second-guessers. The only private comment he made to me during this period was about his lack of protection in the lineup. "I need some help. I can't do it all by myself," he said, then zipped his lips publicly.

Management's view of McRae especially began to sour with his acting of First Amendment rights. But Sosa earned admiration for airing his concerns in private with Riggleman and other management members.

"He never made any statements toward the organization," Riggleman said. "Whereas other players have publicly come out and said—'You know, why didn't we get so-and-so player? We should get this guy. Why didn't we sign this guy? We should have traded for this player. You know, so-and-so wants to play here. Why didn't we get him?'

"Those things, criticizing management, he never did that. He would come to you personally, whether it was Ed Lynch or to me and say, 'I think we should do this.' And it would go no further than that. It wouldn't be to the writers or whatever. He would express himself man-to-man instead of saying something anonymously to the writers and not having guts enough to put your name by it. He would say it to the man.

"Quite often, it would be something we were trying to do anyway or already had explored, and it was not possible. And that's what we would tell him. We'd say, 'Yeah, we wanted to do that, but we couldn't do it because of this.' And he would say, 'Great, I understand that.' "

Sosa couldn't have known that the Cubs were willing to make a huge sacrifice in mid-summer in an attempt to snare crafty left-hander Denny Neagle from the Pittsburgh Pirates. Unknown to any scoopster in the media at the time, Lynch was willing to sacrifice top young relief pitcher Terry Adams along with minor-league right hander Steve Rain for Neagle. In 1996, Adams was considered the closer of the future, in the middle of a fine rookie season in which he sported a 2.94 ERA and 78 strikeouts in 101 innings.

But the Pirates instead chose young right-hander Jason Schmidt of the Atlanta Braves in a deal. The Buccos liked Adams, but front-office assistant Pete Vuckovich liked Schmidt even better. So even though the Cubs offered up a sumptuous package in the Neagle affair, their failure looked like more inaction and paralysis. MacPhail caused only additional frustration by repeatedly vowing that the Cubs would spend money at mid-season on veteran players cast loose by non-contenders. When such moves were not made, it only intensified the feeling that Tribune Co. only cared about making modest profits from a full Wrigley Field in June, July and August, and cared not about spending money to make even more money.

Sosa cooled a little bit in August, hitting only four homers in the first three weeks. Still, the team hung in contention in the National League Central simply because the pace-setting St. Louis Cardinals could not pull away from the pack. On August 18, after the Cubs beat the Houston Astros two consecutive days at Wrigley Field in some rare high-scoring games for them, they were 61-61, but just five games behind the Redbirds.

Two days later, after a 4-3 loss to the Florida Marlins at home, Sosa batted in the first inning against Marlins right hander

Mark Hutton with the bases loaded. Hutton hit him with a pitch on his right hand, and Sosa collected his 100th RBI of the season on the play. He stayed in the game the next two innings, then left due to increasing pain.

Sosa couldn't sleep that night, and had X-rays taken the next morning. He got very bad news: a broken pisiform bone at the base of his right hand. The prognosis: he'd be sidelined four to six weeks. Sosa's 1996 season was over.

At the point of the disablement, Sosa was assembling a season worthy of his achievements of two years later. His 40 homers led the NL. He was on a 52-homer, 130-RBI pace, projected to a full 162-game season. His homers accounted for 28.2 percent of the Cubs' team total, his RBI 17.5 percent, his total bases 14.6 percent. "Wait til next year," screamed the headline on the back sports page of the *Chicago Sun-Times* on August 22. The Cubs players and management put up a brave front, but they knew their slim playoff chances had just been extinguished.

Almost out of sight, out of the baseball consciousness, a super hitter was being born on a pedestrian team—and an ill-placed pitch had cut that off almost at the knees.

"He was on a fast track to accomplish what he did (in 1998)," Ed Lynch said.

"This year is the most unbelievable year I've ever had," Sosa said before preparing to undergo surgery on the hand. "But I'm a young guy." Indeed, he had some inner confidence that he'd get a second chance, someday, some way.

"People were expecting so much out of me, and now I won't be here to give it to them," he added. "But I have to take it like a man."

Sosa's performance had even won over *Sun-Times* columnist Jay Mariotti.

"Sosa has surpassed the Big Hurt (Frank Thomas) in pizzazz," Mariotti penned on the morning of August 22, 1996. "All he lacks is a nickname—but does he really need one, given the way he taps his heart and blows kisses after every home run?...Sosa was popular, enthusiastic and dependable, the kind of power and outfield assists, the new Mr. Cub."

Oddly enough, the day Sosa was officially disabled, the Cubs honored Andre Dawson, finishing his career with the Marlins at age 42, with a special day at Wrigley Field. Dawson took a lap around the outfield, salaaming back to the bleacher fans who had idolized him so much less than a decade earlier. The symbolic passing of the torch from one benchmark Cub to another had been ruined by Sosa's inopportune injury.

The very ordinary Scott Bullett was put into the lineup as Sosa's fill-in. As expected, he fell far short of subbing for the slugger, and Bullett would not endear himself to management with his attitude as the season wound down. The Cubs actually hung around .500 and the fringes of contention, five games out, until a September 17-19 series in St. Louis. The Cubs were swept three in a row, lost 14 of their final 16 games, and finished 76-86. Management ignored the warning signs that this mix of players simply did not work. An overhaul was needed. And halfway, "slow, steady and unspectacular" methods of building a ballclub don't work in a age of risk-taking, mega-spending owners who never could beat out Tribune Co. in a greenback-for-greenback contest.

Conventional wisdom states that one season's results cannot be bottled and transferred to the following year. But in the 1996-97 Cubs' case, that may have actually happened. Sosa's injury brought the team's vulnerabilities to light.

And, again, no big-name home-run hitter came on the shopping list over the winter. The Cubs briefly inquired about the health of Atlanta Braves' slugger David Justice, yet another in a long line of long-ball types who hungered to play at Wrigley Field. Justice even told Brian McRae at a January golf outing in San Diego to pull whatever strings were needed to get him traded to the Cubs. Instead, Justice was dealt to the Cleveland Indians, whom he helped reach the World Series in 1997. The Cubs expected Sandberg to repeat his surprising 25-homer campaign of 1996 without knowing that he already was considering his second, and permanent, retirement after the season. They also brought an older, slower Shawon Dunston back to play shortstop.

Meanwhile, the Cubs, after letting Luis Gonzalez go, opted to throw left field open to a slew of rookies: longtime slugging hopeful Brooks Kieschnick, converted first baseman Brant Brown, all-around hitter Robin Jennings and the speedy Doug Glanville. "We'll get a good player out of whoever plays left field," vowed pitcher Steve Trachsel. Third base belonged to promising rookie Kevin Orie.

MacPhail and Lynch chose to concentrate on pitching after Jaime Navarro jumped to the White Sox as a free agent. Signed up were Kevin Tapani from the White Sox and Terry Mulholland from the Seattle Mariners. Most publicized of the signings, though, was stopper Mel Rojas from the Montreal Expos. Almost every pundit praised Rojas' acquisition to plug up a hole in late-inning relief that Doug Jones, Turk Wendell and Terry Adams couldn't quite fill in 1996.

All the time, the somewhat out-of-kilter feeling that began at the end of '96 was never far away. Sosa, who had taken pains in the previous two seasons to emphasize team goals and proper hitting fundamentals in his comments, suggested 60 homers was a possibility. Tapani suddenly wasn't available to pitch due to pain in his right index finger. Soon he'd be lost for months due to surgery to remove scar tissue around a ligament in the finger. A slick-fielding first baseman throughout the playoffs, Brown expressed trepidation about playing left field, not knowing the fate that awaited him almost two seasons in the future in the late afternoon sun in Milwaukee.

Worst of all was an increasing feeling of distress about the early season schedule. The Cubs were slated to open with six consecutive games on the road at Florida and Atlanta-possessors of the game's two best pitching staffs. Five more games against the Marlins and Braves awaited the Cubs when they opened at home at Wrigley Field. Such team beliefs were echoed in the media, which did everything but forecast doom when projecting ahead to the rough schedule.

Talk about your worst nightmares coming true. The Cubs hitters went cold while the pitchers were shaky, the worst possible combination. Chicago lost all six games on the road, and then dropped the homer opener to the Marlins on April 8. They barely escaped being no-hit for the first time in almost 32 years the next day when Dave Hansen smashed a pitch off Alex Fernandez's leg for an infield hit with two out in the ninth. They lost the rest of the games on the homestand, getting a brief respite from a rainout, to make it a team-worst 0-12 start.

The Cubs went for the all-time worst team losing streak—and all-time worst National League start—on April 20 in the first game of a doubleheader in New York. The mission was accomplished with an 8-2 loss to the Mets. The fact that the Cubs broke the spell with a 4-3 win in the nitecap hardly lifted the ignominy. The Cubs were the nation's laughingstocks, their losing tradition worse than ever. The season was lost before it even got started. Riggleman and his staff had their biggest challenge: Maintaining some semblance of clubhouse spirit with nothing to play for.

Sosa was one of the cold hitters who dragged the Cubs down in April. But, as in previous years, he warmed up in May with 10 homers, 28 RBI and a .333 average. Included was a career-high six-RBI outburst in a 16-7 win over San Diego May 16 at Wrigley Field. Sosa had a homer and a triple in his 4-for-4 day. And, once again, he remembered the past value of hitting to right field.

"At the beginning of the year, I forgot about the other part of the plate," he said. "Now I've tried to make contact and go the other way and stay with the ball. Everyone knows the wind in Wrigley Field. I don't say to myself 'home runs,' but 'just make contact.'"

Unlike past seasons, the hot spell didn't carry over. Almost every Cubs regular suffered through a sub-par year. And whatever leads the team garnered were frittered away by Rojas, who buckled under the pressure of the stopper's role and his big contract. And Sandberg did not immediately recover from his typically lousy April, causing some in the organization to theorize he was finally reaching the end of the line.

"We had nobody," pitcher Steve Trachsel recalled. "It was Sammy hits a home run for us or we lose. That's why we were so terrible."

Sosa had a few good moments, such as a two-out, two-run homer against Todd Worrell and the Dodgers to win a game 4-3 in the bottom of the 12th at Wrigley Field on August 3. But he hit just .219, .232 and .228 in June, July and August, respectively, his strikeouts way up on their way to a club-record and National League-high 174.

"A lot of times in 1997, Sammy Sosa was boring (at the plate)," said one Cubs organization member.

Scouts noted that Sosa had regressed from the performance levels he had achieved in 1995-96.

"I stated in my reports that he struggled with breaking balls," said Alan Hargesheimer, special assistant to Detroit Tigers general manager Randy Smith. "When you were behind in the count, you didn't throw him a strike. One thing leads to the next, and you end up swinging at pitches that are pitchers' pitches."

And he labored under the burden of his new $42.5 million contract signed June 27. That immediately unleashed an undercurrent of clubhouse grumbling that had died down in recent years regarding Sosa's style of play.

"After the contract, especially in this town, all they wanted to do was bring him down," Trachsel said. "He wanted to be the guy. He had to be overly aggressive, and he swung at pitches out of the zone."

"There was pressure to validate that deal," Terry Mulholland said. "It hurt Sammy at the time. He had to prove he was worth the money. That's an awful lot of pressure to put on someone."

The overall atmosphere was so sour that hitting coach Tony Muser made an offhand comment about Cubs players losing faith after he was named Kansas City Royals manager during the 1997 All-Star break. Muser later apologized to the Cubs and manager Jim Riggleman.

Replacing Muser as hitting coach was Jeff Pentland, who soon would begin the work to truly unleash Sosa for the next year. But Pentland first had to help quash some of the backbiting.

"Sammy's one of the most sensitive guys around," he said. "I think there were some petty jealousies around here. I told some players that Sammy wasn't the problem last year. Instead, they should look in the mirror."

Pentland sensed Sosa's unhappiness, a feeling the slugger himself confirmed.

"We lost so many games last year," he said from the safety of 1998, "you couldn't have a good time. I'm the type of player who likes to come here every day and I like to win."

All that was needed was to simply finish up the season without getting hurt, re-group during the winter and start fresh the following spring. At least the Cubs were spared the embarrassment of losing 100 games for only the third time in franchise history. Having sunk to 50-77—close to a 100-loss pace-on August 20—the Cubs avoided the century mark by going 13-12 in September, 1997.

Oddly enough, Sosa somehow would end up with 36 homers and 119 RBI, his identical numbers from 1995. But with the 174 strikeouts and .251 average, the season was considered subpar. STATS, Inc. reported that Sosa hit just .246 with runners in scoring position. His bases-loaded woes continued without letup—just three hits in 16 at-bats.

Ticking down to the finish, the horrid year would not end without one, final watershed event that Sosa had to overcome in establishing himself as Most Valuable Player material for 1998.

Finishing up the lost season in St. Louis, where Mark McGwire was making a belated and eventually unsuccessful assault on 60 homers, Sosa attempted to steal on a "hold" sign put up by Riggleman during a 5-2 Cubs win on September 27, 1997. Sosa was thrown out. Riggleman confronted Sosa in the dugout in full view of the WGN-TV cameras. The incident was played up, and Riggleman vented his frustration with the season. Some seemed directed at Sosa.

"Sometimes you need to do it in front of the team," Riggleman said. "He's done it on a couple of occasions. Don't put this on Sammy Sosa. It's not a Sammy Sosa thing. It's the Chicago Cubs' problem. I saw some other position players doing this, stressing individual over team, since we've fallen out of the race.

"It's crept in. I want them to know if it creeps in next year, they're not going to play."

Riggleman does not hold grudges. He had verbally tussled in the dugout, on camera, with Jaime Navarro in 1996. But even amid the wreckage of his 1997-98 seasons with the White Sox, Navarro always took pains to praise Riggleman.

He settled the issue with Sosa, and all was fine the following day.

"I missed a sign, that's all," Sosa said afterward. "I didn't ignore it; nobody's perfect. Anybody who knows the type of player I am knows I'm not selfish. I'm a gentleman, and I have no problem with Riggleman. I'm trying to steal to set up an RBI situation...People who know me know I only want to win."

Riggleman wasn't finished, though.

"I heard too much 'I, I, I' around here, starting with the bullpen earlier in the year," he said. "It's the type of thing that's been rampant in the Cubs' organization for years, people more worried about personal numbers than what's best for the team.

"It's like they want to...show the world on WGN what a great player they are. I think losing has festered this. They've lost for the last 45 years or whatever."

Unfortunately, Sosa remained the one player linked with Riggleman's blast at the "me-first" attitude. Riggleman did not intend his tongue-lashing to single Sosa out in any way. And during the winter of 1997-98, Riggleman discovered more information about the September 27 stolen-base attempt that he had not realized at the time.

"I'm into team goals," he said. "So, individual tings, when so-and-so hits his 100th home run or gets his 2,000th hit, except for the fact it's flashed up on the scoreboard, I'm very seldom aware of individual things. I can't tell you who made the All-Star team this year. I can't tell you who won the MVP last year.

"The year was going to end and, at the time, Sammy had 199 career stolen bases. I didn't know that. So, as we were in that game, I'm sitting there watching the pitcher work home plate. He's extremely fast to the plate. (Eli) Marrero, catching for the Cardinals, has got a great arm, so I felt this was not a time to run. We really had a very slim chance of getting a stolen base because the pitcher was quick to home and the catcher had a great arm."

Riggleman followed through with his lecture to Sosa in the dugout.

"Sammy ran," he recalled. "So he was out and when he came back in, I said, 'Hey, I make those decisions and you shouldn't have been running there. You disregarded the sign.' The more I talked, the madder I got and so there was a blowup there.

"But, had I been aware that we only had two games to go and it is a milestone number, I may have just said, 'What the heck, we're in last place anyway. Let him try to get it.'"

Riggleman really was directing his comments at players who were on the cusp of staying or going for 1998. Shawon Dunston, Rey Sanchez, and several others already had been let go. More were to follow.

7

Sammy's Ship Comes in on Payday

The collective jaw of the baseball world dropped on June 27, 1997, when the Cubs announced they had signed Sammy Sosa to a four-year contract worth a potential $42.5 million. The deal also had an option for a fifth year.

Talk about bad timing. The Cubs had started out an all-time worst 0-14, packing in the season almost before it got started. And on the morning of June 27, Chicago had sunk to a new low, losing eight of nine games to sink to 30-48. Sosa was in the middle of his worst full Cubs season. He had decent totals of 15 homers and 52 RBI, but batted just .258. He'd go on to record career lows of .251 and a personal- and National League season-high 174 strikeouts. And too many people outside the Cubs' executive suite still thought Sosa was a second-tier star, a fundamentals-challenged player who couldn't help a team win.

Media pundits predictably panned the contract. But for the rest of the '97 season and into 1998, players on the Cubs, their National League opponents and even American League teams shook their heads at the money involved. Nothing against

Sammy Sosa, personally, they said, but you just don't pay that much for a player who wasn't among the game's elite, who had as yet not mastered some of the little things needed to win games. Such feelings were echoed by managers, coaches and executives all over the game.

Sticking their necks out, seemingly fodder for the chopping block, were Cubs president Andy MacPhail and general manager Ed Lynch. They had been dickering with Sosa's agent, Adam Katz, since spring training on a new deal. Almost every 1996-97 Cubs' off-season player move, from the Mel Rojas acquisition on down, had backfired. And there was more to come—this time MacPhail potentially putting at risk with the Sosa contract some of the expected profits of the demanding Tribune Co. stockholders.

"Nobody likes to be criticized," MacPhail said. "The one thing you learn in this game is that you do what you think you have to do. You owe it to yourself and the organization. You're making reasonable decisions after doing your homework. Some are going to work out, some won't. Nobody bats 1.000 in this game. You work hard, make reasonable decisions and you push the odds in your percentage.

"Whatever you do in this particular organization, with the level of scrutiny it has and the size of the city, there are going to be people on either side of the issue. But the only way you're going to make peace with yourself is to know that if it didn't work out two or three years from now, you could look back and say, 'What the hell. We did our homework. We did our due diligence. It just didn't work out.' The last thing you want to do is look in the mirror and suggest you did something that somebody else wanted you to do, and you're heart wasn't in it."

MacPhail, at whose desk the buck stops at Wrigley Field, might have been a stock-market cowboy in another life. He really had a nose for futures. MacPhail would make a monster investment that wouldn't take long to pay off, although the future looked bleak at the time to everyone except him. But in keeping with his low-key approach, he refuses to crow "I told you so" about paying Sosa for potential that would soon be realized and then surpassed along with Roger Maris' home-run record.

"I don't think you've seen anyone from this organization popping off about how smart we were in signing Sammy to a four-year deal," MacPhail said. "We've all kept our mouths shut.

He could break his leg tomorrow. Did we say anything off the record about Jaime Navarro going to the White Sox (where he has failed miserably)?"

Putting his feet up on the desk in his office, MacPhail coolly can recall his motivation for seemingly playing around with the company's profits, at the wrong place at the wrong time and on the wrong player, according to the consensus of baseball people, media and fans.

"Sammy was in the second year of a three-year ($5.25 million annual) contract," he said. "The third year had a mutual option. It was clear to me that Sammy could do better by not picking up the option. The first genesis of that contract was that we were very much aware that Sammy could be a free agent (in 1998)."

MacPhail saw in Sosa's 1996 performance the makings of an elite player. Uncommonly motivated in the first year of a good multi-year deal, Sosa was on a pace for 52 homers and 130 RBI when a pitch broke his right hand on August 20. His final season totals were 40 homers (leading the NL at that point) and 100 RBI, but Sosa had slugged 20 homers and drove in 54 runs while batting .310 in the previous 62 games. He had been showing tendencies of good mechanics, blasting a number of homers to right field.

Cubs brass didn't like their options if Sosa, who had flirted with the Boston Red Sox briefly as a temporary free agent during the 1994-95 strike, jumped ship. There was going to be a huge contract awaiting for him somewhere out there, while the Cubs probably couldn't have found a player of comparable talent to replace him.

"On the free-agent market, there wasn't any corner outfielder remotely up to his ability or production," MacPhail said. "He was enduring a relative off-year, and we had to look at the following to understand his motivation. We really didn't have a lot of players getting on base in front of him. We didn't have people behind him who were offering him a lot of protection. Even so, he scored or drove in over a quarter of our runs while not having a great season."

Sosa wanted to give the Cubs every opportunity to give him the long-term financial security he desired. Money, though, was not his sole object.

"I let it be known he wanted to stay and be treated fairly,"

Sosa's agent, Katz, said after the contract was signed. "He didn't have to have a home run. He wanted a double. You won't be able to tear the Cub uniform off his back. If you try, you better bring two or three very big guys with you."

"People always talk about the millions of dollars," Sosa said. "This is not my type of thing. Money doesn't mean anything to me. The only reason I'm here is because I play good. I always told Andy I wasn't concerned about the money. I don't play for money. That's not my style."

MacPhail believed Sosa was merely in a pause before he stepped to a higher level. He turned out to be a prophet.

"When you make this kind of investment in a player, part of the investment has to be more than just talent and ability. You're making an investment in a person and a philosophy. In our view, Sammy was just 28. We just thought he was going to get better. He had to overcome the hurdle of coming to a different culture and mastering a different language.

"There were precious few people who have the talent to do the things he could do in a game. He played every day. The only injuries that kept him out were broken bones, not a hamstring that was going to stretch into a 15-day affair.

"He wants to play. He likes to play. He likes people. People like him. With the contract (negotiations) behind him, Sammy would be relaxed and be able to perform at a level he already demonstrated he was capable of."

Sosa had agreed with the concept of getting the contract out of the way before it totally distracted him.

"It makes me feel more relaxed," he said with the deal completed. "Talking about a contract in the middle of the season is hard."

And despite the backbiting that nipped at Sosa throughout his Cubs career up to that point, MacPhail had no questions about casting his bottom line, figuratively and literally, with Sosa.

"Our response to that was demonstrated by our actions," he said.

With the megabucks at stake, MacPhail kept in regular contact with Jim Dowdle, the Cubs' overseer at Tribune Co. The actual payroll value of the deal, guaranteed from 1998 to 2001, was actually closer to $40 million, a little less if the structure of deferred money was taken into account. The published value of $42.5 million was considered a "worst-case scenario" for the club by MacPhail—the team opting to buy out the final year of the contract for the year 2002. The deal included a $4 million signing bonus and much smaller bonuses for awards like the Most Valuable Player, a likely payout to Sosa after the glorious 1998 campaign. Sosa got $7 million in 1998. He's scheduled to be paid $8 million in 1998, $10 million in 2000 and $11 million in 2001.

Considering the aura of negativity surrounding the Cubs as the '97 season began, MacPhail ensured that negotiations proceeded in secrecy.

"Negotiations have a better chance of being complete to everyone's satisfaction when they're out of the public eye," he said. "Positions can harden and people feel there's more at stake when they make that position public. It was Ed, myself, Sammy's representatives, and informing Tribune Co. (Dowdle). It was a relatively small circle. This one was better off done as quietly and efficiently as you could possibly do."

Similarly, MacPhail won't tip his hand about how he'll construct the Cubs in the future around Sosa, having quietly suggested he needed more help in the lineup from 1995-97, help that top management somehow did not provide. Sosa responded well to the emotional comfort zone of a beefed-up, home run-hitting lineup. With the baseball cycle swinging so heavily back to the power game, the Cubs cannot afford to stock their lineup with popgun hitters other than Sosa.

"You make the best decisions you can," MacPhail said. "You're always trying to learn, you're always trying to figure out what worked for you and what didn't. I don't know if we're ever going to have the 1927 Yankees here with the payroll. You might be choosing between the power-hitting third baseman and the right-handed starter who you think will give you 240 innings. There's risk in this game. You sit behind these desks and risk is part of what you deal with every day."

However he constructs the Cubs, the one constant likely will be Sosa as the new millennium is about to dawn. Laughing at a *Japan Times* reporter's question of what it will take for Sosa to play for the powerful Japanese League Giants, the slugger replied, "Maybe in 10 years." In truth, Sosa hints he'd be finishing up his last Cubs contract at that point. "I'd like to play my whole career here," he said.

All things being equal, MacPhail would like to oblige Sosa.

"Our interest and belief in Sammy is self-evident by our actions," he said. "Who knows what the future holds? The likelihood is that will be our preference at the time, and we've already demonstrated that."

After Sosa finished his unforgettable season in 1998, the Cubs ended up with a comparative bargain of a deal. Again, timing is everything in baseball.

8

Class in Session with Jeff Pentland

Bespectacled and modest in stature, Jeff Pentland doesn't look like a former great ballplayer in a new incarnation as a hitting coach. He can grab a shower from his workout of throwing left-handed batting practice to his players, comb his hair, get into civvies, and he won't give off the baseball-stereotype image.

Pentland looks like a teacher. He was. And is.

He doesn't hang around with an entourage and bodyguards. After a game at Wrigley Field, you might find him quaffing a beer at Bernie's, a popular watering hole for knowledgeable fans at the corner of Clark and Waveland avenues. Yeah, teachers like their refreshments and mix with just plain folks.

"I taught lower-division (100) level at the University of California-Riverside," said the Cubs' hitting instructor. "History, philosophy, phys.ed. I assisted on biomechanics. I also taught tennis and golf. I really enjoyed teaching."

Present tense, for that statement. For the prize pupil of Jeff Pentland's career is Sammy Sosa. The pair went through a kind of baseball post-graduate course—Sosa, despite his detractors—had gone beyond Baseball 101 by 1997. The end result of this teacher-to-student ratio of one-to-one was the final unlocking of whatever massive talent Sosa had still kept inside via either lack of maturity or lack of a proper way to channel it. The little movement of a "tap step" of his left (front) foot, the lowering of his hands gripping the bat, and the concept of a little more patience went an immeasurably longer way.

The coming together of Sosa and Pentland toward the end of the lost 1997 Cubs season—out of sight, out of mind for most media types turning their attention to the Bears, Bulls or whatever was deemed more interesting than baseball then—was a fortuitous event. Maybe if the two didn't link, Sosa would not have burst onto the scene with one of the greatest offensive years in major-league history.

"I have always felt that things were done for a reason," Pentland said. "Sammy and I came together for a reason. You can call it anything you want. The timing was just right when I came here."

Others have picked up on the same angle.

"It had to happen at the right time—Jeff Pentland being appointed hitting coach just when Sammy was ready to take the next step," former Cubs general manager Larry Himes, Sosa's former patron in trading for him twice.

Pentland was named Cubs hitting coach on July 14, 1997, just after predecessor Tony Muser was named Kansas City Royals manager. He beat out former Cubs left fielder Gary Matthews—at the time Chicago's minor-league hitting coordinator—for the job. Pentland had been plucked from the minor leagues, where he had served as the New York Mets' minor-league hitting coordinator. Matthews did not end up out in the cold in the end, though, being named Toronto Blue Jays' hitting instructor for 1998 under new manager Tim Johnson, who had worked with Matthews in the Cubs' farm system as Class AAA Iowa manager.

The 52-year-old Hollywood, California, product moved up through the back channels of baseball, playing briefly as a first baseman in the San Diego Padres' farm system at the cusp of the 1970s. Assistant coaching jobs in junior college in Mesa, Arizona, and a junior-varsity head coaching job at Arizona State preceded a short stint as assistant athletic director of Wichita

State and a nine-year run as assistant baseball coach at Cal-Riverside, which won two lower-division collegiate baseball championships while Pentland worked there.

Moving on to work as hitting coach at Arizona State, one of the nation's top baseball programs, in 1983, Pentland went on to instruct Barry Bonds. While at ASU, Pentland met the man who would be his connection to his eventual Cubs job—Creighton University baseball coach Jim Hendry.

"He was as well-respected as any hitting coach in college baseball," Hendry said.

Pentland and Hendry finally broke into pro baseball at the same time in the fall of 1991 for the fledgling Florida Marlins organization. He worked at several minor-league levels, and ended up rooming with Hendry, the manager of the team, at Elmira, N.Y., in 1994. The following spring, Hendry, freshly hired as Cubs farm director, introduced Pentland to Lynch in spring training.

In the second half of the '96 season, after original Marlins manager Rene Lachemann was fired, interim manager John Boles—also Florida's minor-league director—summoned Pentland to serve as hitting coach for the parent club through the end of the year. But when Jim Leyland brought his own cadre of coaches to the Marlins for the 1997 season, Pentland left the organization for a better job with the Mets—with Lynch's recommendation to his old boss, New York GM Joe McIlvain. It's indeed a networking game for baseball jobs, but Pentland—without the big name of a major-league playing career—was advancing on merit.

Pentland saw Sosa from afar—and painfully. He was present in Wrigley Field on August 20, 1996, when a pitch from Mark Hutton broke Sosa's hand and ended a potentially dynamite, 50-homer season.

He came to the Cubs charged with somehow fixing the struggling offensive portfolios of not only Sosa, but virtually the entire roster of the last-place 1997 team.

"We saw a guy who was a hitting instructor at all levels, from the lowest minor leaguers to major-league hitters," Cubs general manager Ed Lynch said. "He was a good communicator with hitters. He's patient. That's what you want in a coach, in that he doesn't treat everybody exactly the same or have everybody hit or pitch exactly the same. He works with what he has, and he allows the player to realize that they need to make changes and incorporate them slowly in a very logical manner instead of dumping it on them all at once."

Pentland is flexible, to be sure. But he believes he has to be able to offer up a consistent philosophy that hitters can follow.

"One thing that sticks out is you have a distinct way of doing things," he said. "The player is the end product. He tells you whether you're right or wrong. Talent isn't the end result, but certainly it's the number one in making anyone into, quote, unquote, a superstar player.

"Hitting is natural. You're not going to make anyone into a hitter. Hitters are born. Certainly they can be improved. Hitting is an art form. It's not just a skill. You see that in any great player that they turn a skill into an art form. As a player gets older and matures, he finds out what's unique about himself."

Coming aboard the Cubs, Pentland sized up Sammy Sosa. He was impressed, as any baseball man who gave a first glance at the right fielder would be.

"My first impression of Sammy was, No. 1, he's very talented," Pentland said. "No. 2, very strong. No. 3, he was tremendously aggressive.

"But he was using that aggression as a detriment. His aggressive style was creating problems. He was making mistakes or he was unproductive because he was so aggressive."

Pentland had a load to handle when he arrived at Wrigley Field in '97. Buried by their record-breaking 0-14 start, the Cubs were 38-54 when he was appointed, having lost four of their first five coming out of the All-Star break. Sosa was the sole home-run source playing in a ballpark perfectly suited for big bombers. Mark Grace finished 1997 with his usual 13 homers to rank second to Sosa's 36, while the retiring Ryne Sandberg had to finish with a rush to end up with 12 homers. Whatever progress Sosa had made in 1995-96 was starting to regress.

"In my 2 1/2 months with the Cubs, I wanted to make sure I had a handle on everyone there. I certainly wanted to make sure I had a great feel and understanding. But my No. 1 priority was Sammy, mainly because he had more physical talent than anyone in the National League. My basic premise was you're the most talented person in the league, we have to make sure the numbers match up with that statement.

"I was drooling at Sammy, because I knew this guy was loaded with ability. I've seen him take pitches off the ground and hit 'em 400 feet, some of them 500 feet. I've seen him do some pretty amazing things, even though the consistency was not there."

But before Pentland could tinker with Sosa's hitting mechanics, he had to get into his head—and earn his trust. That was akin to a reliever getting three outs in the ninth with men on base. It can be done, but it's not easy.

Besides, Sosa's mid-season 1997 mood was dour despite the security of a potentially $42.5 million contract.

"I know Sammy was not a very happy camper in 1997," Pentland said.

The coach had to use some careful psychology on Sosa.

"I had to get to know this guy, No. 1," Pentland said. "This guy had to trust me, to some degree. It wasn't easy. I think what came out of the whole thing was that it took me a long time to get to know Sammy.

"On a daily basis, I made sure I said hello to Sammy, made sure he knew that I was around. I really don't know if he knew I existed for most of that season. Sammy and I finally had a relationship. At the end of the season, Sammy and I were talking to one another. That was a big step."

Hendry knew Pentland wouldn't give up trying to get through to Sosa.

"No. 1, he's the kind of guy who will take time to get to know someone," he said. "That's not hard to believe. He's a players' guy. He doesn't force himself down your throat. He has marvelous patience. He takes the time to establish a trust with you."

Pentland also realized that he'd be waved away. But he never gave up.

"The main thing is, I didn't go away," he said. "I kept coming back, and sometimes he'd brush me away. Maybe he didn't trust me sometimes; I don't blame him. Sammy's pride is incredible. Sometimes I don't say the right thing to him, but it doesn't bother me. I'm not afraid to say anything to anybody. Sometimes my humor rubs him the wrong way and I don't realize it.

"But I don't worry about what I say. Shit, I'm a human being. Sammy takes things so seriously, he doesn't understand I'm kidding with him. Even today, we're still finding ways to deal with each other's personalities."

When Sosa fell into a relatively brief dry spell during his duel with Mark McGwire, Pentland would sit in the chair next to Sosa's locker and quietly talk with him. That's not special treatment; the coach worked the Cubs' clubhouse in the same manner.

Once the wall between Sosa and Pentland was gone, the latter was able to break down every facet of his mechanics. That was the typical Pentland *modus operandi*.

"He is a marvelous analyst of players' swings," Hendry said. "He gets to know everyone's style very carefully."

"You want to come up with one or two things that might trigger four or five positive things in a swing," Pentland said. "But when you have that much talent, you don't want them thinking. You want to give them something that will immediately click. That's easier said than done, no question about it."

The first idea Pentland concocted was the "tap step" of the hitter's front foot. Away from the glare of publicity, in the gloomy batting cages underneath the Wrigley Field bleachers, the makings of a record-breaking season was born.

So what's a "tap step?" Baseball folks talk in a jargon of "staying back" and all sorts of insider terms that require translation into layman's language. And if you think the dumb fan and media types need it broken down into the simplest language, think about the explaining of a concept to as prideful a player as Sosa, whose hitting style was almost set in stone.

"A tap step is a mechanism for starting your step with your front foot," began the long Pentland explanation. "You tap back toward your back foot, then step forward.

"It's a mechanism for getting loaded on your back leg. When you're back like that, you're in a position to read and recognize pitches a little bit better and sooner. It also allows you to control your weight transfer. Pitchers are constantly throwing all kinds of pitches—fastballs, curveballs, changeups, split-fingers. The main ingredient is the change of speed. You must have a mechanism in your hitting form that, once you recognize the change of speed, you have control of your weight."

Pentland made sure Sosa understood the rhyme and reason for the little dance at home plate.

"I wanted Sammy to understand the why, the reason, what he was accomplishing," he said. "If you're going to do the tap-step, let's do it the right way. If a breaking pitch comes, he can slow down, and not just be in one speed moving your body toward the ball. You can understand an off-speed pitch coming. He slows down to where he knows he can handle it."

As Sosa began working the tap-step into this stance, Pentland gave Sosa some videotapes of Texas Rangers tap-steppers. He also could point down the clubhouse to a familiar face doing the tap-step, Mark Grace. The Atlanta Braves' Chipper Jones and the New York Yankees' Bernie Williams also are practitioners.

Also offering some informal hitting instruction on the tap-step was Sosa's old friend from their White Sox days, Cubs center fielder Lance Johnson. "One Dog," as the soft-spoken Johnson is called, had to encourage Sosa, who finished '97 in a tailspin.

"Sammy's real comfortable with me," he said. "At the end of the year, he's trying to change his leg kick, and the last thing I said to Sammy was, 'If you go home and work hard on it, Sammy, you're gonna still hit your home runs and you're going to hit for a higher batting average.'" And, let me tell you, when he came into spring training and I saw him the first couple of days hitting, it was unbelievable.

"Pentland was the man who really helped Sammy. I was just trying to keep him on a even keel to get him to continue to do it. Because I knew what was gonna happen."

Next on the agenda was firming up Sosa's own decision to lower his hands in his stance, begun at the start of 1998. The change in how Sosa held his bat was so noticeable that ESPN and other TV networks, analyzing the secret of his success, began showing before-and-after tapes of him batting.

"I told him I liked what he was doing, then he lowered his hands even more," Pentland said. "By lowering your hands, it takes all the tightness out of his body and allows him to be more loose and relaxed. When you have strong people, they're very muscular. There's a fine line in having muscles loose and relaxed. Loose is quick, tight is slow. You have to stay relaxed in order to be able to fire, to create the quickness."

Sosa fined-tuned his batting style changes as the 1998 season progressed. There came a point, though, when he didn't feel the need to tinker with mechanics anymore.

"That's when he hit the mother lode at the end of May," Pentland said. "Then he just solidified what he did. When working with athletes as mentally driven as them, all you have to do is get them going in the right direction and then get out of their way."

But all of the new mechanics of Sosa's feet and hands would go for naught if he didn't somehow acquire a quality in short supply in almost every human being: patience. Noted for being an over-eager hitter, particularly with runners in scoring position, Sosa had earned a reputation around the fraternity of pitchers as a hitter who could be worked with bad pitches.

Pentland did not have to look at raw numbers to see a change in Sosa's approach was necessary.

"I talked to him very early on about particular goals for this season," he said. "I wanted to see him draw 100 walks, get deeper into the count, to be more selective. To read and recognize pitches—that's the key word."

Sosa never realized the 100-walks goal. A notoriously impatient and free-swinging team long before Sosa arrived, only one Cub, Gary Matthews in 1984, had drawn at least 100 walks in the last 20 years. But there were some tangible results.

In 1998, Sosa took more pitches than the previous season. STATS, Inc., one of the two top statistical services used by Major League Baseball, found that in 2,686 pitches thrown to Sosa through September 15, 1998 (two weeks remained in the season), he took 1,444 pitches. Through the entire season of 1997, Sosa had 2,663 pitches thrown to him, of which he took 1,244.

A big increase was on the first pitch. Sosa took 527 in 1998; 428 in 1997. He actually cut in half the number of times he swung at the first pitch, from 266 in 1997 to 135 in 1998. By working the count in his favor to 2-and-0 or 3-and-1, Sosa was able to fashion respective batting averages on these counts of .522 and .412 in 1998.

Sosa took a ton of close pitches in 1998 he might have otherwise swung at in previous years. He seemingly worked the count full more than ever before. Rarely did umpires ring him up on called-third strikes.

Sosa repeatedly said he would take his walks and let the next hitter serve as the hero. Seconding that approach was Cubs pitcher Steve Trachsel.

"He feels if he walks, that's just another run," he said. "Last year, you were throwing to a 25-inch plate against Sammy. "This year, you're throwing to a 17-inch plate like you're supposed to. The more pitches you throw, the odds of making a poor pitch increase."

Opponents took note of Sosa's new look-'em-over tendencies.

"He's taking a lot more first pitches," Pittsburgh Pirates hitting coach Lloyd McClendon, a "patience is a virtue" advocate, said. "He's taking with the game And if that happens to be three walks that day, then he takes them.

"The deeper you can go into the count, the more pitches you see. Obviously, you are gonna have a better idea getting the timing off that pitcher and hopefully he'll give something up. A lot of times we go out there and we swing at first pitches and it really isn't the pitch we wanted. We don't know the type of movement that the pitcher has in the ball. Just how fast it's coming. The timing is just now there. So, it's to our advantage as hitters to try to take them as deep as we possibly can sometime in the count."

Other hitters can benefit in the same manner. But Sosa's new-found high profile made him a textbook case for patience.

"It's showing up bright and clear with one guy because he's got so much talent," Pentland said. "I explained what happens when you read and recognize pitches. You can't go up there and think, because you have to see the pitches. You don't have much time to think. You've got to see it, read it and hit it. If we can give the hitter as much time as possible, by shortening their swing a little bit, by keeping them back a little long, getting them back a little sooner, they'll see it and read it much better than ever before."

Pentland isn't finished analyzing Sosa and his muscle-bound brethren. He believes the ability to hit a ball a long way requires more than just brute strength.

"Sammy has a tremendous gift, just like Mark McGwire, Junior (Griffey), some others—the ability to swing very easy and hit the ball a long way," he said. "When your swing is in sequence, when you coordinate your swing, and you happen to meet the ball at the right time, the ball has no chance. His ability to repeat this swing is so very good."

Sluggers often have their best seasons between ages 28 and 34, when emotional maturity and patience peak while catching up with physical tools in their prime.

Cubs Hall of Famer Billy Williams, for one, had his finest campaign at 32 in 1970 with 42 homers, 129 RBI and a .322 average. Two years later, at 34, Williams won the batting title with .333, to go along with 37 homers and 122 RBI. Williams was joined by another peaking clutch hitter in '70—Jim Hickman, with 32 homers, 115 RBI and .315. At 33, Hickman amassed a season far beyond anything he ever had before.

"Oftentimes they say 28, 29, 30, 31 are the best years you're gonna have and hopefully your experience keeps you a real good player," Pirates manager Gene Lamont said. "Sammy's definitely harnessed his emotions or whatever it might be and become one of those top players in baseball."

So at least half a decade of top production awaits Sosa if he can bottle the lessons of 1997-98. He's not going to get any unhappier. The past season has made him an all-time folk hero in Chicago sports, certainly the most popular Cub since Ernie Banks' heyday.

"He's going to get smarter," Pentland said. "Whether he maintains the hunger for what he's doing, that's something the player has to answer. Right now he's in his prime of hitting.

"What he showed me this year, he can hit any pitch at any time. He can hit the ball high, hit the ball low, hit an offspeed pitch, do anything he wanted to do."

So how does Sosa top 1998? It's not easy, Pentland said.

"Numbers are sometimes misleading," he said. "Home runs are not misleading, of course. They go over the fence. Sammy's RBI total was as phenomenal as his homers. I know in one month, June, poor Mark Grace only had two men in scoring position because Sammy was cleaning 'em off the bases.

"However good you are, you still have to get help from your teammates. Look at the number of men on base in front of Sammy."

Sosa has not graduated from the Pentland school of hitting. No, there's no diploma. Class will be ongoing, and teacher will always give pop quizzes to star pupil. More importantly, though, are the pep talks and refresher courses.

Even amid the glory of 60-plus homers, Sosa's eagerness to please, to take the role of the hero who wins the game, sometimes got the better of him. Pentland came a long way to harnessing such dive. The job is not 100 percent completed. It perhaps never will be.

"He was well on his way to a decent strikeout total for the season until we got into this home-run contest with McGwire," he said. "Then he got so emotionally involved and so fired up, sometimes he was swinging too hard again.

"His ability to stay under control, to swing easy and create timing and rhythm instead of brute strength will be the key to him having great seasons like this year after year."

A rising tide lifts all boats. As Sosa establishes himself as baseball's preeminent all-around hitter and spokesman for the game, the guy with the glasses in the corner of the clubhouse, dressing next to Billy Williams but not sharing his Cooperstown pedigree on his record, will finally get the credit he earned for years among baseball insiders.

"I'm a finesse-type coach," said the man who would harness some of the greatest power in the game.

"I feel very happy for Jeff," said Jim Hendry, waving off credit for his own recommendation of the coach. "The recognition that Jeff is getting is overdue."

Indeed. As with Sosa's breakthrough year, some things are worth waiting for.

Sunday, Aug. 23, 1998

1998 NATIONAL LEAGUE UMPIRES

4 Mark Hirschbeck	13 Larry Poncino	22 Joe West	31 Bob Davidson	40 Jerry Crawford*
5 Angel Hernandez	15 Frank Pulli*	23 Ed Rapuano	32 Dana DeMuth	41 Jerry Meals
6 Bruce Froemming*	15 Jim Quick*	24 Jerry Layne	33 Mike Winters	43 Paul Schrieber
7 Eric Gregg	16 Rich Rieker	25 Charlie Williams	34 Greg Bonin	44 Kerwin Danley
8 Jeff Kellogg	18 Charlie Reliford	27 Steve Rippley*	35 Gary Darling	
9 Brian Gorman	19 Terry Tata*	28 Larry Vanover	36 Wally Bell	
11 Ed Montague*	20 Tom Hallion	29 Bill Hohn	37 Bruce Dreckman	
12 Gerry Davis	21 Harry Wendelstedt*	30 Randy Marsh*	38 Sam Holbrook	

*Crew Chief

Houston

- 3 Carl Everett, OF
- 5 Jeff Bagwell, IF
- 7 Craig Biggio, IF
- 8 Matt Galante, Coach
- 10 Mike Hampton, LHP
- 11 Brad Ausmus, C
- 12 Ricky Gutierrez, IF
- 13 Billy Wagner, LHP
- 15 Derek Bell, OF
- 15 Richard Hidalgo, OF
- 16 Tom McCraw, Coach
- 17 Sean Berry, IF
- 18 Moises Alou, OF
- 19 Doug Henry, RHP
- 20 Tony Eusebio, C
- 21 Dave Engle, Coach
- 22 Pete Incaviglia, OF
- 24 Mike Cubbage, Coach
- 25 Jose Cruz, Coach
- 27 Tim Bogar, IF
- 28 Bill Spiers, IF
- 35 Dave Clark, OF
- 36 Jack Howell, IF
- 36 Shane Reynolds, RHP
- 38 Sean Bergman, RHP
- 39 Jay Powell, RHP
- 42 Jose Lima, RHP
- 45 Chris Holt, RHP
- 46 Trever Miller, LHP
- 48 Vern Ruhle, Coach
- 49 Larry Dierker, MGR
- 50 Scott Elarton, RHP
- 51 Randy Johnson, LHP
- 52 Mike Magnante, LHP
- 59 Ramon Garcia, RHP

No.	Player	Pos.	1	2	3	4	5	6	7	8	9	10	AB	R	H	RBI
7	Biggio	2b														
28	Spiers	3b														
14	D. Bell	rf														
15	Hidalgo rf/7th															
5	Bagwell	1b														
18	M. Alou	lf														
3	Everett	cf														
12	Gutierrez	ss														
11	Ausmus	c														
42	Lima	p														
22	Incaviglia ph															

	Pitchers	IP	H	R	ER	BB	SO			Notes
Lima (13-6)		8	9	3	3	0	3			
Magnante/9th										

CUBS

- 1 Lance Johnson, OF
- 2 Jeff Pentland, Coach
- 3 Dan Radison, Coach
- 4 Jeff Blauser, IF
- 5 Jim Riggleman, MGR
- 6 Glenallen Hill, OF
- 7 Tyler Houston, C-IF
- 8 Sandy Martinez, C
- 9 Scott Servais, C
- 12 Mickey Morandini, IF
- 15 Gary Gaetti, IF
- 17 Mark Grace, IF
- 18 Jose Hernandez, IF-OF
- 21 Sammy Sosa, OF
- 24 Manny Alexander, IF
- 26 Billy Williams, Coach
- 27 Phil Regan, Coach
- 30 Jeremi Gonzalez, RHP
- 33 Don Wengert, RHP
- 34 Kerry Wood, RHP
- 36 Kevin Tapani, RHP
- 37 Brant Brown, OF-IF
- 39 Tom Gamboa, Coach
- 40 Henry Rodriguez, OF
- 43 Dave Bialas, Coach
- 45 Terry Mulholland, LHP
- 46 Steve Trachsel, RHP
- 47 Rod Beck, RHP
- 48 Dave Stevens, RHP
- 49 Felix Heredia, LHP
- 51 Terry Adams, RHP
- 52 Matt Karchner, RHP
- 54 Mark Clark, RHP
- 63 Rick Kranitz, Instructor

No.	Player	Pos.	1	2	3	4	5	6	7	8	9	10	AB	R	H	RBI
1	L. Johnson	cf														
12	Morandini	2b														
21	Sosa	rf														
24	Alexander 3b/4th															
17	Grace	1b														
6	Hill lf/4th															
40	H. Rodriguez lf															
37	B. Brown lf/3rd															
18	J. Hernandez ss															
48	Stevens p/7th															
7	Houston	c														
	E. Gaetti	3b														
48	Stevens p/7th															
46	Trachsel	p														
54	R. Myers p/6th															
4	Blauser ss/4th															
9	Servais ph/9th															

	Pitchers	IP	H	R	ER	BB	SO			Notes
Trachsel (13-7)		5	7	7	7	4	1			
Myers		1⅓	5	5	5	1				

9

An RBI Champ
Needs Support On
and Off the Field

Employing a post mortem for the very dead
1997 season, Cubs general manager Ed Lynch
gave absolution for Sammy Sosa's off-kilter
performance at the plate.

"Unfortunately and I played a long time, any
player tends to probably look at their own performance when you are 0-14, and 30 games under
.500," Lynch said. "Every player, no matter how good
a person he is, no matter how good a team player
he is, tends to focus on individual statistics. Sammy's
a human being just like the rest of us.

"The team's lack of performance in '97 was a
major problem for Sammy. We didn't have anyone
to hit behind him."

Now the ball was in the court of Lynch and
team president Andy MacPhail. Their laughingstock
team was the butt of jokes nationwide. They had to
turn over the furniture in the off-season. The bosses
had no other choice.

They did so, and crafted the biggest one-season improvement in baseball in 1998. The Cubs
jumped from 68 to 90 victories, only the fourth time
since the 1945 pennant season Chicago has reached

the 90-win mark. The additions of Henry Rodriguez, Mickey Morandini, and Rod Beck in the winter helped spur the Cubs to competitive stature, while the mid- and late-season pickups of Gary Gaetti, Glenallen Hill and Orlando Merced provided the additional spark needed to barely scratch out a wild-card play-off berth spot, won in a tie-breaking 5-3 win over the San Francisco Giants in an extra game on September 28 at Wrigley Field.

Finally, Sosa had players getting on base consistently in front of him. He had players picking him up behind him when he suffered an off-day at the plate. The Cubs could even sweep a three-game series with the Atlanta Braves without Sosa in the lineup, employing just enough hitting and sharp pitching.

Sosa immediately perked up when he came to spring training in late February with a new supporting cast of veterans ready, willing and able to do what it took to win.

"Definitely," he said of his improved mood compared to 1997. "When you're happy, it makes a lot of difference. The (bad) situation we had last year, we had to make some moves. We did. We have a much better quality team. We made some good moves in the off-season. When you're playing on a (good) team, it makes a lot of difference. There's no reason to get pissed off."

Lynch actually began retooling the Cubs on August 8, 1997, when he got rid of two albatrosses. Reliever Mel Rojas, an absolute disaster, and slump-ridden center fielder Brian McRae were dispatched along with reliever Turk Wendell to the New York Mets for center fielder Lance Johnson and backup infielder Manny Alexander, two longtime Sosa friends, and starting pitcher Mark Clark. The latter paid immediate dividends, going 6-1 with the Cubs to finish up the '97 season. Johnson promised to fill a hole at leadoff hitter after leading the majors with a career-high 227 hits in 1997 with the Mets.

But Lynch and Co. still had a big job to finish in retooling the roster. Management first had to find and identify players with the right attitude.

"We coined a phrase last year, 'WTP'—winning-type players," Cubs manager Jim Riggleman said. "So we let a lot of people walk out of here and brought in some different players who we perceived as winning-type players. People who were committed to winning. They've been on winning teams. They understood the sacrifices.

"In doing that, we were able to keep Sosa, (Mark) Grace,

some of the mainstays of the organization. (Mark) Clark and (Kevin) Tapani, who had been with us a short time, we were able to keep them. (Steve) Trachsel, (Rod) Beck, who was a winner."

Lynch looked to the Braves, one of the winningest teams in modern times, for his first new "WTP." Shortstop Jeff Blauser, coming off his best season with a .308 average and 70 RBI, was available as a free agent. Never a star, Blauser did the little things that helped fuel Atlanta victories. But he also had hit well against the Cubs with a .351 lifetime average and 15 homers, including 11 at Wrigley Field.

The Cubs, who had acquired Mickey Morandini, completed their big winter moves by signing closer Rod Beck as a free agent on January 15, 1998. Beck was so eager to meet his new teammates and fans that he flew to the Cubs Convention in Chicago the next day. Even though Beck would walk a high-wire act almost all of the 1998 season, he gave the Cubs confidence they often lacked in ninth-inning situations through a variety of closers in recent seasons.

More additions would come later in 1998, such as clutch hitters Gary Gaetti and Glenallen Hill, and pinch-hitter Orlando Merced. Sosa would flip-flop with first baseman Mark Grace into the No. 3 slot in the lineup, with pitchers now forced to throw strikes to Sosa for fear of ending up with a bad matchup with the .320-hitting Grace. But the emotional comfort of a team almost everyone praised as improved put Sosa at ease and enabled him to concentrate on elevating his game as 1998 began.

"He's happier because we have a better team," Rodriguez, who had known Sosa from back in the Dominican, said. "He's more relieved now because of the kind of team we have. Other people are here to take the pressure off him."

Grace offers up a minority report of sorts. No matter how many good hitters were stacked in the lineup, Sosa's time to break through with his big year may not have come anytime prior to 1998, in his view.

"I don't think it was necessarily going to happen because Sammy wasn't the player he is this year," Grace said. "What was he last year? .250 with 30 some-odd home runs. So there was no reason to protect him. Sammy was kind of unprotectable over these last few years. Because he was swinging anyway. Whether it was a ball or strike, he was swinging.

"People would always say that they needed somebody to protect Sammy, to hit behind Sammy. But it didn't matter if it was me. It didn't matter if it was Barry Bonds or Rafael Belliard, Sammy was swinging. But this year, with a whole lot of work with Jeff Pentland and a lot of talks with me and other guys, Sammy realizes that he can still be a 30-30 type of guy. He's done a lot better than that, of course, in the home-run column."

Grace offered a theory as to why pitchers simply did not walk Sosa to get to him. After all, Grace is Grace, never breaking out of the mid-teens range in homers, always more of a threat to tweak a pitcher than bomb him.

"First of all, he's got the ability to steal second base, whereas (Mark) McGwire doesn't," he said. "McGwire clogs the bases. Sammy can not only steal second, but he can also steal third. The second thing is the guy strikes out more than 150 times a year. So, in a big situation, a pitcher will think, 'Well, if I make my pitches here, I can strike Sammy out.' Well, so they try, end up making a mistake and there it goes."

Any Cubs fan and most baseball purists know all about Grace. In the Class AA Eastern League in 1987, he had the best overall minor-league season of any Cubs prospect in memory. That foretold a career as a gifted hitter, and Grace didn't disappoint. You knew what you were getting every year with him.

But fans may not have known the track records and personalities of the players who so ably helped Sosa get enough good pitches to hit 66 homers, got on base enough for him to drive in an astounding 158 runs, and help enable him to finish with a .300 average (.308) for only the second time in his career. The following are profiles of what Sosa has called a "family"—new, significant teammates who helped make 1998 a truly memorable season.

Lance Johnson

Nicknamed "One Dog" by White Sox announcer Ken Harrelson in the early 1990s, Johnson and Sosa met as young players on the South Side during that era. They've stayed in touch ever since Sosa was traded to the Cubs.

"I remember back when we were with the White Sox and I was telling him, 'Hey, man, if you learn how to cut down on your strikeouts and take a softer swing, you're gonna get more hits,'" Johnson said. "After he left and came over here, we would come and play the Cubs once a year (in an exhibition game) and I would talk to him and hug him. One time he told me, 'Hey, Dog, I'm getting ready to get some hits and then after I get my batting average up, then I'm going to start bombing.'" And I said, 'Sammy, now you're learning.' That's when I knew he was starting to mature and he was gonna end up being a very great player."

Johnson's style actually gravitated in the opposite direction compared to Sosa's. A .300-range slap hitter with the White Sox, Johnson began driving the ball while in his last year on the South Side, amassing 10 homers. In spring training, 1998, he had planned to muscle up even more as a Cub. But first a thigh injury, then a lingering hand injury cost him more than a half a season's playing time.

Johnson returned to regular's duty in center field in August, slowly but surely regaining his batting stroke. He batted more than .300 after his return with a pair of four-hit games and a three-hit, four-runs scored outing on August 27 against the Rockies in Colorado. And on a team that hardly ran, he was the only stolen-base threat with Sosa concentrating on hitting. His return was welcomed by Sosa just as he emerged into the stretch drive of the home-run chase.

"He's matured as a hitter," Cubs manager Jim Riggleman said. "Lance just has that great ability to put the big part of the bat on the ball. I'm not concerned about his patience at the plate. He's started to walk more in recent years, and his on-base percentage has been pretty good."

Sosa's not the only Cubs outfielder who feels he's settled into a second home in Wrigley Field. Johnson, a Cincinnati native, became a Cubs fan while attending Triton Junior College in the Chicago suburb of River Grove in 1982-83.

One of Johnson's teammates back then was Kirby Puckett. And he had a special Cubs connection.

"At the time, Leon Durham was a good friend of mine," he said. "I used to come down and watch him play. You ended up becoming a Cubs fan, with the appeal of Harry (Caray) and Wrigley Field.

"I'm here, and I'm happy. I kept my home here (after leaving the White Sox). I didn't sell it. I knew ultimately I'd be coming back. I didn't know whether it would be the North Side or the South Side.

"The fans know me from the White Sox, and they respect how hard I go out and play. I haven't had to change anything."

Johnson also dabbled in music production, at one time co-chairing Lance Productions, a Chicago recording company specializing in jazz and rhythm and blues.

"It was a good experience for me," he said. "Now I'm just like everyone else (off the field). I'll see movies, play golf, things like that."

Johnson has never gotten away from another kind of rhythm. Get on base, set things up for Sammy Sosa. Help out an old buddy. That was sweet music to a lot of baseball fans throughout 1998.

Brant Brown

Momentarily, Brant Brown may have wanted to jump in a hole and cover himself up after he dropped a fly ball with the bases loaded, two outs and the Cubs leading 7-5 in the bottom of the ninth inning in Milwaukee on September 23. That one misplay could have cost the Cubs the wild-card playoff berth.

For several minutes after the game, Brown tried to retreat into his locker in the 1950ish-style clubhouse in County Stadium. He faced away from his teammates, who were trying to console him, and the gingerly approaching media.

But in 1998, Brown had already proved he was made of strong stuff. He had answered the challenge of filling in for Lance Johnson in center field for most of the first half, after Johnson was sidelined with various injuries. And on September 23, he recovered from his own shock to hold back his well of emotions, turn around, and face four waves of media inquisitors.

Lesson one for ad-libbing for Brown. Normally, he's one of the most well-organized Cubs.

"I'm very routine-oriented," he said. "I think I suffer from obsessive-compulsive disorder. Everything's got to be neat, folded this way. My locker's got to be this way. I'm just kind of a neat freak and things just have to go a certain way.

"If I have a certain plan and it gets broken up, it really flusters me. I've got to sit back, take a deep breath and have to re-plan. I have to make a Plan B."

Brown's Plan A was to help the Cubs off the bench for 1998. There was no room as a starter in the outfield with Sosa,

Johnson and Henry Rodriguez set, right to left. Willing to accept any role, he proclaimed in spring training: "If you're a gladi-
ator and they just give you a knife, you take the knife."

He ended up with a war club instead. Brown took advantage of a starting role in center and the leadoff man's job with
gusto, sometimes showing off Sosa-like power, all the time getting on base with a .300 average to provide Sosa with runners
to drive in wire-to-wire throughout 1998.

Brown even took a page from Sosa's hero's script. He
slugged a game-winning, 11th-inning homer off the Braves' John
Rocker—lefty vs. lefty—on May 29 at Wrigley Field. One week
later, he ended the first Cubs-White Sox game at Wrigley Field
with a 12th-inning homer against Tony Castillo. And on June 18
at the Friendly Confines, he momentarily stole that month's
power show from Sosa with three homers against the Phillies.

"When I hit the game-winning homer against the Sox, one
of my favorite songs, by the Beastie Boys, was playing on the
(clubhouse) stereo when they were starting to interview me,"
Brown recalled. "I lost track of what the people were asking me
because I was trying to listen to the song. I was thinking, 'Could
we take a break for three minutes while this song finishes?'

"It seems like every time you're doing good and get on
track, all of a sudden everyone comes out of the woodwork. All
of a sudden, boom! It jinxes you and you go right back in the
crapper."

No, Brown didn't end up there, not even after the mishap
in Milwaukee. The only thing that really marred his season was
injury. A lot of Brown's forward momentum ended when he
suffered a separated shoulder 10 days after his Phillies heroics
in Detroit. But the Cubs still knew they had an up-and-comer
who can augment Sosa's power production in future years. Cubs
general manager Ed Lynch felt Brown had 20-homer potential.
That bore out with his 14 homers in 347 at-bats projected out
over a full season. No wonder Lynch resisted trade overtures for
Brown during the '98 season.

Brown has come a long way from just plain average seasons in the minors, then failing to nail down the left-field job
coming out of spring training in 1997. He also was slightly over-
whelmed by being shifted from first base to the outfield.

"Being in a new position and fighting for a job was a challenge," Brown said. "But my confidence was always there. I never
lost it."

He could have applied that statement to dropping the fly ball in Milwaukee. He never lost confidence, and the Cubs didn't lose the good attitude of a ballplayer. More help for Sosa down the line.

Mickey Morandini

Does a rising tide indeed lift all boats?

Did Mickey Morandini's career season lift Sammy Sosa to rarified heights?

Well, yes and no.

Sosa would have improved to all-galaxy status on his own. But it helped that he had the most productive No. 2 hitter in his Cubs career getting on in front of him in Morandini.

Taking advantage of the prime of his own career and being able to play at home, Morandini might have been the second-most valuable Cub after Sosa with his pesky hitting all season. Only a late-season lull dropped Morandini's average under .300—it was hovering in the .320s for awhile—and his on-base percentage under .400. The .400-plus on-base percentage that Morandini amassed for much of the season was a recent high for the Cubs, a notoriously free-swinging bunch since the mid-1980s.

Ryne Sandberg, a gifted No. 2 hitter, was already starting his decline by the time Sosa assumed a middle-of-the-lineup role in 1993. Except for power—Sandberg being a 20-homer-plus player —Morandini was virtually every bit the hitter the vintage Sandberg had been.

Morandini ensured he'd be on base for Sosa frequently with 172 hits and 72 walks, both numbers third-highest on the team—during the regular season. But he prefers to swing away.

"As much as I'd like to change my game to get on base and see Sammy come up six or seven times a game, I can't alter what's comfortable for me," he said. "I have to be aggressive, look for a fastball over the plate, and try to hack at the first good pitch I see. I feel I have as good of a chance of getting a base hit as a walk.

"There's also not been much of a chance in how pitchers throw to me when I bat in front of Sammy. Pitchers are still trying to get ahead of me with breaking stuff."

Morandini is a true all-around second baseman. He sported Gold Glove-calibre defense at second base in 1998. He believed

eammates greet Sammy Sosa after one of his historic 66 home runs.
o by Ron Vesely)

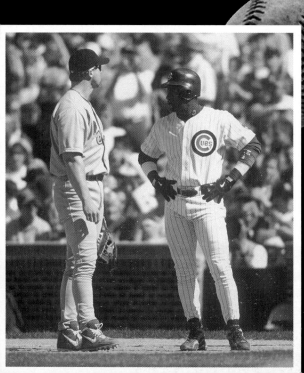

Sammy and Mark McGwire (left), two of the greatest sluggers in the history of baseball, chat during a meeting at first base. (Photo by Ron Vesely)

sammy

Sammy spent portions of three seasons with the Chicago White Sox, but hit just 28 home runs in 947 official at bats. (Photo by Ron Vesely)

Sammy Sosa ...
(Photo by Ron Vesely)

admired by both his teammates ...
(Photo by Ron Vesely)

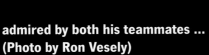

... and his
fans.
(Photo by
Ron
Vesely)

sammy

Sammy Sosa is a ball-hawking right fielder ... (Photo by Ron Vesely)

... and has an excellent arm, too. (Photo by Ron Vesely)

Two down. (Photo by Ron Vesely)

Though he doesn't possess great speed, Sammy always hustles. (Photo by Ron Vesely)

Sammy tags at third. (Photo by Ron Vesely)

sammy

Trumpeters sound a fanfare as the Sammy Sosa Celebration begins on Sept. 20, 1998. (Photo by Ron Vesely)

Members of Sammy's family, including his mother Lucretia (right in white dress), and other honors guests applaud their hero. (Photo by Ron Vesely)

The Dominican Republic's most celebrated citizen speaks to the sellout crowd at the Sammy Sosa Celebration. (Photo by Ron Vesely)

With the theme from "Superman" blaring over the loudspeakers, Sammy Sosa takes a victory trot around Wrigley Field. (Photo by Ron Vesely)

sammy

Sammy Sosa: one of baseball's most popular players. (Photo by Ron Vesely)

he was comparable to the slick-fielding Sandberg.

"Defensively, you can compare me; I'll accept that challenge," he said. "At this point of my career, I'm not going to win nine Gold Gloves in a row, but what I will be is a second baseman who's consistent, who will do the job.

"I've always worked on defense. I take pride in it. It's not natural; you've got to work on it. I'm better now than five years ago, when I had just made the adjustment from shortstop. Fortunately, I had all former middle infielders as managers or coaches, so that made the transition easy for me."

Morandini and his wife, Peg, were thrilled to get the Christmas present of his career—the announcement of his trade to the Cubs two days before the holiday. The family would be able to live most of the season (except when the schedule bunched up with day games following night games at Wrigley Field) in their Valparaiso, Indiana, home, an hour southeast of Chicago.

"I said, 'I'm not that lucky, that kind of stuff doesn't happen to me,'" Peg Morandini said.

Sosa has jumped into the active philanthropy with his "Sammy Claus" Christmas presents distributed all over the United States and the Dominican Republic. He also drew attention to relief for the Dominican Republic, battered by Hurricane Georges in September, 1998. The Morandinis could give Sosa pointers on how to handle philanthropic work.

They're long-time activists in fund-raising efforts for ALS, "Lou Gehrig's Disease." The Morandinis also purchased $20,000 annually in tickets to Philadelphia Phillies games during Mickey's tenure in Veterans Stadium to allow cancer-stricken stricken children to attend games. That program, "Mickey's MVP's," continued in Chicago with the purchase of 16 season tickets for each Wrigley Field game.

"We don't mind donating our time," Peg Morandini said.

Sounds like Sammy Sosa doesn't have to carry the load as a role model on the Cubs. Just like producing in the lineup, he doesn't have to carry the load alone off the field when folks like Mickey Morandini are present.

Henry Rodriguez

Left-handed hitting slugger Henry Rodriguez was credited with providing a comfort zone for Sammy Sosa this year. After all, Sosa's never batted with a 30-home-run man in the lineup. Rick Wilkins had a peak year of 30 homers in 1993, but the catcher had never come close before or since to that total.

Rodriguez will try to soft-pedal his own role in Sosa's upsurge. So will some Cubs organization types. "Maybe Henry Rodriguez got better because of Sammy," said one fellow.

"I don't want to say it's because of me," Rodriguez said. "Sammy has done whatever he's done. Maybe bring more life to his game or maybe he feels less pressure. Maybe he thinks the whole team we have here could compete and that's the way he's taking it."

Rodriguez's peak season was 36 homers for the Montreal Expos in 1996. He had 26 in 1997 in an off year. With the Cubs, he was headed for possibly a 40-homer, 100-RBI season, but several injuries, especially a sprained right ankle that hampered him from late August through the end of the regular season, cost him productive time.

Still, Rodriguez finished with 31 homers and 85 RBI in 415 at-bats. He was able to provide a second power source in the No. 5 slot in the lineup after doubles-slashing Mark Grace protected Sosa in the cleanup job.

Rodriguez praised the overall productive nature of the Cubs' lineup. Even after the 97 homers combined that Sosa and Rodriguez amassed were taken into account, the Cubs still had plenty of long-ball punch, finishing with a team-record 211 homers.

"I was lost for (three weeks) and we didn't lose any ground," he said. "That means we had a good ballclub, and if somebody got hurt, whoever he was, we picked him up."

Rodriguez's power revived an old Montreal custom—the tossing of "Oh Henry" candy bars onto the field. "He had a nice little schtick going," Mark Grace said. The Wrigley Field bleacher bums were just the right kind of people to start littering the warning track with chocolate.

"When you play in front of 20,000, 30,000, 40,000 people, you get more into the game," Rodriguez said of playing in Wrigley Field. "But sometimes you play and there's only 10,000 or 15,000 people (in Montreal), and you hear a lot of things in the stands. It gets kind of boring.

"I love to play in Chicago. I love day games. In Chicago, you see really well. I loved to go to Chicago (as an Expo) to hit, not just hit home runs."

Rodriguez did not mind being platooned in left field. In the second half of the 1998 season, Cubs manager Jim Riggleman used the right-handed hitting Glenallen Hill against left-handers.

"I don't hit great against lefties, only OK," Rodriguez said. "But the more left-handers I face, the better I'll get. I don't think I'm that bad against lefties. I don't want to sit every time I face a lefty."

Rodriguez was a product of the Los Angeles Dodgers' active Dominican Republic scouting efforts. He rose through the LA minor-league system, but eventually found his path blocked by assorted players at first base and the outfield. He began to come into his own in Montreal before finding a homer in Wrigley Field.

A native of the Dominican capital of Santo Domingo, Rodriguez knew Sosa for years. His presence and that of other Dominican players on the Cubs has definitely provided Sosa with an emotional comfort zone.

Along with Rodriguez, Sosa was joined by infielder Manny Alexander, catcher Sandy Martinez and, later in the season, by reliever Felix Heredia.

"For sure that's helped," Rodriguez said. "When you see people from your town, from the Dominican, five, six on the team makes you feel like you're back playing on one of the teams in the Dominican. You relax."

The ability to relax under pressure was a key for a lot of success on the '98 Cubs—from Sosa to his new muscleman partner Rodriguez, to all points of the lineup. At last.

Gary Gaetti and Glenallen Hill

Any team that makes the postseason needs offensive contributions from players who didn't start the season on the club.

That's what the Cubs received from Gary Gaetti and Glenallen Hill. And it's safe to say that without the clutch hitting these cagey veterans provided down the stretch, Sammy Sosa's singularly superb season would have been wasted on an also-ran.

Third baseman Gaetti had been released by the St. Louis Cardinals. Outfielder Hill was let go by the Seattle Mariners. Neither had a flaming ego that was damaged by rejection.

"It's personal character," Gaetti said of his reaction. "I knew I could play. It's something (you handle) in your heart."

Personal character also enables such veterans to not require a Sosa-like, centerpiece starring role.

"Over the course of the years," Hill said, "teams that do well have guys on the bench who also can be starters and have good attitudes. It's a good formula."

Gaetti ensured he'd start with 8 homers and 27 RBI in just 128 regular-season Cubs at-bats. He may have been the majors' best clutch hitter in September, period. Every time the Cubs needed a key hit, he collected it.

"I just know that I've always been a good player in August and September," he said.

He slugged a pinch homer that won a game against ace closer Trevor Hoffman on September 17, 1998. And he gave the Cubs a 2-0 lead with a two-homer off Mark Gardner in the eventual 5-3 win in the wild-card tiebreaking game on September 28 at Wrigley Field. In 34 starts at third base, a position he played superbly defensively, Gaetti was 40-for-125.

Not bad for a man who turned 40 the day the Cubs signed him on August 19. "He's playing like he's 32 years old," Riggleman said.

A native of the downstate Illinois city of Centralia, Gaetti grew up a St. Louis Cardinals fan. But he's also wanted to play for the Cubs for nearly a decade. He tried and failed to sign as a free agent after the 1990 season. Thwarted, he began a career as a Cubs Killer when he played for the Cardinals from 1996 to 1998.

"I knew Wrigley Field is a great place to hit," Gaetti said. "And confidence is a big part of hitting."

Hill, let go by the Cubs after a successful one-plus season of outfield work in 1993-94, did not hold any resentment against management. That's not his style. Instead, Hill calmly went about his business of being a quiet clubhouse leader and producer off the bench and in left field.

"You need 'gamers' on any winning team," he said. "I stay on an even keel. It's not part of my personality to get too high or too low."

Hill was game in a couple of vital pinch-hitting roles. He belted a two-run homer in the bottom of the eighth off the New York Mets' John Franco on July 25, enabling the Cubs to come from behind to win 3-2. Franco hadn't learned his lessons, apparently. That was Hill's third career pinch homer off the reliever.

Then, on August 20, Hill blasted his sixth overall career pinch homer, making it count good this time with the bases loaded. The grand slam off the San Francisco Giants' Julian Tavarez fueled a 7-3 Cubs victory.

So in the end, Sammy Sosa could have the most spectacular single-season season in Cubs annals. But he wouldn't have gotten to the playoffs without a little help from his friends.

Rod Beck

Rod Beck wasn't likely to bat much or contribute to the Cubs' lineup as the team's closer.

But in setting the emotional tone for the 1998 season, the most colorful-looking Cub was as vital as Sosa. His ice-water, high-wire acts in the ninth inning were only the public view of Rod Beck's ability to handle pressure on his way to 51 nerve-wracking saves. Only Randy Myers, with 53 saves in 1993, had more saves in a season in Cubs history.

Beck became almost the centerpiece of the clubhouse. The most down-to-earth and one of the most candid Cubs along with Mark Grace, Beck convened post-game gab sessions by his locker. With Grace, Jeff Blauser, Terry Mulholland and assorted others joining in, Beck—in his skivvies with cigarette and can of beer handy—rehashed the game in the manner of old-time players. We've heard of 25 different cabs for 25 different players in modern times. Don't we wish that the mega-millionaires would hang around together for a little camaraderie after games? Well, that happened on the '98 Cubs.

But Beck didn't just welcome his new teammates into his personal space. In the style of old-time players, he mingled with the fans after games at Bernie's, a popular watering hole just west of Wrigley Field at the corner of Clark and Waveland avenues.

And he served as a "media watchdog" for the Cubs. In one game, Beck suffered a self-admitted brain cramp and was slow in getting over to first base on a grounder to Mark Grace. The runner was safe, and the Cubs lost the game. Afterward, talk-show host Mike Murphy of WSCR-AM lambasted Beck for being too heavy to cover first. Listening as he often does, Beck had the private WSCR studio number. He dialed it, got on the air and set Murphy straight.

Beck became a hero to anyone who has trouble keeping the pounds off. His 238-pound girth didn't keep him from pitching every day, if called upon.

"I look at it this way," he'd often say. "I've never seen anyone on the disabled list with pulled fat."

He said he actually was in better shape than when he started with the San Francisco Giants in 1991.

"I came to the big leagues at 256 pounds, and I had 25 percent body fat," he said. "Now I'm 238 with 14 percent body fat. For me, that's the best I've ever been. I'm probably in the best shape of my career.

"But is that going to make me pitch any better? No. You still have to make the pitches, the ball's got to go where you want it to. I've seen guys running and running and running and running. That may be good for endurance and stamina for starting pitchers.

"The bottom line, I've got about 15 minutes out there for myself. If I'm out there any longer, we're probably going to lose anyway. I'm out there to make my pitches. You're not going to get that done by running five miles."

Okay, you can stand Beck's dangerous style of pitching in the ninth. But that shaggy hair flowing out of his cap and his Fu Manchu moustache have got to go, right?

Keep waiting. You won't see any clippings.

"My dad used to give me haircuts in the garage," Beck said. "Maybe I'm rebellious. I grew my moustache to look older. I've had it since I was 13. This is me. What you see is what you get. I'm comfortable this way."

Oh, by the way, when Beck isn't pitching, he's a gearhead. He's into drag racing. Fortunately, he'll wait until after the end of his career to try to learn how to drive. He just tools with engines now.

"When you're going that fast, you have to learn first," he said. "Auto racing is something I don't think one person can afford on his own. To have a race team costs millions, literally. Right now, I'm not that deep into it. It's a hobby. I'm an engine builder. But I eventually would like to get sponsors and get deep into it like Joe Gibbs did."

Beck got the Cubs deeper than they'd dare to dream back in February, 1998. Someone had to protect those hard-won leads that Sammy Sosa and Co. had fashioned after some good days at the plate. Beck did it, although, to quote the late Jack Brickhouse, "someone please bring me my stomach."

1998 NATIONAL LEAGUE UMPIRES

4 Mark Hirschbeck	13 Larry Poncino	22 Joe West	31 Bob Davidson	40 Jerry Crawford*
5 Angel Hernandez	14 Frank Pulli*	23 Ed Rapuano	32 Dana DeMuth	41 Jerry Meals
6 Bruce Froemming*	15 Jim Quick*	24 Jerry Layne	33 Mike Winters	43 Paul Schrieber
7 Eric Gregg	16 Rich Rieker	25 Charlie Williams	34 Greg Bonin	44 Kerwin Danley
8 Jeff Kellogg	18 Charlie Reliford	27 Steve Rippley*	35 Gary Darling	
9 Brian Gorman	19 Terry Tata*	28 Larry Vanover	36 Wally Bell	
11 Ed Montague*	20 Tom Hallion	29 Bill Hohn	37 Bruce Dreckman	
12 Gerry Davis	21 Harry Wendelstedt*	30 Randy Marsh*	38 Sam Holbrook	
		*Crew Chief		

Monday, Aug 31, 1998

Cincinnati

2 Harry Dunlop, Coach
3 Pokey Reese, IF
4 Jeffrey Hammonds, OF
6 Brook Fordyce, C
7 Ron Oester, Coach
9 Pat Watkins, OF
10 Eddie Taubensee, C
11 Barry Larkin, IF
15 Jack McKeon, MGR
16 Reggie Sanders, OF
17 Aaron Boone, IF
19 Denis Menke, Coach
21 Sean Casey, IF
23 Chris Stynes, IF-OF
25 Dmitri Young, OF-IF
26 Steve Cooke, LHP
29 Bret Boone, IF
30 Ken Griffey, Coach
31 Scott Sullivan, RHP
32 Danny Graves, RHP
33 John Hudek, RHP
34 Don Gullett, Coach
36 Gabe White, LHP
37 Stan Belinda, RHP
38 Pete Harnisch, RHP
39 Eduardo Perez, IF
40 Brett Tomko, RHP
43 Mike Remlinger, LHP
46 Melvin Nieves, OF
47 Tom Hume, Coach
48 Rick Krivda, LHP
49 Dennis Reyes, LHP
51 Jason Bere, RHP
54 Keith Glauber, RHP
57 Roberto Petagine, IF-OF
58 Steve Parris, RHP

No.	Player	Pos.	1	2	3	4	5	6	7	8	9	10	AB	R	H	RBI
16	R. Sanders	rf	K		Go 6-3	K		Go 6-3	K							
11	Larkin	ss	sing.		sing. R	F8	E-6									
57	Petagine	1b	E-8		BB R		sing.	F7								
25	D. Young	lf	sing. RBI		HR 3RBI	K			Go 5-3							
4	Hammonds	cf	F9		K		sing		K							
29	B. Boone	2b	Go 6-4		Go 5-3		WP K		BB							
10	Taubensee	c		K	F7		Go 4-3		Go 4-6							
17	A. Boone	3b		Go 2-3		K		K	Go 3							
43	Remlinger p/5th															
40	Nieves ph/5th															
40	Tomko 3b/7th			K		K		F9	Go 5-3							
23	Stynes 3b/7th															
33	Hudek p/8th															
			1/3	0/0	3/2	0/0	0/0	0/0	0/0							

Pitchers	IP	H	R	ER	BB	SO		Notes
Tomko	5⅓	6	5	2	3	8		
Remlinger/6th								
Hudek/8th								

CUBS

1 Lance Johnson, OF
2 Jeff Pentland, Coach
3 Dan Radison, Coach
4 Jeff Blauser, IF
5 Jim Riggleman, MGR
6 Glenallen Hill, OF
7 Tyler Houston, C-IF
8 Gary Gaetti, IF
9 Scott Servais, C
12 Mickey Morandini, IF
15 Sandy Martinez, C
17 Mark Grace, IF
18 Jose Hernandez, IF-OF
21 Sammy Sosa, OF
24 Manny Alexander, IF
26 Billy Williams, Coach
30 Jeremi Gonzalez, RHP
33 Don Wengert, RHP
34 Kerry Wood, RHP
36 Kevin Tapani, RHP
37 Brant Brown, OF-IF
38 Mike Morgan, RHP
39 Tom Gamboa, Coach
40 Henry Rodriguez, OF
43 Dave Bialas, Coach
45 Terry Mulholland, LHP
46 Steve Trachsel, RHP
47 Rod Beck, RHP
48 Dave Stevens, RHP
49 Felix Heredia, LHP
52 Matt Karchner, RHP
54 Mark Clark, RHP
59 Rodney Myers, RHP
63 Rick Kranitz, Instructor

No.	Player	Pos.	1	2	3	4	5	6	7	8	9	10	AB	R	H	RBI
1	L. Johnson	cf	BB R		sing. R			4-3								
12	Morandini	2b	K		F7	Flo 7		Go 6-3								
21	Sosa	rf	F9		HR #55 2RBI		K	K								
17	Grace	1b	BB		Go 4-3		2b	F7								
37	B. Brown	lf	K		Go 1-3		K	F10								
18	J. Hernandez	3b		F9	2b	K		K								
7	Houston	c		Go 1-3	Go 6-3		K	BB								
8	Gaetti	3b		F7	E-7 R	2b	F10									
34	Wood	p			HR 2RBI											
52	Karchner p/7th															
45	Mulholland p/8th															
47	Beck p/9th															
			0/0	0/0	2/2	3/3	0/0	0/0	0/0							

Pitchers	IP	H	R	ER	BB	SO		Notes
Wood	6	4	4	3	1	10		117 p, 76 k's — Wood
Karchner/7th								
Mulholland/8th								A - 36,700
Beck/9th								

Track Kerry Wood's Strikeouts K K K K K K K K K K K K K K K K K K K K K K K K K K K K K K

8/31/98-9/2/98

10

A Quiet Start to a Great Season

After a winter of rest, with Jeff Pentland's new-fangled hitting style on his mind and with the problems of 1997 receding in the past, Sammy Sosa prepared to report to the Cubs' 1998 spring training camp in Mesa, Arizona.

He would welcome an old friend, Henry Rodriguez, from the Dominican, and a cast of new characters acquired over the off-season. The usual aura of negativity about the Cubs' chances for the new season had been dampened down. It never goes away completely, though, and never will until the Cubs win the World Series.

And the last negative angle before his great season got underway would rear its ugly head ever-so-briefly.

Eager to get ready with the revamped roster, every Cub reported early to Fitch Park, the minor-league facility used before spring games actually began at HoHoKam Park, four blocks north on Center Street in Mesa. The majority of players were working out by Wednesday, February 18. Sosa had contacted Cubs management and asked for permission to report on Monday, February 23, so he could spend a final few days with wife Sonia and their four children in the Dominican. The collective bargaining agreement with the Players Association had set Wednesday, February 25, as the deadline for players to report before being subject to fines for tardiness. Yet most teams, the Cubs included, considered it good form to report early, family matters or not. The team had requested the players report on Friday, February 20.

"I don't consider it a big deal," Cubs general manager Ed Lynch said. "He has young children and he wanted some family time before he started working seven days a week for eight months. It's a very long season and I see no reason why he can't have a couple of extra days."

Some Cubs players raised their eyebrows about Sosa's delayed arrival. They, too, had families they had to leave behind, but they had reported early nonetheless. Cubs manager Jim Riggleman worked to prevent the usual clubhouse dissension from bubbling over.

"I have to make sure we don't let it creep in," Riggleman said. "The less said the better, because in three or four days, we won't remember this. In a perfect world, everyone would show up on the designated day. But it's not a perfect world and we have to adjust accordingly. It'll go away when Sammy gets here and shows he's working hard."

But it didn't go away until Sosa himself had his say on the day he arrived at camp. Usually mum on the clubhouse tenor, even when it was directed at him, Sosa spoke out.

"Definitely there's been sniping," he said, refusing to name players. "We have to help each other, pick up the other guy, rather than do that. I always hear there are some people who have a problem with me and what I do. Well, they know where to find me. Come to me. If I have a problem with someone, I go and tell them. That's all I'm asking. If there's a problem, come to me, man to man.

"We weren't all together last year. That has to change this year. People who know me know I don't play for myself. I'm a team player. Everybody has to get along and play for each other. I'm here to win a championship.

"This year is going to be better. We're not going to be in the same situation (last place). If we all play together, if I have a great year, if we play like a family, we should be good."

That did not turn out to be an idle prediction.

But after that brief monologue, smiles returned to Sosa's face. He laughed when both he and several reporters suggested a lascivious method for his staying in shape over the winter. This indeed would be a new year, and a new player attitude in the clubhouse—toward themselves, and toward Sammy Sosa.

The coaches picked up on the change. Sosa's demeanor was, of course, of particular interest to Jeff Pentland, in the middle of the reconstruction project to perfect the "tap-step" in his swing.

"When he got to spring training," Pentland later remembered, "he was the happiest person on the face of the earth."

Baseball and clubhouse issues temporarily took a back seat to the wall-to-wall coverage of Harry Caray's funeral in Chicago on February 27, 1998. Sosa, Lynch, Riggleman, first baseman Mark Grace, catcher Scott Servais and coach Billy Williams missed the team's first pre-season game at the Seattle Mariners' ballpark in Peoria, Arizona. The next day, Kerry Wood got some publicity for his first stint against big-league hitters, pitching two shutout innings against the Milwaukee Brewers in Phoenix. Wood fanned John Jaha, the first batter he faced; Jaha claimed he never even saw several of the fastballs.

Honoring Caray, in fact, dominated all the early going. It was the theme of the home opener on Friday, April 3, at Wrigley Field. Never mind that the Cubs had won two of the first three games at Florida, wiping out the bad memories of 1997. Or that Sosa showed off his new "short game," doubling in the first Cubs run, then singling for the third tally in the 10-3 win over the Marlins on Wednesday, April 1.

This was going to be the fans' first mass tribute to the biggest attraction the Cubs had possessed over the previous 15 years. Balloons were sent skyward, the fans roared in tribute, and Harry's widow, Dutchie, sang "Take Me Out to the Ballgame," as the 39,102 fans went along in true heartfelt fashion as the Cubs beat the Montreal Expos 3-1. The Cubs' home uniforms debuted a caricature of Caray on the sleeve, one that would be joined by a patch with Jack Brickhouse's "Hey Hey" home-run call four months later.

"I pointed to the patch of Harry as I was leaving," Cubs starter Steve Trachsel said, "because I wanted the fans to know we were going to be thinking about him all season. I'll remember this day for a long time."

But more indications of the season that lay ahead were being picked up by the players.

"This is a much more relaxed team than in the past," Servais said after the game. "If we get behind, we still think we can come back."

Good Cubs starting pitching continued the next day as lefty Terry Mulholland beat the Expos 3-1. Finally, Sosa got his power bat untracked, slugging his first homer of the year off Marc Valdes in the third inning. But, starting a pattern he would continue for a long time, Sosa began his post-game thoughts talking about others.

"We have some people who know how to play and come through in the right situations," he said. "I still have to not swing at the bad pitches, because there are people who can hit behind me. But the way we've been going is great."

The Cubs eventually got off to an 8-2 start, best in a generation and establishing the tempo for the '98 season. Rodriguez got off to a hot start, the whole lineup produced, and the pressure was finally taken off Sosa. He responded well, hitting around .340 and making contact with men on base. He had six homers in April altogether. But his improved overall offensive game took a back seat to the arrival of wunderkind Wood, who had started the season in the minors.

Inserted into the rotation in place of Mulholland, who moved to the bullpen, Wood showed flashes of both his strikeout potential and wildness in his first four starts, going 2-2. When he took the mound against the Houston Astros at Wrigley Field on a rainy day, Wednesday, May 6, at Wrigley Field, he had no idea he would pitch a game for the ages.

Matched against the Houston right-hander Shane Reynolds, Wood struck out Craig Biggio, Derek Bell and Jeff Bagwell in the first, and then Jack Howell and Moises Alou in the second. Meanwhile, Reynolds fanned Brant Brown, Mickey Morandini and Sosa in the Cubs' first. Eight batters up, eight down, all by strikeouts. The Cubs pushed across a run in the second on a double, an error and a sacrifice fly, and then Wood continued his date with destiny.

The rookie fanned Brad Ausmus in the third, and Bagwell and Howell in the fourth. Bell had flied out to Sosa leading off the fourth. Only one other Astro would hit the ball to the outfield on this day. In the fifth, Wood mowed down the side on strikes—Alou, Dave Clark and Ricky Gutierrez—for the second time in this contest. Eleven K's! He had the Cubs' single-game strikeout record of 15 well within sights, if the rain did not get any heavier. Mark Grace jokingly told umpiring crew chief Terry Tata, working first base, that he'd better not delay the game if he knew what was good for his health.

Somehow the heavy rain held off. Wood fanned Reynolds for No. 12 in the sixth, knocked off Bagwell, Howell and Alou in the seventh to tie the team record, and picked up even more momentum by whiffing Clark, Gutierrez and Ausmus in the eighth. Wood now had tied the all-time rookie strikeout record of 18 set by Bill Gullickson of the Expos against the Cubs in 1980. Now the all-time record awaited him.

Bill Spiers pinch hit for Reynolds, who had pitched a masterful game in his own right—two runs, eight hits, 10 strikeouts. Reynolds had gotten out of a bases-loaded jam (singles by Brown and Sosa and walk to Grace) in the third, and allowed just one more run in the eighth. But that was all forgotten as Wood, employing his combo slider-curve, one of the trickiest pitches seen in years, had the Astros baffled all day. He punched out Spiers for No. 19, tying the National League record. But Biggio, a great all-around hitter, managed to make contact and grounded to shortstop Jeff Blauser for the second out.

Bell, a real pro of a .300 hitter, was the last man. The slider-curve bore in again. No. 20, attaining the absolute outer limit of pitching achievement reached only by Roger Clemens, once each in 1986 and 1996. Wood pumped the air with his fist and pandemonium reigned first on the field, then in the clubhouse.

Comparisons with Sandy Koufax, a man whose stuff dictated he should have pitched in a higher league, were rife. Wood was now baseball's overnight sensation, and press conferences awaited him on the upcoming road trips as he set the two-game record of 33 strikeouts in his next start, fanning 13 Arizona Diamondbacks.

Wood mania shared baseball with Mark McGwire's uncommonly hot power start in the merry month of May 1998. On May 25, McGwire became the quickest major-leaguer ever to reach 25 homers with a 433-foot first-inning blast against the Colorado Rockies' John Thomson at Busch Stadium. Through May 25, McGwire had hit nine homers in his last seven games. Sure enough, McGwire, not yet enjoying his spokesman's role, soft-pedaled the feat.

"It's great for historians," he said. "We didn't play very well today (a 6-1 Cardinals defeat). So for all you historians, take it. Records are no good to you while you're still playing the game. Period."

On the night of May 25, Sosa slugged two homers off the Braves in Atlanta. He belted a solo shot off Kevin Millwood in the fourth, then a three-run blast off reliever Mike Cather in the eighth. The Cubs lost 9-5, but the headlines focused on a bench-clearing brawl in the fifth, provoked when catcher Sandy Martinez tossed the Braves' Curtis Pride off of him after a home-plate collision.

Two days later in the Cubs' next game, Sosa had two more homers, giving him 13 for the season to go along with 38 RBI, in a 10-5 loss to the Philadelphia Phillies at Wrigley Field. He was hitting .338, yet did not attract much notice. Nice improvement in the batting average, Sammy, but will you keep it up? He was headed for his typical 36-homer, 120-RBI type season. The Cubs had kept their heads above .500 through some roller-coaster times while Wood, still just 20, was the mule pulling the wagon. Those were the news angles of spring, 1998.

Oh, Sosa got in the headlines, all right—for an old-fashioned Cubs foible. On May 28, the Cubs trailed the Phillies 8-7 in the bottom of the ninth after the Phillies had trailed 7-1 at one point. Sosa was the tying run on first. Mark Grace doubled to the right-center wall. Sosa barreled around third while third base coach Tom Gamboa continued to wave him in. Suddenly, Gamboa put on the stop sign—too late. Sosa jammed on the brakes four steps past third base. He slipped and jammed his left thumb sliding, trying to break his fall. The relay came in fast. Sosa was caught in a rundown and was tagged out.

"If the relay throw is to the side of the cutoff man or short of him, I'm sending him," Gamboa said. "But it was a perfect throw. In fairness to Sammy, I think I gave him the sign too late."

Sosa believed he would have scored if Gamboa kept him coming. But he wouldn't be doing any baserunning, batting or fielding for the next few days. His thumb was sore.

Any great season has its glitches. Sosa is normally a fast healer. And did he ever get well. And his name, conveniently short for headline writers, would take center stage very soon.

11

The Kerry and Sammy Show

Maybe it didn't have the international star power of the Mark and Sammy Show. But for Cubs fans—and any baseball purists desiring the see the peaks of human performance—The Kerry and Sammy Show was good enough.

Making its debut at Wrigley Field early in the 1998 season, the tag-team partnership of Kerry Wood and Sammy Sosa is destined, given good health, to serve as one of the game's top attractions well into a new millennium.

See Kerry blow 'em down. See Sammy hit 'em a mile. And, lo and behold, see Kerry hit 'em at least one foot over the fence. They count just the same.

Who can beat that combination? Whatever the Cubs' fates in the future, they possess the game's top young fireballer in Wood, a kid whose stuff was comparable to Sandy Koufax at its best. And, backing him up is the newly minted 60-homer man/baseball spokesman in Sosa. Is there a better one-two gate attraction on the same team in baseball? And was there ever a time when Cubs fans could take comfort in watching two of the top five most sensational players in blue pinstripes?

Kerry helped Sammy's quest for the postseason with a rookie-best 13-6 record and an astounding 233 strikeouts in 166 2/3 innings. Long before Sosa caught fire with his 20-homer June, Wood was baseball's certifiable sensation after his record-tying 20-strikeout spree against the Houston Astros on May 6 at Wrigley Field. Cubs coaches Billy Williams and Phil Regan, along with broadcaster Ron Santo, compared Wood's fastball and breaking pitch in the 20K affair to Sandy Koufax's at his best. And Koufax possibly is the greatest pitcher of all time.

Wood's debut was one of the most eagerly awaited in Cubs' history. Hyped ever since the Cubs plucked him as their first-round draft choice out of Grand Prairie High School in suburban Dallas in 1995, he caused the countdown due to his strikeout feats in the minors. Only 20 when spring training 1998 began, Wood increasingly showed he was ready for the majors while the Cubs brass acted with caution. Anaheim Angels manager Terry Collins said that if the Cubs had five starters better than Wood, they'd be going directly to the World Series.

With a combination slider-curve he developed in the minors in 1997, Wood thought he had the arsenal to break in successfully.

"It's fast enough. I'm happy with my fastball," he said. "I love the slider. I'll throw it anytime. It helps the curve. The last five feet, it dives toward the left-handed hitter's box. It's a pitch that looks like a fastball coming in. It's a pitch I throw when I need a ground ball with a man on base."

Wood desired to evolve into a pitcher from the thrower he had been in the minors.

"I want to be able to go to other pitches," he said. "If I see a situation where I've got a 3-and-1 count on a left-handed batter with two outs and a guy in scoring position, I'm not going to give it (fastball down the middle) to him and give up a run. In any one start, you won't have all four pitches working. I'd like to be able to have three working. Marty DeMerritt (Cubs' Triple-A pitching coach) told me that out of every five starts, you have one with your really good stuff."

After one start in Triple-A, Wood was promoted to the Cubs' rotation and never looked back. An elbow injury in the final month was the only factor that slowed him down. He impressed in his first Cubs starts. Then came the 20K game, in which he made a whole mess of great Astros hitters look silly with that slider curve. Many people who watch baseball believe was the best game they had ever seen pitched, a game with better stuff shown in no-hitters. After all, in 1969, the Cubs' Ken Holtzman no-hit Henry Aaron and the Atlanta Braves without one strikeout.

As at the season grind wore on, Wood—despite a fastball topping out at 100 mph—realized he couldn't do it all himself. He couldn't strike out everybody. A number of hitters tagged him good as he served up 14 homers. And he realized he needed help from his friends, namely Sosa.

Sammy was eager to oblige. He slugged seven homers in Wood's victories, including his rooftop blast, one of a pair in the June 20 game against the Philadelphia Phillies at Wrigley Field. Wood made his long-ball debut with a homer into the center-field shrubbery.

In Wood's August 26 start in Cincinnati, he showed he had no ill effects from a "tired arm" earlier in the month by striking out 16 Reds, his second-highest game total. Sosa, of course, obliged with his 52nd homer. Then, in his last regular-season start on August 31 at Wrigley Field, Sosa blasted No. 55 in the third. Not to be outdone, Wood collected his second homer in the 5-4 Cubs victory. The fans demanded a curtain call from Wood. But, unwilling to show up the Cincinnati Reds, Wood stayed put in the dugout while Sosa took the bow in his place to the roar of the crowd.

Sosa came around at just the right time—not only to bail Wood out in some of his starts, but also to take the pressure off the 21-year-old who was experiencing major-league life for the first time.

"I think it definitely could have," Wood said of Sosa bailing him out from melting down from all the attention. His emergence onto the world stage at midsummer prevented Wood, mature for his age but still inexperienced in the bright lights of attention, from burning out prematurely, and possibly ruining a good persona.

"It was pretty hectic there for a couple of weeks," Wood said of the press conferences in every road city after the 20K game. "Sometimes it's hard to concentrate. That's why I think Sammy did such a great job with all this stuff going on and he was still able to go there and perform knowing that before and after each games, he was going to have press conferences. He had two a day."

"He was a poster boy and he handled it well. He's definitely taking a lot of the tension and pressure off me, which definitely couldn't hurt."

A reporter was interviewing Kerry outside the Cubs' minor-league spring training complex in 1997. They sat on the grass under a tree and talked about the far future, about how Wood could handle fame if, and when, it ever came. He said he'd be ready. But he never could have foreseen the media mobs descending after his starts as a dress rehearsal for the Sosa spectacle later. Then, after his first appearance in a big-league spring training game at the Milwaukee Brewers' spring home in the Maryville section of Phoenix, Paul Sullivan of the *Chicago Tribune* and another reporter were the only ones to talk with Wood by his locker, in a deserted clubhouse. He would never be that alone in public again.

So the kid needed a break from the inquiring hordes. Sosa gave it to him. And Wood actually learned from the smooth way Sosa handled the media.

"In the situation that came up here and all that stuff that happened so quickly, I did a pretty OK job with handling that stuff," he said. "But after seeing the way Sammy handled it, if it does come around for me again, I'm just gonna have fun with it.

"Who knows, five years from now, I might be begging to talk to reporters."

Wood was amazed Sosa was able to handle the attention through the inevitable down moods any human experiences.

"Everybody has a time when they don't want to talk, on a particular day or when they're having a bad week or something," Wood said. "They just don't want to talk to anybody and forget about everything that's going on and just relax and get refocused. You know Sammy liked it. I promise you he liked it and he's having fun with it."

Handling the heavy media load distracted Wood from some simple everyday tasks, so Sammy was like some super-closer, coming in to give him relief.

"For me coming up in that situation with all the attention I was getting there early on, there were just so many things going on I was forgetting all kinds of stuff," he said.

"I came to the field one day and left the stove on at the apartment. I was pitching that day. I'm sending for fire trucks while I'm on the mound. I had to go have somebody call the apartment."

But Wood's feeling was different when he could simply concentrate on baseball—on the mound and at the plate.

On June 20, Cubs manager Jim Riggleman gave him the green light on the first pitch in his at-bat. Wood, of course, soft-pedals his feet.

"The wind was blowing out," he said. "I had a pretty good breeze blowing out and if he throws an offspeed pitch there, first pitch I'll probably go out to the training room. I was guessing fastball. The ball was up, I put good wood on it, and the wind blew it out."

On August 31, when Wood came back to the dugout after rounding the bases, Sosa gave him a big bear hug. Then he stepped out the dugout with a big grin to doff his cap as Wood's fill-in.

"They didn't come to see me take the curtain calls," Wood recalled. "I was pumped. I mean, we were down by one run, we had a guy on first base and I put us up (one run). It was uplifting not only for me just hitting a home run, but to go back out the next inning knowing we go the lead and it's time to shut the door."

Wood's a confident young man. He's also a budding analyst of pitching. Another pitcher who flat-out knew the game cold was Greg Maddux. Wood would cherish just being in Maddux's class as a mound craftsman.

He can actually dissect Sosa's game. Think ahead five years, with all the experiences Wood will absorb in the interim, to see how much smarter he'll be at the time.

"You can't make a mistake the way he was swinging the bat (in 1998)," he said. "Now, last year (1997), not being up here and seeing him in person, but watching a lot of games on TV in the clubhouses where I was playing, anytime you got two strikes to hit, or even one strike, you could throw two sliders in the dirt and he was swing at them.

"This year, even though he's going to get his hacks in, he's been 100 percent more patient than I've seen in the past. He's a completely different hitter."

So how well could Wood pitch against Sosa? The kid's confidence—and practicality—show up side by side here.

"I think seeing Sammy all year that I would have the edge," he said. "But if I faced him 10 times, he would get me a couple of times."

The Cubs have emotionally fed off Sosa. Wood said no other kind of player is acceptable on a winner.

"We have a lot of players on this team and we feed off the fact that guys go out there and give 100 percent every day," he said. "To see guys, either up by 11 or down by 11, diving for balls, you appreciate it. For me, I want all my teammates to look at me and say I gave 110 percent when I was out there every time.

"I could say that about a lot of guys out there and Sammy is definitely one of them. He plays every day, he plays hard, he has fun and he loves the game."

Wood and Sosa are obviously the cornerstone for a Cubs contender that might break the decades-long losing syndrome.

"I think it's time to build," he said. "The fans deserve it. The city deserves it. A winning baseball team here would be great. And if people say Sammy and I have started that, then I'm glad to be a part of it.

"We've definitely gained a lot of respect this year. Not only from the fans here, but from other teams. People see we're serious about this.

"Not only the fans enjoyed us winning, the players enjoyed us winning, but I also think management and the guys in the front office are enjoying it more than anybody. They're enjoying it, so I think they're gonna keep it going. They're having more fun winning, I'm sure, than they did losing in the past. I have a good feeling that we'll continue this for awhile."

Sosa worked his way up the hard way. Wood was seemingly dropped from the sky as the Cubs finally got a shot at a pitching phenom, after Koufax went to the Dodgers, Nolan Ryan went to the Mets and Roger Clemens—having been passed up by the Cubs in the 1983 draft—was snapped up by the Red Sox.

The Kerry and Sammy Show. Get your tickets early. They'll go fast.

12

June 1998 and Record-Busting

The Cubs' team and Sammy Sosa's personal indicators didn't exactly coincide as May 1998 ended.

After a roller-coaster month, the Cubs suddenly caught fire, sweeping the Atlanta Braves in a three-game series at Wrigley Field.

The coup de grace was a 4-2 triumph on Sunday, May 31. Momentum had swung so powerfully to the Cubs that manager Jim Riggleman could get away with using Jeff Blauser, in the middle of what turned out to be a lost season on the field for the shortstop, as the cleanup hitter in place of Sosa in the opening game on Friday, May 29. All of this was headline news. The Braves had been so good while the Cubs had been mediocre or worse, both for so long, that the last three-game broom brigade effort over Atlanta had taken place in 1989.

Amazingly, the Cubs nailed the Braves without Sosa. He had bruised his left thumb sliding on May 28 against the Philadelphia Phillies and sat out the entire Braves series. These would turn out to be three of the four games Sosa would miss—all to injury—the entire 1998 season.

Sosa finally returned to the lineup on Monday night, June 1, against the Florida Marlins at Wrigley Field. If the thumb bothered him, he didn't show it. After second baseman Mickey Morandini walked in the first, Sosa slugged his 14th homer off Marlins starter Ryan Dempster. Then, in the eighth, Sosa homered again with two runners on to add nothing but gravy to the Cubs' 10th consecutive win; it would be their longest winning streak since 1970.

"I guess I'm lucky," he said. "I'm not 100 percent, but I can hold the bat pretty good."

The 2-for-5 night maintained Sosa's good start. He finished the game batting .344.

But Sosa wasn't the main Cubs story. Kerry Wood was still sizzling in the wake of his 20-strikeout game. On Wednesday, June 3, at Wrigley Field, Kid K increased his record to 6-2 with a nine-strikeout, five-hit victory over the Marlins. Sosa homered in the fifth, making it seven homers in his previous six games— broken up, of course, by the thumb injuries. But he could continue to dress without much media pestering him at his locker. Across the clubhouse aisle, Wood was being inundated again.

At the other end of the locker room, first baseman Mark Grace was running out of adjectives to describe Wood.

"Outstanding. Unbelievable. He's something else. Damn kid," Grace said.

Over the next three games, Sosa would light his own fire like never before. But with the White Sox in Wrigley Field for a ballyhooed three-game series and the Bulls playing the Utah Jazz in the National Basketball Association Finals, most of the media attention was directed elsewhere.

Sosa belted his 17th homer, a two-run shot, off Sox rookie Jim Parque in the fifth on Friday, June 5. But the blast rated only afterthought status as a result of the fluky nature of this game.

With the Sox's Wil Cordero on first in the eighth inning and the score tied at 5, Magglio Ordonez slashed a drive into the right-field gap between Sosa and center fielder Jose Hernandez. But the ball was swallowed up by the ivy. Both Sosa and Hernandez knew the ground rules. Cordero would have easily scored the lead run, but he was called to third on the ground-rule double.

"I almost went to pick it up, but I was thinking quick," Hernandez said. "I got there before Sammy. I saw it go in the vines and I put my hands up."

The late Harry Caray's heavenly interference was cited by some for the kicking of the ball into the vines. "We got lucky," Hernandez said. And then Brant Brown wrote a storybook finish to the game with a home run leading off the bottom of the 12th, giving the Cubs a 6-5 victory.

Still another hero of the day took attention away from Sosa when he homered in the seventh inning against the Sox on Saturday, June 6. Career minor-leaguer Derrick White, recently called up as an extra man off the bench, blasted a Sosa-like homer onto Waveland Avenue as a pinch-hitter in the sixth inning, the key hit in the 7-6 victory.

"Sammy had been talking to me about looking for a ball to swing at," White said. "He said it's easier to hit something up than something down. He was right. ...The pitch I got was up."

That was White's first, and last, hurrah with the Cubs. He was optioned down to the minors soon after, and then released by the organization despite impressive Triple-A numbers.

Perhaps figuring he'd have to rack up more RBI than anyone else to rate a line, Sosa drove in five in the Sunday, June 7, finale in which the Cubs swept the Sox out of the Friendly Confines in a 13-7 victory. He slashed a two-run double in the first, then belted a three-run homer (No. 19) in the fifth.

"I'm practicing by playing Nintendo baseball with my daughter and my wife," Sosa said. "They usually beat me, so I have to take it out on other teams."

By now, his teammates began to take notice.

"I don't think I've ever seen anything like that," Grace said of Sosa's budding power surge. "Maybe Mark McGwire. But I've never seen McGwire do it. Sammy's just locked in. It's impressive."

He hadn't seen anything. Sosa quieted over the next few days. He then collected homer No. 20 for the season on Saturday, June 13, in a 10-8 Cubs win at Veterans Stadium in Philadelphia. Two days later, Sammy ensured he'd be in position to make history by lowering the boom against Cal Eldred and the Milwaukee Brewers at Wrigley Field.

A crowd of 37,903 gathered to see the newly formed geographical rivalry between the Cubs and Brewers on Monday night, June 15. By now, Sosa had bulled his way onto center stage. He lashed an Eldred pitch into the right-field bleachers in the first. In the third, he blasted a serve onto Waveland Avenue.

Finally, in the seventh, Sosa gave the ball hawks on Waveland yet another souvenir with No. 24, prompting a curtain-calling crowd to bellow "Sammy! Sammy!" in unison. In true 1998 Cubs fashion, though, his teammates had to scrape by to win, 6-5.

"I wasn't trying for home runs," Sosa said. "I'm trying to hit to right field more. When I do that, the home runs come."

Statistics crunchers began to tackle their databases on Wednesday, June 17, when Sosa nailed No. 25, his 16th homer in his past 18 games, in the third inning against the Brewers. The Cubs lived by the sword and died by it, however, in this game as John Jaha slugged a three-run homer off Cubs starter Kevin Tapani in the seventh to give Milwaukee a 6-5 win.

The strong-armed Sosa unfortunately could not pitch for the Cubs. Chicago pitching, especially the bullpen, was getting increasingly shaky by this point. Six Cubs pitchers combined to allow 19 hits in a 9-8, 12-inning loss to the Philadelphia Phillies at Wrigley Field on Friday, June 19. But Sosa soothed the sting of defeat a bit by shifting into overdrive toward the all-time record for homers in June. He belted two homers, giving him 14 for the month.

"Sosa has never hit more than 40 homers in a season, making him an unlikely prospect to unseat Maris," Michael Rosenberg wrote in *The Chicago Tribune* the following morning. But Rosenberg had been among the first to pop Sosa the magic question about breaking Roger Maris' home run record after the June 19 game.

"No, no, nooooo," Sosa said, while also professing lack of awareness about the June home run record. "Well, you never know. I'll let you know after the season is over." It would be a long time until Maris' name disappeared from postgame questioning.

Dress rehearsal No. 2 for the homer-quest media crunch took place a little more than 24 hours later, on Saturday night, June 20. And in front of the sellout Wrigley Field throng of 39,761, Sosa launched his most spectacular home run of the season—an all-time Wrigley Field heat-seeker.

He tuned up for his long distance effort with a two-run homer onto Waveland Avenue off Phillies starter Matt Beech in the third. But he far outdid most of his previous tape-measure shots in the sixth against side-arming reliever Toby Borland. Breaking the June record for homers with style, he launched the blast far into the night. The ball appeared headed toward the roof of the three-story apartment building on the northwest corner of Waveland and Kenmore avenues. But the ball hooked to the left and landed in the middle of partygoers on the roof of a two-story building next door. Almost everyone in Wrigley Field was speechless.

"The homer he belted onto the rooftop was the most exciting homer I've ever seen, and I've seen some great ones," Cubs second baseman Mickey Morandini said. "For him to hit the ball as hard and as far as he did made everybody in Wrigley Field awestruck."

The homer onslaught was contagious. To top off the festive evening, strikeout phenom Wood belted his first major league homer into the shrubbery in dead-center field. Some kind of magic was in the night air.

Now, finally, Sosa's name was linked with Babe Ruth—a fact that elicited an "Oh, God, no" response from Sosa when it was brought up to him. The Bambino had set the record of 15 homers in June in 1930, later matched by Bob Johnson in 1934, Maris in 1961 and Pedro Guerrero in 1985.

"I've never seen anyone hit like this for power," Cubs manager Jim Riggleman said. "Sammy's so hot, I don't even have the words to describe it. He's setting standards I don't know if anyone is going to meet." Especially in such a short period of time in Cubs' history.

Sosa slugged still another homer, No. 30 for the season, against the Phillies in a 7-2 loss on Sunday, June 21. For the second time in 1998, Sosa had collected 10 homers in nine games. No other Cub had ever hit 10 in a period of time of less than 17 games. By now, Sosa had 21 homers and 43 RBI in his last 22 games. And, finally, he'd be linked up with McGwire for the remainder of the season, statistically and emotionally. McGwire had become only the second National Leaguer to hit 30 homers before the end of June. Sosa was the third.

"Right now, I'm not going to lie to you," Sosa said, allowing himself some time to enjoy the moment. "I'm feeling pretty good. I'm in my zone."

Then, suddenly, the Cleveland Indians yanked Sosa out of it. A tense and exciting two-game interleague series commenced at Wrigley Field on Monday, June 22. The Indians, playing before thousands of vocal partisans—some garbed in full Cleveland uniforms—shut down Sosa. He went 0-for-9 in the series. But his lineup protection, with the exception of Henry Rodriguez, also was stifled by cagey Indians pitchers like Doc Gooden.

"I'm a human being. I'm not Superman," Sosa said after the second game, in which he left two runners on in the fifth and the bases loaded in the sixth.

"They pitched me tough. What do you want me to do? I can't do it every day, and I can't do it alone."

The blanking against the Tribe turned out to be just a momentary detour in Sosa's journey through the records book. On the night of Wednesday, June 24, at Tiger Stadium in Detroit, he tied old-time Tiger Rudy York's record for homers in a month with 18, set in August 1937. Morandini warmed Sosa up for his feat by homering in the first, and then the slugger made it a back-to-back job. But the Cubs lost again when Bobby Higginson slugged a two-run, two-out homer in the ninth off Rod Beck to tie the game at 6, two innings before Gabe Alvarez put the finishing touches on the victory with an RBI single off Dave Stevens. Riggleman saw fit to give the Cubs a tongue-lashing after their 11th loss in 15 games, almost negating the positive momentum of the long winning streak three weeks earlier.

Five days remained in the month. Sosa didn't want to wait to smash records. On Thursday, June 25, he blasted his 19th homer of the month in the seventh to pass up the old York mark. Once again, though, dialing long distance wasn't enough in the Cubs' 6-4 loss.

"I'm happy I'm in the book, but for me it won't mean nothing now because we lost the game," Sosa said. "It would have been much better if we'd have won."

But why stop there? No. 20 for June was recorded on Tuesday night, June 30, against the Arizona Diamondbacks at Wrigley Field. Sosa sure knew how to excite the fans. Two of them intruded onto the field and caught up with Sosa as he trotted between second and third. He practically had to use an old Gale Sayers hip fake to get around the intruders at third base. Afterward, Sosa smiled about the fans, an interesting emotion considering the security problems other athletes have suffered in different sports.

"I picked them up (noticing them) just before I reached third," Sosa said. "I don't have a problem with nobody. They just said congratulations."

Sosa knew no other way to handle even a security breach in 1998. As with most other aspects of his transformed life, he did it with a smile and a couple of quips.

And there was far more to come.

Wednesday, Sept. 2, 1998

1998 NATIONAL LEAGUE UMPIRES

4 Mark Hirschbeck	13 Larry Poncino	22 Joe West	31 Bob Davidson	40 Jerry Crawford*
5 Angel Hernandez	14 Frank Pulli*	23 Ed Rapuano	32 Dana DeMuth	41 Jerry Meals
6 Bruce Froemming*	15 Jim Quick*	24 Jerry Layne	33 Mike Winters	43 Paul Schrieber
7 Eric Gregg	16 Rich Rieker	25 Charlie Williams	34 Greg Bonin	44 Kerwin Danley
8 Jeff Kellogg	18 Charlie Reliford	27 Steve Rippley*	35 Gary Darling	
9 Brian Gorman	19 Terry Tata*	28 Larry Vanover	36 Wally Bell	
11 Ed Montague*	20 Tom Hallion	29 Bill Hohn	37 Bruce Dreckman	
12 Gerry Davis	21 Harry Wendelstedt*	30 Randy Marsh*	38 Sam Holbrook	

*Crew Chief

Cincinnati

No.	Player	Pos.	1	2	3	4	5	6	7	8	9	10	AB	R	H	RBI
23	Stynes	3b	F10 8	FC 4-6		F10 8		H0 2								
21	S. Casey	1b	F10		sing.		sing.									
16	R. Sanders ph/8th rf															
11	Larkin	SS	sing		DP 6-4-3		G0	BB								
25	D. Young	lf	G0 3			G0 3-1	K		K							
36	a. White															
57	Petagine	rf-1b/8th		G0 4-3	F10 9		F8		K							
4	Hammonds	cf	BB		sing.		K		sing.							
29	B. Boone	2b	F10 9	F10 8			K		K							
6	Fordyce	c	K			G0 4-3		F10 8		K						
33	Hudek p/7th															
51	Bere	p		BB	K			2b F10 8							
12	Taubensee c/7th															
9	Watkins rf/8th															
46	Nieves ph/8th															
			0	0	0	0	0	0	0	0	0			2	7	

Pitchers	IP	H	R	ER	BB	SO		Notes
Bere	6	5	1	1	3	5		
Hudek /7th	1	0	0	0	1			
White /8th (5-3)	1	4	3	3	0	1		

CUBS

No.	Player	Pos.	1	2	3	4	5	6	7	8	9	10	AB	R	H	RBI
1	L. Johnson	cf	F10 7		3b		F10 9		BB F10 5							
12	Morandini	2b	K		F10 9		K		K							
21	Sosa	rf	G0 6-3		sing.		HR #58	F8								
17	Grace	1b	G0 6-3	BB		BB		F10							
37	B. Brown	lf		2b	F10 3		out	sing.							
6	G. Hill ph/8th															
8	Gaetti	3b	F10 7	K		8	HR 2-31	BB							
24	M. Alexander	ss	G0 1-3		G0 6-4		F10 4									
9	Servais	c		F10 8		F10 8		HBP HR							
46	Trachsel	p		K		K		S 1-3	2b						
50	Maxwell ph/7th															
45	Mulholland /8th															
52	Karchner p/8th															
49	Heredia p/8th															
18	J. Hernandez ph/8th															
	ph/8th															
47	Beck p/9th	lf	0	0	0	0	8	1	0	3			4	9	

Pitchers	IP	H	R	ER	BB	SO		Notes
Trachsel	7	4	0	0	2	5		A-55,761
Mulholland /8th	⅓	1	1	1	0	0		T-2:44
Karchner /8th	⅓	1	0	0	0	0		
Heredia /8th (4-2)	1⅓	1	0	0	0	1		

Track Kerry Wood's Strikeouts K K K K K K K K K K K K K K K K K K K K K K K K K K K K K K

Beck /9th (42) 1 1 0 0 0 2

8/31/98-9/2/98

Cincinnati roster
- 2 Harry Dunlop, Coach
- 3 Pokey Reese, IF
- 4 Jeffrey Hammonds, OF
- 6 Brook Fordyce, C
- 7 Ron Oester, Coach
- 9 Pat Watkins, OF
- 10 Eddie Taubensee, C
- 11 Barry Larkin, IF
- 15 Jack McKeon, MGR
- 16 Reggie Sanders, OF
- 17 Aaron Boone, IF
- 19 Denis Menke, Coach
- 21 Sean Casey, IF
- 23 Chris Stynes, IF-OF
- 25 Dmitri Young, OF-IF
- 26 Steve Cooke, LHP
- 29 Bret Boone, IF
- 30 Ken Griffey, Coach
- 31 Scott Sullivan, RHP
- 32 Danny Graves, RHP
- 33 John Hudek, RHP
- 36 Don Gullett, Coach
- 36 Gabe White, LHP
- 37 Stan Belinda, RHP
- 38 Pete Harnisch, RHP
- 39 Eduardo Perez, IF
- 40 Brett Tomko, RHP
- 43 Mike Remlinger, LHP
- 46 Melvin Nieves, OF
- 47 Tom Hume, Coach
- 48 Rick Krivda, LHP
- 49 Dennis Reyes, LHP
- 51 Jason Bere, RHP
- 54 Keith Glauber, RHP
- 57 Roberto Petagine, IF-OF
- 58 Steve Parris, RHP

Cubs roster
- 1 Lance Johnson, OF
- 2 Jeff Pentland, Coach
- 3 Dan Radison, Coach
- 4 Jeff Blauser, IF
- 5 Jim Riggleman, MGR
- 6 Glenallen Hill, OF
- 7 Tyler Houston, C-IF
- 8 Gary Gaetti, IF
- 9 Scott Servais, C
- 12 Mickey Morandini, IF
- 15 Sandy Martinez, C
- 17 Mark Grace, IF
- 18 Jose Hernandez, IF-OF
- 21 Sammy Sosa, OF
- 24 Manny Alexander, IF
- 26 Billy Williams, Coach
- 27 Phil Regan, Coach
- 30 Jeremi Gonzalez, RHP
- 33 Don Wengert, RHP
- 34 Kerry Wood, RHP
- 36 Kevin Tapani, RHP
- 37 Brant Brown, OF-IF
- 38 Mike Morgan, RHP
- 39 Tom Gamboa, Coach
- 40 Henry Rodriguez, OF
- 43 Dave Bialas, Coach
- 45 Terry Mulholland, LHP
- 46 Steve Trachsel, RHP
- 47 Rod Beck, RHP
- 48 Dave Stevens, RHP
- 49 Felix Heredia, LHP
- 52 Matt Karchner, RHP
- 54 Mark Clark, RHP
- 59 Rodney Myers, RHP
- 63 Rick Kranitz, Instructor

13

Guardian Angel of Sammy and the Cubs?

Even as teammates and assorted media members took shots at him from 1992 to 1997, Sammy Sosa had one consistent fan, the one with the highest profile of all at Wrigley Field: Harry Caray.

Sosa obviously passed the toughest tests. The late Caray, who knew baseball cold, saw his natural talent and hustle. The great broadcaster chose to overlook any Sosa fundamental lapses as he learned on the job on the majors. That was a radical change from Caray's St. Louis Cardinals and Chicago White Sox days, when he'd jump any players who failed consistently in the clutch or didn't put forth a decent day's effort.

Why did Caray take such a great liking to Sosa, who provided him with some of his last, best "Holy Cow" home-run calls?

"It's the way I played and went out there and took care of my business," Sosa said. "I consider myself a good person and he liked the way I played. That was the key."

Chip Caray, Harry's grandson and successor, confirms such feelings.

"He loved Sammy, loved the flair he had for the game," Chip said. "He saw all the tools, he saw the talent. Guys like my grandfather, Jack Brickhouse, Jack Buck, they know guys who can play and guys who can't.

"For myself, I likened Sammy to an apprentice master carpenter. He's got brand-new tools: the saw, the ax, the hammer, brand-new shiny nails. But until he learned how to use those tools, the things he builds aren't going to be all that great. Once he learns how to put those tools to their best use, look out, because he's going to build a mansion. I think we saw in 1998 Sammy become a master carpenter, a master craftsman at what he does, playing baseball.

"He (Harry Caray) was right, the Cubs were right, in evaluating the immense talent Sammy has."

Sosa's stature in Cubdom and connection with Caray were honored during the broadcaster's memorial service back in February, the equivalent of a state funeral in Chicago. Sosa, Mark Grace and Scott Servais—the latter the Cubs' player representative—were the three players excused from spring training for a day to attend the funeral.

But Sosa's tribute did not stop there. Sosa dedicated the 1998 season to Caray. All year long, he made references to the spirit of Caray perhaps influencing some of the crazy-quilt Cubs' wins. And, indeed, baseballs sticking in the vines and gutters or bouncing off a pitcher's rear end to an infielder do seem like they've been guided by higher powers. When Brickhouse, Caray's predecessor in the Chicago TV booth and an even more ingrained part of Cubdom, died on August 6, so many folks believed the Cubs and Sosa now had two guardian angels.

Conversely, when the Cubs lost, sometimes blowing the game in spectacular fashion, one press-box wise guy suggested Caray and Brickhouse were out playing cards upstairs.

No matter what the oddball outcome of every game, the 66 Sosa homers each featured a tribute to Caray. When he got back to the dugout, Sosa would begin his famed body English of hearttaps, the first one to his mother in the Dominican Republic, the second one, by Sosa's definition, to all the mothers in the audience. Then he held out his fingers in a "V" gesture. Not for "victory"-but for Harry Caray.

That gesture has won more generations of Sosa fans in the Caray family, starting with Chip.

"I've never heard of a player doing anything like that," Chip Caray said. "Our whole family is in awe of it. I can't say 'thank you' enough."

"I was quite surprised to hear Sammy dedicate the year and do the 'V' gesture for Harry," said Dutchie Caray, his widow. She talked to Sosa about the tribute during Harry Caray Day ceremonies at Wrigley Field on August 2, 1998.

Caray mangled players' names, Sosa's included, in his last decade on the air. Melding his own baseball broadcasting memories with the present—sometimes they ran together, anyway—Sosa was at various times called Sammy Cepeda, Sammy Sofa and Sammy Segui. But neither Sosa nor his legion of fans tuning in domestically or in his native Dominican Republic seemed to mind.

"They loved Harry in the Dominican," Sosa said. "They understood what he said; a lot of people are bilingual."

Caray's fans everywhere would have loved to hear the great warbler call Sosa's historic homers. Had Caray lived, he would have called Mark McGwire's 61st and 62nd homers, too. Although he did not make regular road trips anymore, he probably would have worked the games in St. Louis, his hometown.

Such sentiment was prevalent the entire year. Harry Caray broadcasting a contending team that specialized in memorable wins and horrific defeats. No even keel. Perfect for his everyman-fan style.

"He lived for the moment," Chip Caray said. "He loved the big players, loved the World Series, loved the playoffs. The fact all those games were so meaningful, he would have really risen to the occasion. He was at his best when the game was on the line. Even in his later years, when people liked to take shots at him mispronouncing names from time to time, he was still without peer in describing the moment.

"Sammy had a great quote: 'They probably would have killed him all over again had he been here.' We've seen so many emotional moments (in 1998) that it would have been an unbelievable ride for my grandfather.

"In some small way, I know he experienced it."

Without Caray's corporeal form, there were no "Holy Cows" on the air, except for one solitary time Chip Caray used it. Considering the drama of Sosa's home-run hunt, wouldn't it have been appropriate to use the famed call, especially by someone with Harry's bloodlines? Special circumstances require special action, it seemed.

But even then, Chip Caray did not want to appropriate someone else's trademark, not even on an inherited, special-case basis.

"I know I lot of folks miss it," he said of "Holy Cow." "But as much as I'd liked to have broken it out every now and then, I just didn't think I could. It's his call, it's his thing. I'm not him. It's not right for me to have done it. I wouldn't use 'Hey Hey' after Jack Brickhouse."

The Sosa-Caray connection continued to work both ways in 1998. Harry Caray's Restaurant in downtown Chicago set up a display of Sosa's autographed bat and jersey at the entrance to the dining room. Sosa and his wife, Sonia, used to drop by to eat at least once every other week.

But such visits wouldn't have been practical once homer No. 60 began drawing near. One of the fun aspects of Harry Caray's is jostling with the throngs, who sing take me out to the ballgame at 7:30 p.m. nightly, the equivalent on the clock of the seventh-inning stretch (7 1/2 innings). If Sosa suddenly showed up, a madhouse would have ensued. A home-run king should enjoy the delicacies there and not spend his time getting writer's cramp with autographs.

Sosa need not break bread with her at the restaurant to have done more than was possible to pay tribute, according to Dutchie Caray. Just the way he conducted himself throughout the 1998 season was honor enough.

"Sammy's a fine young man," she said. "Just the same way I think about Mark McGwire. Neither one is cocky. They are down to earth, and they have a great feeling for the fans and the game of baseball. They conducted themselves extremely well."

In the end, Sosa doesn't need to dive into the restaurant's Italian delicacies to think of Caray. Sosa's has a heart full of soul, and there's a reserved section for the broadcaster who gave him a break on the air.

"He gave everything for the game, for the fan," Sosa concluded. "He always had a smile on his face. I'll miss him."

14

Blessings From the Hall of Famers

Throughout 1998, Sammy Sosa climbed the statistical ladder with ease. He zoomed past the single-season highs of so many Hall of Famers that it made their numbers look like someone's halting rookie campaigns.

But Sosa knows all too well that the time to compare himself with the all-time players who preceded him won't come until well into a new millennium. "When I retire," was his succinct answer when queried as to when folks will allow him to walk with the immortals of our grand ol' game.

"I'm not here to take anyone's place," Sosa said. Having moved up a few levels in the way he handles himself publicly, the slugger realizes that any proclamation that he's the best in Cubs history, or one of the best all-time in the majors, would backfire royally. And his handling of self-ratings has filtered back to the all-time Cubs whose places atop the statistical mountain were obliterated by the Sammy Sosa World Tour 1998.

They like what they hear, and let Sosa know that all the time. Cubs Hall of Famers Ernie Banks and Billy Williams, surely No. 1 and 2 in team history in all-time ranking among fans, have psychically welcomed Sosa into the fraternity of real, old-fashioned pros that seemed in so much short supply in the 1990s.

Williams, of course, has been with Sosa since he came to the Cubs in 1992. The Sweet Swinger from Whistler, Alabama, served as Cubs hitting coach for Sosa's first five seasons before switching over to bench-coach duties. Sosa always has taken pains to give Williams credit for his development as a hitter amid all the countless hours the pair spent in pre-game batting-cage sessions.

Banks, better known as "Mr. Cub," blows in and out of his favorite Friendly Confines on his whims, still light of foot when curious interviewers want to corner him, and still spreading good cheer even in the bleakest of Cubs moments.

Meanwhile, looking on from afar was a worthy opponent of both Banks and Williams in the 1960s. Former San Francisco Giants pitcher Juan Marichal, a fellow enshrinee in Cooperstown, is now the Dominican Republic's minister of sports. A member of the first generation of great Dominican players to star in the majors, Marichal finally got a chance to praise Sosa face to face during the latter's special day on Sunday, September 21, 1998, at Wrigley Field. A few feet away were Williams and Banks, the latter waving a Dominican flag while helping unveil a painting of Sosa. Marichal has joined Banks and Williams in developing a strong rooting interest in Sosa's performance—and off-the-field persona.

Banks has tried to entertain Sosa in the same manner as millions of Cubs fans since 1953. One September afternoon, "Mr. Cub" played interior decorator in the Cubs' clubhouse, trying to place a huge color photo of Sosa and Mark McGwire, taken in St. Louis, over a wall hanging of an old newspaper story about Hack Wilson. Sosa, of course, had just broken Wilson's all-time single-season Cubs homer record of 56. Earlier, Banks, who is famous for his off-key singing attempts did the absolute worst version of *Take Me Out to the Ballgame* during the seventh-inning stretch all season.

Sosa may break Banks' all-time Cubs records before he's through. Six or seven seasons of peak production may enable Sosa to reach Banks' career total of 512 homers. With 139 homers since Opening Day 1996, Sosa already broke Banks' three-year total of 135 homers from 1957 to 1959. And long before the end of the season, Sosa left Banks' season career highs of 47 homers (1958) and 143 RBI behind.

"I have no problem with that," Banks said. "I really like to see people reach goals, move on, go to high levels and set standards. That's what Sammy has done here. There will be standards that he will set throughout his career. This is not just one year. Sammy is just at the start of the greatness we'll see in this young man."

Williams' top season was 42 homers and 129 RBI in 1970. He won the NL batting title with a .333 average in 1972 after hitting .322 in 1970.

"It's just showing the prediction people made about him," Williams said. "You saw great talent in this individual. When he surpassed Ernie and me, two guys who performed a long time over the years, it shows he's already been a great ballplayer."

And what if Sosa matches or surpasses all of Banks' career numbers? Should he be the new Mr. Cub? That's a tall order. In addition to his homer total, Banks ranks first all-time in Cubs history in total bases (4,706) and games played (2,528) and second in hits (2,583) and RBI (1,636).

Bulletin: Banks is willing to bestow his title on Sosa.

"Yes. He will be Mr. Cub," he said. "That's why I want to establish a relationship with him, because he was going to do it. When he was going for the (homer) record, he was always praising Mark McGwire. Yet he played so hard, and realized the team was more important than anything we do."

Williams, though, believes Banks has earned "Mr. Cub" on a permanent basis.

"I think Ernie always will be 'Mr. Cub,'" he said. "The people have made that choice. A lot of people asked me when I started, 'Do I mind Ernie being Mr. Cub?' I said no, that Ernie was here almost 10 years before me. He was here when no other player was hitting homers for the Cubs. Hey, I call Ernie 'Mr. Cub' myself.

"But the way Sammy's going now, he will have some great numbers when he takes off the uniform. He'll be considered one of the great Cubs along with Ernie, myself and Ron Santo."

Marichal is an expert of Hall of Famer numbers, too. He went 243-142 with a 2.89 ERA over his 16-season career. He won 25 games in 1963 and 26 in 1968, when he also completed 30 of his 38 starts. That earned him the nickname "The Dominican Dandy." He joins Banks in flat-out predicting Sosa could be making a trip to upstate New York to move in alongside them sometime in the future.

"If Sammy continues to play the game the way he plays today, the way he's hitting, throwing and fielding, he can be rated a complete ballplayer," he said. "If he plays like this five or six more years, he's a Hall of Famer."

Comparisons with the greats of the past are inevitable, no matter how much Sosa tries to soft-pedal the issue.

Sosa himself idolized the great Roberto Clemente. And, to make things a little haunting, immediately after Sosa's 62nd homer, a replica cereal box with Clemente's photo appeared in the Wrigley Field locker next to Sosa's. All Sosa has to do is turn one way and the greatest Latin player of all time is staring him down. For years Sosa had a photo of Clemente in his own locker, and acquired uniform No. 21 in his second Cubs season after wearing No. 25 in his first three-plus big-league seasons.

"When I spoke of Roberto to him, he wanted to know everything about him, what kind of ballplayer he was, what kind of person he was," Williams said. "Whenever I came across an article or a tape, I gave it to him, because I know he idolizes him. We all have got to idolize people to inspire us.

"I think he has done Roberto proud."

Marichal, who tried to get Clemente out for more than 10 years, agrees.

"I see in Sammy more like Roberto, not only because he's so aggressive like Roberto, but also because he's a right fielder like him. He can be like Roberto, only with more power."

But Marichal stops short of linking Sosa with Willie Mays, his longtime Giants teammate and the one man rated by many as the best all-around ballplayer in history.

"To me, nobody is going to be like Willie," he said. "But Sammy's very, very close to being a great, great ballplayer."

The name Mays brings up yet another comparison. Of all the great sluggers who came up in the 1950s—Banks, Williams, Henry Aaron, Frank Robinson, Harmon Killebrew and Eddie Matthews—only Mays ever exceeded the 50-homer mark, in 1955 and 1965. Sosa exceeded that mark with ease.

"The difference is that Sammy has everything going in the right direction," Banks said. "The pressure of today with the wild-card playoffs and winning the divisional titles creates more pressure, more at stake, for the players to be at their best every game.

"But for me, Hank and the guys who played in that time, if we were out of the race, you didn't have that extra incentive to play hard. You played hard, but not hard enough. Now, everything counts, everything means a lot, and they rise to the occasion."

What completes a great ballplayer is how they handle themselves. Sosa gets an "A" from the greats.

"The more he does, the more humble he gets," Williams said. "That's the sign of a good athlete, the sign of a good ballplayer."

Sosa can draw all the credit to himself if he wants. Williams believes he's already had his good run, with his name recorded for posterity.

"My joy is to see the individual perform and do well, not to see my name in the paper," he said. "I tell people, I'm already in the Hall of Fame. I don't need this (more publicity). I just want the guys to remember and do things right to make themselves better."

Banks appreciates Sosa's acknowledgment of the players who preceded him.

"I was the same way, having respect for people before me, people who accomplished things before me," he said.

Marichal once was a role model for young Dominican players. Now Sosa can easily take over that role.

"What amazes me is the way he's composed himself with all his fame and money," Marichal said. "He's still a very nice kid. I hope and I wish that most of the players from the Dominican Republic imitate what Sammy's doing now. I love the way he praises his teammates."

There's no reason for Sosa to change, because he'll continue to toil in the positive atmosphere of Wrigley Field. To Banks, the fans feed off Sosa—and vice versa.

"When I saw him play, it reminded me of my own personal feelings as a Cubs player," he said. "He has a lot of humility, he's hard-working, he loves playing here, he truly loves it.

"I used to try to figure it out when I played. What is it about playing in Wrigley Field that's different than most parks? If you do love the game, fans can see that. If you do not love it, fans can see it, too.

"If you're into it, they're all behind you. It's a remarkable place to play baseball. To me, it's the perfect place for Sammy. It's a perfect place for me. It's a perfect place for Mark Grace. He said he wants to retire as a Cub."

Sosa, who wants to play for the Cubs for the rest of his career, may get that chance. And, like Mr. Cub, he'll always be beloved if he continues the same style of play.

"The thing that I admire about Sammy is he plays this game with tremendous joy. Sammy's main thing is he wants to be the best player who ever plays the game."

Building upon 1998, don't put it past Sosa. And those that preceded him wouldn't mind a man with that kind of character being their next-door neighbor in Cooperstown.

15

The Home Run Race

Sammy Sosa's locker was like a calm oasis amid the maelstrom around him. You wouldn't know at first glance that it belonged to the star of stars on the Cubs, lacking ostentation and distinguishing features.

Several years ago, Sosa had a photo of Roberto Clemente in the locker, but that's gone, replaced by a photo of wife Sonia and their four children. A box of Flintstones vitamins, a prop he'd used for comic effect in 1998, and a bottle of Ginseng Gold were on the top shelf. There was an extra, unused locker cubicle next door, a privilege often given to a top star. Kerry Wood had an extra locker for much of the 1998 season, using the space to store boxes of mail he hadn't processed. Wood lost the additional elbow room when September rosters were expanded and Orlando Merced took the locker. But Sosa retained the space, which was adorned with an old, old sticker: "Have You Hugged Your Kid Today? Richard J. Elrod, Sheriff."

Three hours before games, Sosa and locker mate Jose Hernandez would sit side by side, dressing, conversing softly. Sosa spent a couple of minutes each time slapping talcum powder on his legs and thighs before he pulled on his uniform pants for batting practice. He also used this time to attend to the minutiae of stardom—filling out names for tickets or passes, signing autographs, engaging in a bit of horseplay with teammates.

At this time, Cubs marketing department aide Javier Bedolla would bring assorted items for Sosa to sign. One day Bedolla had Sammy signing napkins for the gala commemorating the 100th anniversary of George Gershwin's birth at Chicago's Fairmont Hotel. The Cubs players were asked to write down their favorite Gershwin tunes. Sosa, who couldn't have possibly been a Gershwin devotee in this youth in the Dominican Republic, listed "Love Is Here To Stay" for Bedolla.

"I hate bugging these guys," Bedolla said. But it's a necessary job, and Sosa and the Cubs usually are cooperative. The signings often continue after batting practice, ending 90 minutes prior to the start of home games. Cell phones permit last-minute conversations with loved ones and business associates, and Sosa sometimes jumped on the phone. Off the line, he'd wander halfway down the clubhouse to sit with fellow Dominican players Manny Alexander, Sandy Martinez and Henry Rodriguez, whose lockers were all clustered. That was his form of relaxation as the first pitch neared, and he'd continue that pattern even as his home-run total climbed into the 60s.

But on July 1, 1998, Sosa still could not have conceived of an impending journey into the record books, despite his historic 20-homer June, despite the fans' expectations. Kerry Wood seized the headlines from Sosa on his day, fanning 13 Arizona Diamondbacks while allowing three hits in eight innings, upping his record to 6-4 in the Cubs' 6-4 victory at Wrigley Field. Sosa contributed by slamming RBI doubles in the third and seventh innings, the latter touching off a two-run burst that held up as the winning margin. Sosa's first double rocketed toward the fence in right center, but fell short of clearing the wall. The fans wanted more. A mass groan emanated from the crowd of 31,002 when the would-be homer stayed in play. When's the last time Cubs fans were disappointed when their big hero drove in a key run?

The Cubs had their ups and downs at this point, a season-high 38-24 record receding to 44-39 after the win over Arizona. But Sosa was convinced it was a new year, and it would end far differently than 1997.

"We're winning together and staying together," he said. "We know we can go out and play good against anyone. I'm really happy now, and all the problems (of 1997) are gone. I go home at night and can sleep. We pick each other up. Let's be happy now because everything's going great."

Sosa would not homer in the next three games, all Cubs victories, as the All-Star break loomed. He was human, after all. And on the morning of July 5, a chill went through Cubdom when Sosa was scratched from the Cubs lineup for the game against the Pittsburgh Pirates at Wrigley Field. That would turn out to be the fourth and final game he would miss all season.

Sosa's left shoulder was stiff; he claimed he had slept wrong the night before. He'd have to miss his second All-Star Game. He had been chosen as an outfield reserve, his June power spree coming too late to influence the voters. With Sosa's absence, no Cub was on the active roster at Coors Field, upsetting second baseman Mickey Morandini, who was eminently deserving of selection. Morandini had been hitting .331 to .287 for the Reds' Bret Boone, who was picked due to a rule mandating all teams must have one All-Star representative. Cincinnati reliever Jeff Shaw, his team's lone All-Star, had just been traded to Los Angeles.

Sosa still showed up in Denver to partake in ceremonies, sign autographs and clown around in the dugout.

"I can't play, but I want to represent Chicago," he said. "Was I disappointed? Yes. But it's much better for this to happen to me now with three days' rest coming."

Sosa had gone into the All-Star break with 33 homers, four behind Mark McGwire and two in arrears of Ken Griffey Jr. The expected McGwire-Griffey duel for the Roger Maris record was still the angle favored by the media. Sosa had an incredible June, but was he a real contender or just a flash in the pan who'd fade, like his team, as the weather heated up?

In fact, most of the publicity still centered on McGwire. Even Dr. Joyce Brothers, noted advice columnist and analyst of the human condition, jumped into the fray. She suggested the wound-tight McGwire, who complained he felt like a "caged animal" and wondered why his batting-practice sessions were all the rage, find a quiet room, close his eyes and envision himself swinging for the fences.

"Time spent visualizing you making all those homers—doing it just right—sends a message to your mind and your muscles that you can get into the flow and routine, and that it will happen," Brothers told the Bloomberg News Service.

Sosa needed no such advice. Having enjoyed the hoopla of the All-Star Game and with his shoulder soreness gone, he jumped back into the lineup for a four-game series against the Milwaukee Brewers at County Stadium starting July 9. Huge crowds, inflated by thousands of Cubs fans making the short trek to Brewtown, filled the creaky ballpark for every game. Sosa didn't disappoint, slugging No. 34 against Jeff Juden during a 12-9 Cubs loss on July 9. The next night, he came back with No. 35, also in the second, off Scott Karl. Sosa thus became only the second Cub after Ernie Banks to belt at least 35 homers in four consecutive seasons.

But now his pace of power slowed, even as the Cubs' pace of winning picked up. Sosa would not hit another homer for a whole week. And, once again, the focus would shift from him as the Cubs moved into Atlanta for a two-game series July 20-21. Kevin Tapani's grand-slam homer, the first by a Cubs pitcher since Burt Hooton in 1972, shocked the Braves in the first game. Then came a hyped matchup of once and future Cubs aces— Greg Maddux vs. Kerry Wood. Despite control problems that gave the Braves prime scoring opportunities, Wood held firm, fanned 11 in 7 2/3 innings, and bested The Master, 3-0. The Cubs knew they had arrived by taking the season series 6-3 against the Braves.

Not until another week passed did Sosa really seem to energize himself for a real duel with McGwire. That took place in an unlikely location—the air-conditioned cocoon of Bank One Ballpark in Phoenix. Sosa would get a long-time monkey off his back and launch himself into direct competition with the St. Louis slugger.

Obviously overanxious as a less mature player, Sosa had a big hole in his game with the bases loaded. He had belted 245 homers going into the first game of a four-game series against the Diamondbacks on July 27. None had ever come with the bases loaded. Sosa possessed an ignominious record: most homers from the start of a career without a grand slam. The Braves' Bob Horner had held the previous dubious mark with 209 slamless homers. His overall performance with the bases loaded was poor: a .156 average from 1995 to 1997 during his consecutive 100-RBI seasons.

Against the D-Backs' Willie Blair, Sosa warmed up with a two-run shot in the sixth inning. Two innings later, with the bases loaded, he broke the 4,428 at-bat spell with a long shot to center field off Alan Embree. A thrilled Sosa had to contain himself from dancing around the bases. He drove in all the runs, reaching the 100 mark for the fourth consecutive season, in the Cubs' 6-2 victory.

"I'm not going to lie to you," Sosa said. "I'm not going to hear about that (bases-loaded failures) anymore, and it feels great.

"I'm sure he's glad he got that monkey off his back. It was a fluke thing," Jim Riggleman said.

But to ensure the grand slam was no fluke in and of itself, Sosa came through again the next night with a fifth-inning grand slam off Bob Wolcott into the packed left-field seats. Now he recorded the first of numerous entries into the Cubs' record book—first player in team history to slug grand slams in consecutive games (and the 18th major-leaguer overall to accomplish the feat). And he set a season high with his 41st homer. The Cubs' defeat almost seemed secondary to the awesome feat.

"It gets easier with the first one out of the way," Sosa said.

Wise guys stepped up with their one-liners. "Sammy can retire now that he's hit his grand slam," closer Rod Beck joked.

To paraphrase Joe Garagiola, baseball's a funny game. Here Sosa was virtually inept with the bases loaded, earning a mark of distinction—in reverse—by never connecting with the bases loaded. And now he had three grand slams in a season. No Cub had a trio of such blasts since Ernie Banks had five in 1955. It truly was going to be a different year for Sosa.

One day after returning home from the four-game trip to Phoenix, Sosa came to the ballpark to hear some bad news on the morning of August 1. Just 10 minutes to midnight on July 31, Houston Astros general manager Gerry Hunsicker made one last call to Woody Woodward, his Seattle Mariners' counterpart. Woodward had held on to dissatisfied fireballer Randy Johnson too long. The New York Yankees and Cleveland Indians had played a game of chicken for Johnson's services over the previous week. Neither blinked, and Johnson stayed put in the Kingdome. Woodward took what he could get, obtaining three minor-leaguers for The Big Unit.

The Cubs had been rejected early in the process, having lost top trade-bait pitcher Jeremi Gonzalez to injury and unable to interest Woodward in prospects from a still-sagging farm system. Cubs general manager Ed Lynch then busied himself trying to shore up his terrible bullpen, making deals for Matt Karchner from the White Sox and, at the same time as the Johnson trade, lefty Felix Heredia from the Florida Marlins. Lynch had used up his tradeable material in No. 1 draft picks Jon Garland and Todd Noel in the deals for the relievers. But no one will ever know what might have happened had Lynch, on a hunch, made a late-night phone call to Woodward on July 31.

Sosa wasn't discouraged at all by the news of Johnson going to the Cubs' top rival in the National League Central, a team that already had proved itself superior in the standings to the Cubs without the left-hander. But life, pennant and home-run races had to go on.

Two months remained. Two good months of power, not sensational, just no long dry spells, and Sosa could reach the Roger Maris record. Suddenly, like the proverbial ocean liner somehow successfully turning around in the bathtub, the nation's attention began to focus on Sammy Sosa as Mark McGwire's top challenger.

Strangely, the two sluggers began a kind of communication with one another during their interviews. McGwire suddenly loosened up a bit as August commenced, while Sosa began deferring to the red-goateed giant as "The Man," turning back all suggestions that he could break the Maris record and beat out McGwire for the home-run crown.

Whatever inspired McGwire, his petulance diminished and his inner thoughts suddenly were shared with the world. Instead of pushing it away and downgrading its impact, he began to embrace the home-run chase.

"It's excellent for the game," he said of the budding derby. "It's fantastic. I totally realize that. I think everyone realizes the game is on an uprise now."

And McGwire finally realized the entertainment value of his batting-practice sessions.

"It's taken a life of its own," he said. "A lot of these owners should be real happy. They're making a lot of money. It's definitely great for the game. But, let's realize, I'm just one person who plays this game. There's a lot of other great guys who hit home runs, and I hope they would go out and watch them in batting practice, too."

McGwire's own mid-season power lull enabled Sosa to creep up on him in their first head-to-head duel from August 7 to 9 at Busch Stadium in St. Louis. It initially had to share headlines in Chicago with the death at age 82 of all-time Cubs TV broadcaster Jack Brickhouse, Harry Caray's predecessor. McGwire had 45 while Sosa had 43. Both were blanked the first night. Then, in a nationally televised game on Saturday afternoon, August 8, both sluggers and their teams displayed what true entertainment really was as they continued to revive baseball.

McGwire ended a 29 at-bat homerless drought, his longest of the season, with a homer in the fourth. Sosa saved his blast for when it really counted. With the Cubs trailing 5-3 and two outs in the ninth, he connected off Rick Croushore to tie it up. Tyler Houston slugged a two-run homer in the top of the 11th to give the Cubs a 7-5 lead.

But after an error by Jeff Blauser on a Brian Jordan grounder in the bottom of the 11th, Ray Lankford slugged a two-out, game-tying homer off Rod Beck after striking out in each of his previous five at-bats. Sosa then showed off his all-fields hitting style with an RBI single to right to put the Cubs ahead 8-7 in the top of the 12th. Cardinals catcher Eli Marrero answered that with a homer off Beck in the bottom of the 12th to make it 8-8. Lankford finally ended the wild affair with an RBI single in the bottom of the 13th.

"I've never seen anything like it," Cardinals manager Tony La Russa said after the game. Indeed he hadn't, but neither he nor anyone else in the ballpark could know that the Cubs would soon play some even wilder contests.

McGwire would hit only one more homer in the next week, while Sosa slugged three, including two in one game on August 10 against the Giants. Now for the real big show—both tied at 47 going into the night of Tuesday, August 18, at Wrigley Field amid a torrent of national media chronicling the matchup.

But, as overhyped affairs often are, the first game was a bust. Both Sosa and McGwire each struck out three times apiece as the Cubs won 4-1, with catcher Scott Servais driving in three runs on three infielder groundouts.

Sosa finally pulled ahead for the first time in the home-run race in the fifth inning the next afternoon. He launched a two-run homer (No. 48) in the fifth off ex-Cub Kent Bottenfield. But Sammy's edge lasted less than an hour. McGwire tied him and the game with a solo shot onto Waveland Avenue off Matt Karchner in the eighth. In the 10th, the situation might have called for lefty Cubs reliever Terry Mulholland to pitch around McGwire with nobody on base. Servais confirmed that was the battle plan: "We didn't execute the pitch." Mulholland got too much of the plate with one pitch and McGwire got too much of the ball. No. 49 gave the Cardinals the lead, Lankford followed with another homer, and they eventually won 8-6.

"They've been coming after me since last night," McGwire said of the Cubs throwing him strikes. "I got a hitters' pitch."

That blast seemed to touch off a vintage McGwire home-run binge, and Sosa gamely tried to keep up. He collected No. 49 two days later against Orel Hershiser of the San Francisco Giants. Then, on Sunday, August 23, Sosa's two-homer performance, to reach and pass the 50 mark, was marred by accusations against Houston Astros' pitcher Jose Lima grooving the pitch hit out for No. 51.

Sosa became only the second Cub ever and the first Latin player to reach 50 with a titanic fifth-inning blast off Lima. "I'm not going to lie to you. I'm proud," he said of the feat of being the first Hispanic at the historic power number.

But the powerful Astros blew open a close game in the two innings after the Sosa homer. With the Cubs trailing 12-2 in the bottom of the eighth, Lima gave up No. 51 into the left-field bleachers. Something about Dominican Republic native Lima's body language gave some press box observers pause to believe he might have laid it in there. But both Sosa and Lima immediately denied it.

"Just because I know Jose Lima doesn't mean he'll give me everything to hit. Lima was throwing fastballs all day," Sosa said. "Look, no one is grooving any pitches. I know Lima, but in baseball, you don't have any friends like that. He's trying to get me out, and I'm trying to do my job. It's a mistake to say that.

"To me, it's extremely disrespectful," Cubs manager Jim Riggleman said. "I can't believe anyone would have the nerve to suggest that in any way."

Implications of race and racism didn't sit well with Sosa. Weeks later, he would put the issue of American vs. Dominican to rest once and for all.

"To me, color doesn't make any difference," he said. "It's all about human beings. It's all about who you are inside."

After the game, word filtered down that McGwire stayed ahead with his 53rd homer in Pittsburgh.

"He's 'The Man,'" Sosa said, repeating his mantra. "He's the type who can hit five, six homers in a couple of days. I put my money on him.

"I'm not thinking about the record. I'm coming here thinking about the game. If I think about the game, I'll play better."

He had to think about the game and the Cubs. Another 12-3 pasting at the hands of the Astros the next afternoon at Wrigley Field, then a 10-9 loss in Cincinnati on August 25, put their momentum in reverse as the Cubs tried to stay tied with the hated New York Mets in the wild-card race. The Cubs were bumping along at around 10 games over .500, but needed a boost.

Sosa tried to provide that with four more homers from August 26 to 31 as the Cubs won five of six from the Reds and Colorado Rockies. On Monday night, August 31, Sosa collected No. 55 in the third inning off Brett Tomko at Wrigley Field, tying McGwire once again. Tomko also had surrendered No. 52 five days previously in Cincinnati. For good measure, Kerry Wood belted his second homer of the year, a two-run shot in the fourth that gave the Cubs a 5-4 lead. Sosa took an extra curtain call for the crowd of 36,700 when Wood did not want to show up Tomko.

"The people were getting excited and I said, 'Hey, I'm jumping up there," Sosa said. "It's a free country."

Further showing his joy, Sosa trotted out his bottle of Flintstones vitamins after the game to show from where his power emanated, a contrast to the raging controversy over McGwire's use of androstenedione pills.

McGwire, of course, wasn't far from his mind.

"The reason I say he's The Man is because every time we tie he jumps up there right away," Sosa said. "I was tied for about six hours. After that—boom!—he's back on top. I'm happy for him. He seems real happy. The last few interviews he has been enjoying it, and that's what you have to do. If you do that, it's going to be easier for him."

The next meeting with McGwire began to approach quickly —Labor Day, September 7, and September 8, a night game, both in Busch Stadium in St. Louis. And after the game on September 2 at Wrigley Field, pitcher Steve Trachsel, whose next turn on the mound would come up on September 8, was asked how he would react if he gave up a record-breaker to McGwire. Always full of hiss and vinegar, Trachsel put forth a scowl and said he wouldn't want to stand around the mound for 15 minutes while a gleeful celebration over the clout broke out around him. Unfortunately, Trachsel would turn out to be unusually clairvoyant.

At that moment, few others wanted to project that far ahead. Sosa was busy knocking down Cubs and National League records. In the sixth inning of the September 2 game, he tied Hack Wilson's all-time team and league record of 56 homers with a line-drive homer into the waiting glove of Barb Reichert in the first row of the right-field bleachers. Reichert and co-worker Mary Ullmer had elected to sit in that spot to be as close as possible to Sosa. Although Sosa had hit a decent number of homers to right field, that was not a likely spot to snare one of his shots.

But this was a true example of expert place-hitting-and giving the media a first-person story. Reichert and Ullmer had held up a sign that read: "Sammy, hit us No. 56 and we'll give it back free." Ullmer hollered at the right fielder and pointed to the sign earlier in the game. Reichert said Sosa nodded briefly to Ullmer in recognition of the sign.

Reichert, a former New Mexico State softball third baseman, used a 1980-vintage Reggie Jackson glove to snare the baseball. She was able to write about it twice in the next few days in the *Chicago Tribune*, where Reichert worked as a sports department copy editor. Ullmer was an associate sports editor.

Reichert and Ullmer fulfilled their promise, meeting Sosa under the left-field stands, near the players' exit to their parking lot. They returned the ball. Sosa took it, signed it to her utter surprise, and gave it right back to Reichert. Radio talk shows inundated her with interview requests.

"A media darling," Reichert wrote on September 6. "The words sound sarcastic when they drip off my tongue, but what they heck. It's been fun being on the other side. ... My former newsroom, the *Colorado Springs Gazette*, gathered around the TV each half-hour and cheered every time I made that catch. At the *Tribune*, the sports staff roared during the planning meeting when they saw Mary Ullmer and me high-fiving the bleacher bums."

No. 56 and Reichert's glove ended up on display 10 days later in the lobby of Tribune Tower at the behest of Tribune Co. chairman John Madigan.

"The next day (September 3), Mr. Madigan called me at home—I had the day off—and asked me to come see him in his office," Reichert said. "I met him, showed him the glove and ball, and he came up with the idea for the display."

But as creatively as Sosa ended up providing souvenirs for public consumption on the cusp of September 1998, he couldn't stop the inexorable march of McGwire. Hours after Sosa provided his special souvenir to Reichert and Ullmer, the Cardinal crept ever closer to the record by belting Nos. 58 and 59. Sosa would have to play some heavy catch-up in Three Rivers Stadium the following weekend. He tried, he really tried.

On the night of September 4, Sosa waited three pitches before he belted a Jason Schmidt pitch to right field to send him past Wilson on the all-time lists. No. 57 drew him within two of McGwire, who went 0-for-3 against the Reds in St. Louis. McGwire had ducked out on a prearranged pre-game media session, apparently upset that the baseball commissioner's office wanted the Cardinals to remove barricades erected to keep reporters away from the batting cage before the game.

Like Trachsel, Sosa inadvertently proved he could see into the future. Prior to the September 4 game, he told reporters that McGwire would finish with 70 homers. He also would have to watch McGwire play another game before he'd have a chance to get even closer. The Cardinals were scheduled to play a Saturday afternoon nationally televised contest on September 5, while the Cubs did not start until 7 p.m., Eastern time, in Pittsburgh.

McGwire came through again, not wasting any time. He connected for No. 60 in the first inning off Reds lefty Dennis Reyes, tying Babe Ruth's best. "Let's just accept what is happening," he said. "Enjoy it. Ride the wave."

Not discouraged, Sosa belted yet another homer to right field. No. 58 came on a 3-and-1 pitch by Pirates lefty Sean Lawrence in the sixth inning. He was pumping 'em out almost as fast as in June. The blast was Sosa's ninth homer in 13 games.

"To me, I'm a winner already," he said. "I've gone so far this year and a lot more (home runs) are going to come. To me, just being behind Mark McGwire is being a winner."

He couldn't wait until he got to St. Louis.

"People have been waiting for this moment," Sosa said. "It's going to be tremendous. I'm sure they'd like to see Mark and I together for the last time this year. ... I'm willing to have a good time, like always."

Sosa had one more chance to close the gap before the Labor Day matchup. But he went 2-for-5, both singles, as the Cubs lost to the Pirates 4-3 on Jason Kendall's 10th-inning homer as the bullpen blew yet another eminently winnable game. Meanwhile, McGwire went 0-for-3 against the Reds.

September 7 opened with a nationally televised pre-game press conference with both Sosa and McGwire. Both men enjoyed each other's company, both laughed it up, and Sosa hammed it up. "Baseball's been berry, berry good to me," Sammy blurted out without warning, cracking up McGwire and the audience. That would truly start a final month of belly laughs from the newest comic sensation wearing No. 21 in blue pinstripes.

McGwire wasted no time in providing the hot afternoon's drama. He connected for a 430-foot drive to left on a 1-and-1 pitch from the Cubs' Mike Morgan in the first inning. The media had a field day with the symmetry—the 61st homer came on McGwire's father John's 61st birthday. And, suddenly, McGwire invoked references to higher powers.

"Hopefully, the day that I die I can, after seeing the Lord, I can go see him and Babe Ruth and talk to them," he said.

Sosa applauded the homer from his station in right field, tapping his right hand into his gloved left. He hugged McGwire when he reached first on his solitary single. But he also struck out three times, including with the tying run on third and two out in the ninth in the Cardinals' 3-2 victory.

But all the while, the St. Louis crowd of 50,530 gave Sosa rousing ovations for each of his at-bats. That would continue the next night as both sluggers continued their duel.

"Nobody ever said anything nasty about Sosa here," said lifelong St. Louis baseball fan Jim Rygelski, who attended games since the mid-1950s, when the old Busch Stadium was the Cardinals' home on Grand Avenue on the city's North Side. "Cardinals fans were genuine in their applause for Sosa. They had a lot of respect for him. Some of the women even said he was cute. The fans here always appreciate opponents' best feats, and have applauded good plays in the field even when they were against the Cardinals."

The Cubs and Sosa could hardly concentrate on the concept of the wild-card race in the circus atmosphere enveloping McGwire. A World Series-sized contingent of more than 700 media members was in attendance, and the pack threatened to trample one another to get close to McGwire and Sosa. They got their wish on September 8. Steve Trachsel's worst scenario came true on his first pitch in the fourth, which McGwire blasted on a line just 341 feet over the left-field wall, his shortest, yet most memorable, homer of the season. Just as Trachsel figured, the game stopped. "There's nothing cool about it," Trachsel later said, but he was a majority of one. His Cubs infielders congratulated McGwire as he toured the bases. And, after hugging his son and jumping into the stands to greet the children of Roger Maris, McGwire held court in ceremonies near home plate.

Sosa at first hesitated, then ran in from right field. He leaped into McGwire's arms. McGwire gave him a bear hug and twirled Sosa around in his arms like he was a kid. The pair gave each other Sosa's trademark heart-taps.

"When he hugged me, it was a great moment I am not going to forget," Sosa said.

Later in the Cardinals' 6-3 victory, Sosa and McGwire talked at first base when Sammy reached on a single.

"I said to him, 'Maybe you can go home now and relax and take it easy and wait for me.'"

That sounded like bravado at the time. But it would turn out to be oh-so-true. With only 2 1/2 weeks to go in the season, he wasn't finished chasing McGwire. And the sheer weirdness of the Cubs' season would only step up in intensity.

Saturday, Sept. 12, 1998

1998 NATIONAL LEAGUE UMPIRES

4 Mark Hirschbeck	22 Joe West	31 Bob Davidson	40 Jerry Crawford*
5 Angel Hernandez*	23 Ed Rapuano	32 Dana DeMuth	41 Jerry Meals
6 Bruce Froemming*	24 Jerry Layne	33 Mike Winters	43 Paul Schrieber
7 Eric Gregg	25 Charlie Williams	34 Greg Bonin	44 Kerwin Danley
8 Jeff Kellogg	27 Steve Rippley*	35 Gary Darling	
9 Brian Gorman	28 Larry Vanover	36 Wally Bell	
11 Ed Montague*	29 Bill Hohn	37 Bruce Dreckman	
12 Gerry Davis	30 Randy Marsh*	38 Sam Holbrook	

13 Larry Poncino
14 Frank Pulli*
15 Jim Quick*
16 Rich Rieker
18 Charlie Reliford
19 Terry Tata*
20 Tom Hallion
21 Harry Wendelstedt*

*Crew Chief

Milwaukee

1 Fernando Vina, IF
2 Jose Valentin, IF
3 Phil Garner, MGR
6 Geoff Jenkins, OF
7 David Nilsson, IF-OF
8 Mark Loretta, IF
9 Marquis Grissom, OF
10 Marc Newfield, OF
12 Chris Bando, Coach
13 Jeff D'Amico, RHP
16 Jesse Levis, C
20 Jeromy Burnitz, OF
21 Cal Eldred, RHP
22 Mike Matheny, C
24 Darrin Jackson, OF
26 Jeff Cirillo, IF
27 Bob Wickman, RHP
28 Mike Myers, LHP
29 Jim Lefebvre, Coach
30 Bob Hamelin, IF
31 Bronswell Patrick, RHP
32 John Jaha, IF
33 Bobby Hughes, C-OF
35 Bill Castro, Coach
36 Joel Youngblood, Coach
37 Steve Woodard, RHP
38 Doug Mansolino, Coach
39 Eric Plunk, RHP
40 Chad Fox, RHP
41 Jose Mercedes, RHP
42 Scott Karl, LHP
45 Don Rowe, Coach
46 Bill Pulsipher, LHP
47 Al Reyes, RHP
48 Brad Woodall, LHP
49 David Weathers, RHP
52 Rafael Roque, LHP
58 Valerio De Los Santos, LHP

No.	Player	Pos.	1	2	3	4	5	6	7	8	9	10	AB	R	H	RBI
1	Vina	2b														
8	Loretta	ss														
7	Nilsson	1b														
26	Cirillo	3b														
20	Burnitz	rf														
9	Grissom	cf														
5	G. Jenkins	lf														
10	Newfield ph/9th															
33	B. Hughes	c														
27	Wick															
52	Roque	p														
30	Hamelin ph/7th															
58	De Los Santos p/7th															
40	C. Fox p/9th															
27	Wic															
22	Matheny c/9th		0	0	1	8	0	1	2	0	0		2	0	0	

Pitchers	IP	H	R	ER	BB	SO	Notes
Roque	6	9	5	5	2	3	
De Los Santos /7th							
C. Fox /8th							
Wickman /9th							

CUBS

1 Lance Johnson, OF
2 Jeff Pentland, Coach
3 Dan Radison, Coach
4 Jeff Blauser, IF
5 Jim Riggleman, MGR
6 Glenallen Hill, OF
7 Tyler Houston, C-IF
8 Gary Gaetti, C
9 Scott Servais, C
12 Mickey Morandini, IF
15 Sandy Martinez, C
17 Mark Grace, IF
18 Jose Hernandez, IF-OF
20 Matt Mieske, OF
21 Sammy Sosa, OF
24 Manny Alexander, IF
25 Orlando Merced, OF-IF
26 Billy Williams, Coach
27 Phil Regan, Coach
28 Pedro Valdes, OF
30 Jeremi Gonzalez, RHP
33 Don Wengert, RHP
34 Kerry Wood, RHP
36 Kevin Tapani, RHP
37 Brant Brown, OF-IF
38 Mike Morgan, RHP
39 Tom Gamboa, Coach
40 Henry Rodriguez, OF
43 Dave Bialas, Coach
45 Terry Mulholland, LHP
46 Steve Trachsel, RHP
47 Rod Beck, RHP
48 Dave Stevens, RHP
49 Felix Heredia, LHP
50 Jason Maxwell, IF
51 Terry Adams, RHP
52 Matt Karchner, RHP
54 Mark Clark, RHP
59 Rodney Myers, RHP
63 Rick Kranitz, Instructor

No.	Player	Pos.	1	2	3	4	5	6	7	8	9	10	AB	R	H	RBI
1	L. Johnson	cf														
18	J. Hernandez	ss														
47	Beck p/9th															
17	Grace	1b														
21	Sosa	rf														
6	G. Hill	lf														
8	Gaetti	3b														
12	Morandini	2b														
9	Servais	c														
7	Houston ph/8th															
38	Morgan	p														
48	Stevens p/4th															
49	Heredia p/7th															
37	B. Brown ph/8th															
45	Mulholland p/8th															
24	M. Alexander ss/8th	0	2	0	0	1	2	4	1	5					
25	Merced ph/9th															

Pitchers	IP	H	R	ER	BB	SO	Notes
Morgan	3	8	8	5	1	1	A - 39,170
Stevens /4th							
Heredia /7th							
Mulholland /8th							

Track Sammy Sosa's Home Runs	59	60	61	62	63	64	65

9/11/98-9/13/98

16

Sammy Showbiz and Media-Relations Mastery

There's the well-timed pause for comic effect. Laughs erupt. Then there's a sideways look. Sometimes the eyes roll to evoke surprise at the one-liner.

Jack Benny? Johnny Carson? Groucho Marx?

Well, maybe he took inspiration from all of 'em. No, this is Sammy Sosa, 1998, providing warmup lines or nightcap entertainment for the main event, his front-row-center role in the greatest home-run chase in history.

It was well worth the price of admission.

The act had been playing on a low-profile basis out in the provinces until Labor Day, September 7, 1998. Here was Sosa, doing a dual pre-game press conference with Mark McGwire as Sosa sat on 58 homers and McGwire on 60. And, suddenly, out of the clear blue, came the line that set off the belly laughs that accompanied almost every Sosa interview session through the end of the season.

"Baseball's been berry, berry good to me," Sosa blurted out, as McGwire and the media mob cracked up.

Sosa's too young to have remembered Garrett Morris' origination of that line playing a Hispanic player-turned-sportscaster on "Saturday Night Live" two decades ago. But somehow it got carried down through the years to the slugger, who ad-libbed it at just the right time, in just the right place.

Suddenly, Sosa's mass-gab sessions became the best show in sports. And McGwire, ahead of him most of the time in the power column but behind Sosa in media relations, had to play catch-up ball. A star was truly being born—and so was the man who, by a combination of words and deeds, put himself in a position to be Major League Baseball's top spokesman.

He started out by displaying a box of Flintstones vitamins to the mob around his locker after games. In the wake of the controversy over McGwire's performance-enhancing boosts, Sosa grinned and claimed that Fred and Barney provided him with his pep.

Then came a torrent of one-liners, with accompanying sideways looks and smiles, never a sour moment among any of them:

Asked for his reaction when he slid into home plate in Milwaukee, and Brewers catcher Bobby Hughes' shin guards caught him in the groin:

"I was pretty hurt. He hit me in the wrong part of my body."

On the Brewers' shift to the National League, just in time for their pitchers to serve up 12 homers to him in 1998:

"That was a good move there."

On the reaction of his family when he initially forgot to mention them during his remarks on Sammy Sosa Day on September 20, 1998 at Wrigley Field:

"My wife is a little bit pissed off because I forgot to mention her. She got me that night."

On whether the 61st and 62nd homer performance was the best day of his life:

"The best day of my life was when I was born."

On the literal street-fighting for his No. 62 home-run ball:

"If I wasn't playing, I'd be fighting for the ball, too."

Responding to a youthful correspondent from "Nickelodeon", asking if he had any superstitions:

"Yeah. 0-for-5."

Asked about his next goal:

"To go to heaven."

Nobody could script those comments, which made even

the most cynical media types laugh and write favorable stories about Sosa.

"You sit in a room and listen to him, and you can tell from the way he talks and the words he uses, that he's an instinctively nice person," said Dave Anderson, Pulitzer Prize-winning sports columnist for *The New York Times*.

"There's no meanness in this guy," Anderson added. "He doesn't have that type of ego that turns people off, that people resent. To a great extent, he's a little kid, a little boy with a mischievous smile. And he's doing it in another language. The English words he uses are just right. When he said his next goal was to go to heaven, you couldn't script something like that.

"He's got great values, spiritual and moral values. This is a nice man."

Obviously, Sosa made a quantum leap forward off the field as well as at the plate in 1998. But the seeds for his crowd- and media-pleasing persona were sown as a kid in the Dominican Republic, when he worked his way onto the good side of shoe-factory owner Bill Chase after Sosa shined his shoes. Chase now is Sosa's business partner. Later, the street-wise Sosa, with only two years of organized baseball under his belt, knew exactly how to impress Texas Rangers scouts and get himself signed in a tryout in San Pedro de Macoris in mid-1985.

Bit by bit, the Sosa personality was constructed from the late 1980s on, when he began learning about English and American customs as a Rangers' minor-leaguer and a young White Sox player. Just as he did on the field, developing from a sheer raw talent, Sosa came a long, long way with his personality and confidence in his life. And his ability to wise-crack in English was nothing short of phenomenal, mastering one-liners in a language he only began learning a decade previously.

One witness to the early Sosa experience in Chicago is Steve Grad, a producer and sometime air-personality for One on One Sports, the national all-sports radio network. Grad got to hang with the wet-behind-the-ears Sosa in his two-plus seasons with the White Sox from 1989 to 1991.

Grad met Sosa through mutual friends—the Sox's Latin players like Ivan Calderon, Melido Perez and Carlos Martinez. Sosa was outgoing, but in another language at the time. His English was quite rudimentary even though he tried very hard starting in the Texas Rangers minor-league system to pick up the language.

"The first time I met him was at a party at Melido Perez's house," Grad said. "I took him home, and it took 45 minutes to find his apartment. He couldn't explain where he lived, so we drove around looking at buildings to see which one was his."

Grad became a frequent companion. He helped Sosa pack up and go home to San Pedro de Macoris at the end of the season. "I would take care of some stuff, go out and get medicine, take him to my parents' house for dinner," he said. Sosa's brother, Jose, nicknamed Nino, lived with Grad for two months in the off-season.

Grad and Sosa used to go out clubbing in Chicago; Excalibur was a favorite Sosa destination. They'd also go out on the road in Milwaukee. Sosa's nighttime travels were typical for a young player, and he was hanging with the fellow Latin players on the White Sox.

He also endured a stormy and short first marriage prior to meeting his present wife, Sonia, at a disco in the Dominican Republic. Sosa raised eyebrows in the Sox front office, particularly when new general manager Ron Schueler took over in 1991. "The front office's concerns about Sammy were legitimate," Grad recalled. "He couldn't harness himself."

His upward move into gentleman status began, Grad theorized, with his trade to the Cubs on March 29, 1992. He finally found a baseball home with supportive fans. "He really changed when he went to the Cubs," Grad said. "When he was with the Sox, they looked at him as someone who had to produce instantly. There was a lot of pressure on him."

Sosa immediately responded to the almost-always adoring Cubs fans. "It's like I've been here all my life," he said in the spring of 1992. He began saluting the fans in the right-field bleachers before every game, earning their everlasting devotion. That's a practice that continues today, and Sosa gave the right-field bleacher bums a champagne shower on September 29, 1998, after he and the Cubs beat the San Francisco Giants 5-3 in the wild-card tiebreaker game.

"What impresses me about Sammy is in the outfield, after each warm-up session at the start of the inning he always throws a ball into the bleachers to the fans," said Red Mottlow, dean of Chicago's radio sportscasters and an instructor in broadcasting at Columbia College.

"And often when he catches a fly ball in foul territory down the line, he'll flip the ball into the stands," Mottlow said. "I think that's a wonderful gesture on the part of a ballplayer, and it makes the fans happy. It gets them closer to the ballplayer and gives them a better impression of the game and the players themselves."

More importantly, a Sosa autograph became an accessible commodity at Wrigley Field. He became one of a minority of Cubs to go outside the VIP parking lot after games to sign. Sosa also signed after batting practice, and several times was spotted sitting atop the dugout roof signing before games. That practice couldn't continue amid the tumult of 1998, but Sosa had already put plenty of goodwill in the bank.

"The fans are right behind me," Sosa said of his post-game sessions of yore. "They support me a lot, and that's why I take a lot of time to sign.

"They know I want to stay here. I will do anything to prove I want to stay here. This is where I got the opportunity to play. This is where people love me."

The great players who preceded Sosa took notice and approved.

"Things like that go unnoticed," Cubs Hall of Fame inductee-to-be Andre Dawson said of the autograph sessions. "It's always the dirt, the bad things, that are dwelled on more. He can do a lot of positive things for you."

By that time, he had settled down with his second wife, Sonia, and began starting his family that eventually would grow to four children: Keysha, Kenia, Sammy Jr., and Michael.

"When I am at the ballpark, I'm a baseball player," he said. "When I'm at home, I'm a family man."

Sonia couldn't often bring their brood out to games. "It's a problem now a little bit," she said. "Little babies. The oldest is only five years old." But he had a support system at home, and he thus curtailed his night life. "I'll go home and have a glass of wine with my wife," was his usual post-game comment about celebrating a homer in 1998.

Sonia helped console him after failures at the plate.

"I tried to," she said. "He came to the house after a bad day. I tried to say only, 'Don't worry about that because they just sometimes happen. This is the game. So don't worry about today. Worry about tomorrow because tomorrow is better. It's important to you. Today's already happened, so don't worry about today. Just get better and think about what you can do, and you can do it better tomorrow.'"

Better yet, Sosa's happiness extended to his media relations. Barry Rozner, columnist for the suburban *Daily Herald* of Arlington Heights, had covered the Cubs beat home and road for Sosa first six seasons. Rozner wrote in his September 17, 1998, column that "he has learned to handle the media with smiles and giggles instead of glares and stares. This makes lots of friends and wins you lots of votes."

Sosa's slowly improving fluency in English did not stop him from trying to communicate with the media. Instead, it would have worked the other way around. A lot of TV and radio sports and news directors would have told their reporters and camera operators to shy away from Latin ballplayers who couldn't give them clearly understandable sound bites. Sosa always tried to come through loud and clear, though. Mottlow, the first sportscaster to take a tape recorder into locker rooms in Chicago in the mid-1960s, never believed it was a problem.

"I didn't have any hesitancy taping him," he said. "I've had tougher jobs."

"He's always been cooperative with a teasing nature," Chicago regional CLTV cable channel sports anchor-reporter Jill Carlson said. "He's been fabulous to me, far more than any other Cubs player. Of all the big-name Chicago athletes, he's been No. 1 in terms of accessibility. Here's a kid who tries hard, not being used to the English language and being able to put humor in his comments."

Sosa even allowed curious reporters close-up looks at his broken hand on August 21, 1996, the day after his budding great season was ended by a pitch from the Florida Marlins' Mark Hutton. He's never had a problem with small talk around his locker, which is not too ostentatious for a home-run king with just a photo of his family and few slogans favored by other players as adornments.

Sosa even handled the challenges of live talk-show appearances on WSCR-AM with former hot-dog stand owner Mike North, a kid from the North Side Edgewater neighborhood. Under a management dictum to provide "entertainment" on the air, North never hesitated to fire on players and management, even chasing Bears owner Michael McCaskey off his show once. But even when Sosa endured his strikeouts and foibles in the field, North gave him every break in the world. He welcomed him as "The Panther"—his 1990-91 White Sox nickname—to his show as Sosa played along with the fun, usually via a cell phone from the Wrigley Field dugout before batting practice.

"The reason (he gave him a break) is because he hustled," North said. "You put up with his bad fielding. He always hit 30 to 35, or more, homers. People didn't get on him about his striking out like they did with Shawon Dunston, because Dunston never put up the numbers.

"Sammy's a likable guy, but I'll get on him tomorrow if he strikes out four times." True to his wild-man nature, North was rooting for Mark McGwire to win the home-run title. Nothing against Sosa, "but I had to root for the American guy," North said.

North's producer, Jesse Rogers, rates Sosa in his "top five percent" in accessibility in booking big-name guests.

"You don't want someone who's friendly for a couple of games, and then he isn't," he said. "That doesn't work. But Sammy's been fine. Our first interview (in 1992), he just answered questions. Then he got comfortable."

Sosa's biggest test was handling media criticism. Critical players funneled comments about Sosa's fundamental lapses through the *Daily Herald*'s Rozner and several other reporters, while WSCR's Mike Murphy repeatedly called him "Roberto Clemente without a brain." Sosa wasn't pleased with such barbs, but he didn't go into the tank mentally or become hostile to media a la Albert Belle.

"They can talk about me all they want," Sosa said in 1995. "But they can't take my game away from me. My game is mine.

"Nobody likes to hear negative things. But I feel they will give me my due someday. It doesn't bother me."

That style of two wrongs not making a right rested well with CLTV's Carlson and others who covered Sosa.

"It takes a real man to ignore all that back-biting and back-stabbing," Carlson said.

And it took a real man to meet his critics one-on-one, in private, away from others. So many baseball players have tried to confront media, either verbally or physically, giving the game a black eye. Sosa showed far more polish than that at a relatively early age.

Joseph A. Reaves, covering the Cubs for the *Chicago Tribune*, recalled one such private encounter in 1994 in Houston.

He detailed the meeting in his 1997 book, *From Warsaw To Wrigley*, about his time with the Cubs after working as a *Tribune* foreign correspondent.

Reaves was walking around the Westin Galleria Hotel one day when Sosa waved at him from inside a Chinese restaurant. "Tsssss, compadre. Come here a second," Sosa beckoned.

In the book, Reaves had recalled writing a game story detailing that Sosa swung from the heels and struck out in a first-and-third, one-out, ninth-inning situation with the Cubs down by just one run. His lead: "Let Sammy be Sammy." Reaves continued: "Discipline doesn't suit Sosa's game. Try to rein him in and you risk losing the power and speed that occasionally flash like a bolt of lightning and break open a baseball game."

Reaves went on in his book: "I also mentioned the rap against Sosa, whispered by his teammates and those outside the Cubs organization, that many of his statistics were selfish. That he would steal a base in a lopsided game to pad his numbers or that he would swing from his heels for a home run every time, regardless of the game situation..."

Sosa wondered why he wrote what he did as he sat down to talk with Reaves in the Westin Galleria restaurant.

"Because it's true, Sammy," Reaves replied.

"I'm not trying to hurt nobody," Sosa said to him. "I'm trying to do my best. Sammy always tries to do his best. I thought you were my friend. How come you write something like that about me?"

From there on was dialogue that Albert Belle should crave, but would never endure.

"For the next 30 minutes, we had a surprisingly frank and enjoyable discussion—both of us coming to grips with the confusing concepts of team play, sports journalism, and perception versus reality," Reaves wrote. "Sosa didn't agree with a lot I said about critical writing. I didn't buy into his still-evolving thoughts on winning baseball. But we both talked. And we both listened. And we both came away appreciating ech other a little more."

Reaves added that he had "newfound respect for Sosa. ... He's already a winner. He came to a strange land with a strange language when he was still a kid. He was saddled with expectations few could ever hope to meet and was told to exceed them under an unrelenting spotlight. He stumbled along the way, but never for lack of trying.

"When all is said and done, Sosa could go down as one of the greatest players to wear a Cubs' uniform."

Four years after the meeting with Sosa, Reaves' positive opinion of Sosa grew even more. Reaves had left the Cubs beat and quit the paper in 1995, moved with his wife to Hong Kong, then came back to the United States to teach at Arizona State University. From his perspective covering foreign cultures from the Philippines to eastern Europe, Sosa has conquered tremendous numbers of obstacles.

"Sammy is one of the most admirable guys I've seen," Reaves said. "I spent my career living in foreign cultures. I know how difficult it is to assimilate into a different culture. To have to do that and perform at the peak of a profession that's still new to you, I only wish I could handle it as gracefully."

To prove he still could handle sticky media relations without excessive rancor, Sosa pulled aside another *Tribune* sportswriter to discuss a story on August 24, 1998.

That morning, baseball writer Phil Rogers had written a feature speculating whether the Houston Astros' Jose Lima might have grooved a pitch that Sosa had belted for his 51st homer the eighth inning the day before in Wrigley Field. The reasoning was that Lima might have wanted to help a fellow Dominican chase the most hallowed of baseball records. Sosa had hit No. 50 earlier in the game off Lima, but then the Astros turned it into a 12-2 rout before he connected again. The angle of the story caused brief controversy to flare with the undercurrent of racial antagonism.

Never mind that in a blowout game, a starter's role is to throw fastballs for strikes, avoid walks that could give the near-vanquished foe some life, and get the batters to hit the ball, somewhere, anywhere, hopefully inside the ballpark. Sosa obviously had Lima's number in any situation. A month later, he belted No. 66 off Lima in the Astrodome. But on this day, controversy had to rear its ugly head in the middle of the home-run chase.

Several press-box types had thought they had picked up some body language from Lima tipping them off to his real intentions. And they had long memories of Denny McLain, he of the poor character that would later land him in jail twice, grooving a pitch to idol Mickey Mantle at the end of the latter's career in 1968. Not long after the Lima-Sosa matchup, former pitcher Milt Pappas claimed that he grooved a fat pitch to Roger Maris for homer No. 59 in 1961 while Pappas played for the Baltimore Orioles.

Both Sosa and Lima denied anything unusual had happened. And, as batting practice finished on August 24, a perturbed Sosa spotted a reporter in the clubhouse. "Where's Phil Rogers? I want to talk to him!" he said. Trouble was brewing. The reporter quickly ran out near the batting cage, summoned Rogers, and got him to go back in to see Sosa. The pair met behind closed doors, and neither would comment afterward. But the issue apparently was settled without lasting rancor.

The Lima incident was the only smudge on Sosa's joyful journey into the public's consciousness. As the media attention grew after his 20-homer June, he continued his locker-room business as usual. On the morning of August 1, 1998, a writer approached him, bleary-eyed from having worked the trade-deadline stories until well after midnight, to ask his reaction to big news—the Astros had traded for Randy Johnson at the deadline, while the Cubs settled for lefty reliever Felix Heredia.

Sosa hadn't heard of the Johnson deal, either late the previous night or waking up on that morning. The reporter explained the deals, Sosa listening intently. Finally other media arrived, surrounded the duo, and Sosa began to analyze the trades. No, he wasn't afraid of Johnson's arrival; he wasn't unhittable. Heredia would help the Cubs. When you have confidence, jolting news like this doesn't shake it easily.

Sosa wasn't the most demonstrative clubhouse type like former Cub Shawon Dunston, one of the game's loudest-decibel fellows and a skilled trash-talker. But he could make himself heard when he wanted to. One day after batting practice, Cubs pitching coach Phil Regan walked buck naked from the shower back to his locker to change into his game uniform. No women reporters were present. But Sosa, sitting with his fellow Dominican players as is his usual custom after batting practice, feigned mock outrage. "Hey, Phil, you can't do that! Put some clothes on!"

Women, men, foreigners, New Yorkers, everyone seemingly was present the night of August 18 at Wrigley Field. The Cubs issued some 200 media credentials for the first head-to-head matchup of the home-run race centerpieces with the St. Louis Cardinals and Mark McGwire in town. Sosa was trapped at his locker for 40 minutes after batting practice by some 50 writers, broadcast reporters and TV cameras. There had never been such a jam for one player in recent Cubs history. Sosa finally broke away from the mob and went over to sit with the other Dominican players for a breather with the game less than an hour away.

The Cubs' method of handling Sosa was starting to change—by necessity.

"I haven't seen anything like the St. Louis series for a non-playoff or non-(first) night-game situation," said Chuck Wasserstrom, the Cubs' media information coordinator, who typically stands watch, ready to keep order, in the locker room after games.

At the time, Wasserstrom and Cubs media-relations chief Sharon Pannozzo wanted to avoid press conference-style arrangements to handle Sosa. "The key thing to do is to keep Sammy on as much of his routine as possible," Wasserstrom said. Sosa vowed not to resort to once-a-series pre-game press conferences, a la McGwire. "Three or four times a day," was his projected interview-access time.

He wondered if Sosa was distracted and tired by the August 18 pre-game ordeal. Sosa struck out three times that night against the Cardinals. "He was so flat," Wasserstrom said. Sosa denied he was drained by the media demands.

But with the media pressing in tighter, and in greater numbers, Wasserstrom was forced to clamp the first restriction down on Sosa access. After a 20-minute post-game session, he announced Sosa would take three more questions.

Soon Wasserstrom was regulating five-minute waves of post-game reporters by Sosa's locker, before the Cubs cleared out an old storage room under the first-base stands and converted it to a media interview area. And, still, the situation would worsen, without any change in Sosa's personality.

The worst of all came during the second Sosa-McGwire matchup on September 7-8, 1998, in St. Louis. "It had been manageable up to that time," Wasserstrom said. "But St. Louis was a nightmare."

With a World Series-sized media contingent on hand, expecting McGwire to tie and/or break the 61-homer record, Wasserstrom at times felt like the kid with his finger in the dike. It was going to burst any time.

It did.

Sosa and McGwire posed for a pre-arranged photo shoot for Major League Baseball. Reporters surrounded the area and were closing in.

"I asked people to back up, and I was getting no help from security at all," Wasserstrom said. "As soon as it ended, there was this huge media crush. There were way too many people jumping in there way too quickly. When you hit me in the back of the head with a camera, I'm not going to be too happy. That's when I had to get ballistic."

But some measure of order was restored when Sosa returned home. Pre-game sessions unfortunately were curtailed, and he started getting off his one-liners in the post-game press conferences, alone at a podium, able to breathe and shine without a mass of humanity hovering. Sosa continued to do the post-game sessions even during an 0-for-21 slump going into the season's last week.

"It's embarrassing to take someone to an interview room four straight days after oh-fers because people are going to run to his clubhouse spot anyway if you don't," Wasserstrom said. "A lot of guys would not go there four or five straight days. They're going to be surly. But Sammy realizes this is part of his job.

"I tried to do as much as I could to have him do as little as he could. But he did very well under the circumstances. He treated the media well, and 98 percent of the media have treated him well. It's the 2 percent that have caused problems, not really for him, but for everyone else in general."

Grace under fire earned him plaudits from his media chroniclers.

"Almost any of us would have buckled under the pressure and said go away for a few days," said Mike Bauman, sports columnist for the *Milwaukee Journal Sentinel.*

Sosa's view of the situation? Great, "especially the way you guys supported me," he said before the September 22, 1998 game in Milwaukee.

"I couldn't believe that," said Bauman. "When's the last time you heard an athlete say that?"

Sosa's inclusion of everyone is what made the season so memorable. Not only for extraordinary home-run achievements, but also for extraordinary statements and behavior from one nice Dominican.

"It's made covering the Cubs so much more enjoyable," CLTV's Carlson said of Sosa's trip through history. "Giving chase to one of the most glamorous records in sports, and doing it with such style, it makes you really admire him."

The real test is yet to come. Sosa's life will never be the same.

"He'll have to handle everything in moderation," former Sosa running-mate Steve Grad said. "He'll constantly need people around him to handle the fan crush. He can't walk around Michigan Avenue anymore, or go to a nightclub. Otherwise, he'd get mobbed. But I think he'll handle it, just like he's handled everything else pretty well."

Few could handle such a load so well.

"It's unbelievable," Grad said, using one of the player's own catchwords.

"It's like watching a baby grow up into a man."

Sunday, Sept 13, 1998

1998 NATIONAL LEAGUE UMPIRES

4 Mark Hirschbeck 13 Larry Poncino 22 Joe West 31 Bob Davidson 40 Jerry Crawford*
5 Angel Hernandez 14 Frank Pulli* 23 Ed Rapuano 32 Dana DeMuth 41 Jerry Meals
6 Bruce Froemming* 15 Jim Quick* 24 Jerry Layne 33 Mike Winters 43 Paul Schrieber
7 Eric Gregg 16 Rich Rieker 25 Charlie Williams 34 Greg Bonin 44 Kerwin Danley
8 Jeff Kellogg 18 Charlie Reliford 27 Steve Rippley* 35 Gary Darling
9 Brian Gorman 19 Terry Tata* 28 Larry Vanover 36 Wally Bell
11 Ed Montague* 20 Tom Hallion 29 Bill Hohn 37 Bruce Dreckman
12 Gerry Davis 21 Harry Wendelstedt* 30 Randy Marsh* 38 Sam Holbrook

*Crew Chief

Milwaukee

1 Fernando Vina, IF
2 Jose Valentin, IF
3 Phil Garner, MGR
6 Geoff Jenkins, OF
7 David Nilsson, IF-OF
8 Mark Loretta, IF
9 Marquis Grissom, OF
10 Marc Newfield, OF
12 Chris Bando, Coach
13 Jeff D'Amico, RHP
16 Jesse Levis, C
20 Jeromy Burnitz, OF
21 Cal Eldred, RHP
22 Mike Matheny, C
24 Darrin Jackson, OF
27 Jeff Cirillo, IF
27 Bob Wickman, RHP
28 Mike Myers, LHP
29 Jim Lefebvre, Coach
30 Bob Hamelin, IF
31 Bronswell Patrick, RHP
32 John Jaha, IF
33 Bobby Hughes, C-OF
35 Bill Castro, Coach
36 Joel Youngblood, Coach
37 Steve Woodard, RHP
38 Doug Mansolino, Coach
39 Eric Plunk, RHP
40 Chad Fox, RHP
41 Jose Mercedes, RHP
42 Scott Karl, LHP
45 Don Rowe, Coach
46 Bill Pulsipher, LHP
47 Al Reyes, RHP
48 Brad Woodall, LHP
49 David Weathers, RHP
52 Rafael Roque, LHP
58 Valerio De Los Santos, LHP

No.	Player	Pos.	1	2	3	4	5	6	7	8	9	10	AB	R	H	RBI
1	Vina	2b														
8	Loretta	ss														
7	Nilsson	1b														
26	Cirillo	3b														
20	Burnitz	rf														
9	Grissom	cf														
5	G. Jenkins	lf														
10	Newfield ph/8th															
33	B. Hughes	c														
30	Hamelin ph/8th															
48	Woodall p															
31	Patrick p/3rd															
58	De Los Santos p/6th															
25	B. Banks ph/7th															
49	Weathers p/7th															
24	D. Jackson ph															
39	Plunk p/8th															
28	Myers p/9th															

Pitchers	IP	H	R	ER	BB	SO	Notes
Woodall	2⅔	6	6	6	1	0	Myers p/9th
Patrick /3rd	3⅓	2	2	2	0	3	A. Reyes p/9th
De Los Santos /6th	1	0	0	0	0	0	
Weathers /8th		1	0	0	0		
Plunk /8th							Myers p/9th

CUBS

1 Lance Johnson, OF
2 Jeff Pentland, Coach
3 Dan Radison, Coach
4 Jeff Blauser, IF
5 Jim Riggleman, MGR
6 Glenallen Hill, OF
7 Tyler Houston, C-IF
8 Gary Gaetti, IF
9 Scott Servais, C
12 Mickey Morandini, IF
15 Sandy Martinez, C
17 Mark Grace, IF
18 Jose Hernandez, IF-OF
20 Matt Mieske, OF
21 Sammy Sosa, OF
24 Manny Alexander, IF
25 Orlando Merced, OF-IF
26 Billy Williams, Coach
27 Phil Regan, Coach
28 Pedro Valdes, OF
30 Jeremi Gonzalez, RHP
33 Don Wengert, RHP
34 Kerry Wood, RHP
36 Kevin Tapani, RHP
37 Brant Brown, OF-IF
38 Mike Morgan, RHP
39 Tom Gamboa, Coach
40 Henry Rodriguez, OF
43 Dave Bialas, Coach
45 Terry Mulholland, LHP
46 Steve Trachsel, RHP
47 Rod Beck, RHP
48 Dave Stevens, RHP
49 Felix Heredia, LHP
50 Jason Maxwell, IF
51 Terry Adams, RHP
52 Matt Karchner, RHP
54 Mark Clark, RHP
59 Rodney Myers, RHP
63 Rick Kranitz, Instructor

No.	Player	Pos.	1	2	3	4	5	6	7	8	9	10	AB	R	H	RBI
1	L. Johnson	cf														
18	J. Hernandez	ss														
17	Grace	1b														
21	Sosa	rf														
6	G. Hill	lf														
37	B. Brown pr/7th-lf															
8	Gaetti	3b														
12	Morandini	2b														
9	Servais	c														
7	Houston ph/8th-c															
46	Trachsel p/7th															
45	Mulholland p/7th															
25	Merced lf/8th															
24	Alexander ph															
20	Mieske ph/8th															
52	Karchner p/8th															
49	Heredia p/8th															
33	Wengert p/8th															
44	Haney p/9th															

Pitchers	IP	H	R	ER	BB	SO	Notes
Trachsel	6	7	5	5	0	2	A - 40,846
Mulholland /7th	1⅓	3	4	4	1	3	Sammy's 61st HR
Karchner /8th							@ No. 62 HR
Heredia /8th							

Track Sammy Sosa's Home Runs

59	60	61	62	63	64	65
	Wengert /8th Haney /9th		40 H. Rodriguez ph/9th 50 Maxwell pr/9th	Beck		

9/11/98-9/13/98

17

A Story Angle . . . and a Spokesman

Sammy Sosa's off-the-field persona in 1998 enabled him to gain prime consideration as one of Major League Baseball's top player spokesmen, if not the spokesman. For confirmation, just ask baseball commissioner Bud Selig.

"I've never seen anything like it," Selig said of Sosa's gab sessions that charmed a world. "I think he's one of the nicest human beings I've ever known. He's everything people say he is.

"The more I'm around him, the more I like Sammy Sosa. He will be a great spokesman for baseball on the North American continent. He's absolutely remarkable."

With such great qualities (Where has Sammy Sosa been all these years?), look at Wrigley Field. He slugged 160 homers between 1993 and 1997, certainly a total that would attract attention.

But until June 1998, when he blasted an unheard-of 20 homers in a month, Sosa hardly was publicized outside Chicago. And it had nothing to do with shortcomings.

The Cubs were .500 or worse, sometimes a lot worse. Other elite players, usually performing on better teams, garnered airtime and headlines. Sosa? Outwardly nice numbers, but what's the angle?

"Sammy was just a silly millimeter before the top of the league," said George Will, syndicated columnist, author, and Cubs fan. "Ninety percent of the attention in any sport in our country goes to 3 percent of the players. Sammy was at 4 percent. This was the year where he broke through to the top level.

"They can be absolutely Grade-A players, but they're not A-plus. Look at the NBA. There are about five guys who get all the attention, and then there are five guys below that.

"And the fact he was on the Cubs hurt him. People associated the Cubs with disappointment."

That's the view from Washington. What about the hinterlands?

"Well, there's always something to write about everybody if you look," said the *Dayton Daily News*' Hal McCoy, the most senior traveling baseball beat writer. "I've covered baseball for 26 years, and I can't recall ever searching out Sammy Sosa for a story like I might have Mark Grace or Ryne Sandberg, Ferguson Jenkins or Ernie Banks or somebody like that."

Sosa was considered below elite level, a member of a group of second-tier slugging outfielders who didn't rate any kind of special angle, regionally or nationally.

"He was like a Greg Vaughn when he was with the Padres the last couple of years," said Mike Sansone, sports editor of *The Times* of northwest Indiana, and formerly sports copy chief of *The Sacramento Bee*.

Sosa wasn't worth writing about in media-capital New York.

"He was one of maybe 10 or 15 outfielders in the majors, maybe who would make an All-Star team once in awhile," said Joe Gergen, sports columnist for Long Island *Newsday*. "He didn't have the complete package. He hit .250 or .260 with a lot of strikeouts. The last few years there have been a whole flood of players like him with 35 or 40 homers."

Sosa had a lot of ifs, ands and buts. That does not make consistent "A" material.

"We always thought he was untapped potential," said Drew Olsen, Brewers beat writer for the *Milwaukee Journal Sentinel*. "Everybody saw him as the guy who struck out a lot. Low batting-average guy. Not a guy who could carry a team. People saw him get hot in bursts like he used to, hitting bunches of home runs, and they they dismissed that as well. It's just Sammy getting hot, but next week he'll probably strike out 20 of 25 at-bats again. He'll go back to normal."

But has the world ever turned in less than a year. Mark McGwire may earn the top headline with his other-worldly 70-homer outburst. But Sosa may end up with the more compelling rags-to-riches story when all is said and done. And, in the process, he may have passed up players with better-known pedigrees to become a much-needed spokesman for Major League Baseball.

"He's the first real Latin-American player to capture the nation," said Dave Anderson, sports columnist for the *New York Times*. "Roberto Clemente was the first great Latin in baseball, but he basically was a Pittsburgh player. As good as he was, he never got into the national spotlight. Juan Marichal was the best Dominican player, a terrific pitcher. But he didn't capture the national stage because he was always in Sandy Koufax's shadow. Orlando Cepeda never had it."

Sosa's Dominican background began to draw different parts of the world together.

"His story is great because of its rags-to-riches theme," said Bauman, sports columnist for the *Milwaukee Journal Sentinel*. "But also because he represents the wave of the future. It's part of the globalization of baseball. He's opened doors the way he's carried himself. It's bigger than the numbers, bigger than the (home-run) feat itself. It's symbolic of the changes in the game, and it's all good."

In a nation of diversity, Sosa's story had prime appeal, according to pundit Will.

"It is a greater story than McGwire," he said. "It appeals to our nation of immigrants. The fastest-growing immigrant group in the country is Spanish-speaking. The fastest-growing group in baseball, with a disproportionate share of the young talent are Hispanics."

Was the Sosa story bigger than Michael Jordan?

"When I came to Chicago covering the Phillies in June, I thought at the moment Sammy was the biggest athlete in Chicago," said *Wilmington News-Journal* sportswriter Doug Lesmerises, who had previously covered the Chicago Bulls for *The Times* of northwest Indiana.

"I thought Sammy would beat Michael Jordan. I think for that time period, he absolutely replaced Jordan. Who was thinking of the Bulls? (after their sixth NBA title and during the league's summer-fall lockout). Thank God for Sammy in Chicago. Frank Thomas sucked, and the Bears sucked."

Almost any baseball-watcher was never going to connect Sosa with the elite group of Barry Bonds, Ken Griffey, Jr. and McGwire prior to this season. But not only has Sosa passed up these top-flight players' peak years with his 66-homer, 158-RBI season, but he also may have grabbed the spokesman's mantle for a game that desperately needs a masses-appealing front man.

"He so obviously emotionally reciprocates the country's affection for him," Will said.

Think of it. When baseball needed someone to step up to speak out for its basic goodness after the disastrous strike of 1994-95, the elite group fell short. Meanwhile, a whole slew of NBA and NFL players amassed higher profiles and the resulting endorsement income. Impressionable kids began forging allegiances with the other sports, leaving baseball behind.

The top level of baseball stars figured the golden goose would keep spewing forth their mega-millions, and they didn't have to do anything other than step to the plate to keep the cash flow coming. They seemed wrapped up in themselves, often keeping the media-and the resulting fan identification with them-at bay.

Griffey had the most potential as the game's leading commercial endorser. But the most accessible player on his own Seattle Mariners is shortstop Alex Rodriguez. In the spring of 1997, Griffey said he would not do radio interviews because a Seattle shock jock announced he sexually coveted Griffey's wife on his radio show. The proverbial one bad apple spoiled it for the whole bunch. One year later, Griffey said in spring training he was "cutting down his press" for 1998.

McGwire always has been standoffish, an "introspective" personality, according to Joe Gergen.

"I can recall approaching McGwire twice for interviews in the spring of 1997 in Phoenix and being rebuffed. On April 30, 1998, I again approached McGwire in the Cardinals' clubhouse in Wrigley Field, 3 1/2 hours before the game and just as the locker room had opened. 'Mark?' was the only word out of my mouth before McGwire barked, 'No!'

"No, indeed, not a sentence, a paragraph, not even the decency to hear out one question before a respectful rejection. McGwire would be smoked out later in the season due to the enormity of his 70-homer feat and a gentle nudge from the media-friendly Sosa style."

Said Will: "It took him a little while—and I don't hold it against him—to figure out how to handle this pressure. He figured it out in time. And he'll tell you one reason he did was Sammy Sosa. He saw the other guy was having more fun than he was."

If only Albert Belle of the White Sox could have some fun. Baseball's most menacing figure seemingly has no reason to be hostile to the world, with riches beyond compare and assured jobs with teams willing to put up with his acidic personality. Yet he continues to be baseball's Sphinx, a mystery man who does nothing but promote negatives for the game's image with his anti-social behavior. You simply steer clear of the man; he could have an outburst at any time.

One Sunday morning at Comiskey Park, a reporter sat waiting for another player for an interview. Some distance away, Belle suddenly burst up from his locker toward the clubhouse TV set. The ESPN show *The Sports Reporters* was on. Belle quickly flipped channels and announced to nobody in particular, "We don't need this shit!"

Bonds may be the most frustrating case of not grabbing the mantle of leadership for baseball. He's had a starring role for a decade, a 40-40 man, and possesses a great baseball name and lineage as the son of former Giants star Bobby Bonds. He's a good speaker when he chooses to be one.

After some fancy maneuvering, a reporter managed to land Bonds for a one-on-one interview on his syndicated Diamond Gems baseball radio talk show in mid-summer 1996. The interview was set up in a corner of the visitors' dugout at Wrigley Field, the tape rolled, and one of the most unusual interviews conducted unfolded.

"I wasn't the golden child, and I wasn't picked to be one," Bonds said. Huh? "Not too many famous children of famous people are. How many fathers' children have become the marketable stars? None, except for Griffey. And his father wasn't the main guy on the Big Red Machine. Johnny Bench and Pete Rose overshadowed him publicly."

Bonds went on to say he didn't "see why he couldn't" become baseball's spokesman. But in the same breath, he explained why his media relations were so poor.

"I rebelled against the media," he said of his early baseball days. "I have a cousin named Reggie Smith, a cousin named Reggie Jackson, a godfather named Willie Mays, a father named Bobby Bonds. Here I am a young kid trying to make it. 'Can you be Mr. October like your cousin?' 'Will you ever be as great as your godfather?' 'Will you ever do 30-30 like your father?' The media came up and said, 'Bobby...oops, Barry, I relate to your father.' The media never grasps Barry Bonds.

"That's where the misunderstanding came, that's where the tangles came in. I wanted to mingle when I first started in the minor leagues when I was so accessible. I came to them with open arms. But they never embraced Barry. They always embraced the son of great family. When Michael Jordan makes a great move, they say, 'Oh, Michael!' With Barry Bonds, it's, 'Bobby, oops, Barry, but I relate to your father or godfather.' 'He does things just like his godfather, but he hasn't been able to come through in the playoffs like his cousin, Reggie, yet.

"I never gave them (media) the time back. I refuse to, because I think it's their turn."

With the interview done, the tape was halted. The inquisitor wondered, 'Why not take this opportunity to speak Harry Truman-like, common sense to Barry Bonds?'

"Why can't you be like Mike (Jordan)?" Bonds was asked. "Look how much money he's made by being a good person, looking you straight in the eye, talking to the media." Indeed, if Bonds had $10 million or $15 million as a result of his high profile, why wouldn't he want $30 million or $40 million by employing his natural abilities to talk?

"Because I don't need to give $100 million to each of my kids like Jordan," came Bonds' shocking reply.

That was sad, that the motivation of riches beyond compare would spur Bonds to act decently and become the front man for baseball.

"Barry doesn't want it," said Cubs closer Rod Beck, a Bonds teammate in San Francisco for five seasons and a Truman-like plain speaker himself. "Barry preaches all the time that his job is not to be a role model, his job is not to sign autographs. His job is to help the Giants win ballgames.

"Barry's very media unfriendly. He goes by his own beat. Sammy has embraced the role of spokesman for baseball. I respect Sammy Sosa very much. I respect Barry for his abilities and talents, but not how he presents himself to the public.

"You see how he grew up in the game the way he did, seeing things he saw as a child in the (Giants) clubhouse with Willie Mays, Willie McCovey and Juan Marichal. I heard stories about the way things were then. Barry goes about it the same way the old timers did it way back when, only there wasn't as much media and press. So those players didn't look as poorly to the public.

"It's not that hard to be nice, it's really not. And Sammy's naturally a nice guy."

During the Diamond Gems interview, Bonds himself defined just who would grab the loyalty of the public. It sounded like a perfect description of Sosa.

"Always the marketable people, the ones who are loved, are the unknown names," he said of stars who aren't second-generation athletes. "They're the ones who shock people by surprise.

"The Michael Jordans, the Magic Johnsons, the Shaquille O'Neals, the Muhammad Alis, the Joe Montanas, the unknowns, they take people by surprise."

That's a good group to run with, Sammy. The job as baseball spokesman and No. 1 nice guy was wide open. No employment agency could fill it. Sammy did, and nobody's going to argue now about his job qualifications.

CHICAGO CUBS vs. MILWAUKEE BREWERS
Wednesday, September 23, 1998

CHICAGO CUBS (88-70)

AVG.	HR	RBI	PLAYER	POS.	1	2	3	4	5	6	7	8	9	10	AB	R	H
.279	2	21	1-Lance Johnson	CF	2b	BB		Flo 1	Flo 8		Flo 9						
.258	23	74	18-Jose Hernandez	SS	Sc 2-3	BB RBI		Go 5-3		Go 6-3		Flo					
.312	17	89	17-Mark Grace	1B	sing	BALK K						Flo 9					
.303	63	154	21-Sammy Sosa	RF	BB		BB		HR	HR 65		BB					
.376	8	23	6-Glenallen Hill	LF	DP 5-4-3	Flo 8		K	64	Go 6-3							
.280	18	66	8-Gary Gaetti	3B		BB	7-M E-7	Fc 6-4		sing		Go 3-1					
			Alexander ss/8th														
.301	8	53	12-Mickey Morandini	2B		Fc 3-45	Go 4-3	sing.		Flo 9		K					
.222	7	35	9-Scott Servais	C		Go 3-3	Flo 3	sing RBI		Hbp	sing					
.267	1	7	46-Steve Trachsel	RHP		BB R	Flo 9	sing RB		Fc 5-4	K					
				R	0	2	0	1	0	3	1	9	0	0			
				H													

PITCHER	WLS	IP	H	R	ER	BB	SO	HB	WP	BK	HR
Steve Trachsel (14-8)		6⅓	6	4	4	1	4				
Heredia /7th											
Karchner/7th											
Beck/9th											

SH —
SF —
SB —   CS —
DP —   HB —
GDP —

MILWAUKEE BREWERS (72-85)

A – 45,35

AVG.	HR	RBI	PLAYER	POS.	1	2	3	4	5	6	7	8	9	10	AB	R	H	R
.307	7	43	1-Fernando Vina	2B	Flo 9		BB			CC 4-3	sing		Go 43					
.320	6	52	8-Mark Loretta	1B	Flo 8		sing.			Go 6-3	Flo 9		sing					
.326	14	67	26-Jeff Cirillo	3B	K		Go 5-3			Flo 8	Flo 8		2b					
.263	38	124	20-Jeromy Burnitz	RF		K		K			sing R	BB I BB					
.269	8	58	9-Marquis Grissom	CF		2b		Go 6-3			sing R	Flo 8 Flo 5					
.232	9	28	5-Geoff Jenkins	LF		Flo 9		Flo 9			BB R	Fc 4-6 E7					
.221	15	46	2-Jose Valentin	SS		Go 3			Flo 6		Go 6-3 2RB	sing RBI					
.240	9	28	33-Bobby Hughes	C			E-b 4-3		Flo 3		SF 3 RBI	sing. RBI					
.083	0	1	52-Rafael Roque	LHP			K		K		sing RB	Flo 8					
			47 Reyes p/5th														
D. Jackson			Banks ph/7th	R		0	0	0	0	0	0	4	1				
				H		0	1	0	0	0	0	5	2				

18

59 and Beyond: A Wild, Wild, Wild-Card Finish

Even after losing the race for 61 homers, Sammy Sosa won a more important prize after everything he endured in his life: the respect and adoration of the public.

As his home-run total climbed into the 50s, a mural appeared on the size of the Bigsby & Kruthers warehouse at Ashland Avenue and the Kennedy Expressway on Chicago's near northwest side. A visage of Dennis Rodman had formerly gazed down on commuters from this wall, backing up traffic for miles. But now Sosa's outstretched batting form, complete with an updated sign denoting his home-run totals, would offer a little more pleasing and less outlandish landmark on the way to or from work. You don't get a Bigsby & Kruthers mural unless you've reached the top rank of celebrityhood.

Better yet, Sosa, either largely ignored or ridiculed by the mass of media in the past, was now attracting them like a magnet. *Chicago Sun-Times* weathervane sports columnist Jay Mariotti began following Sosa in every game, blowing off the Bears and the Michael Jordan Watch, two beats that were sacrosanct in the eyes of both sports editors and broadcast sports directors.

"You do find yourself appreciating him more than McGwire," wrote Mariotti, who 6 1/2 years previously had ripped then-Cubs GM Larry Himes for trading for Sosa. "McGwire is the comic-book dominator, the monster who was supposed to be here all along. Sosa is the fairy tale."

Given a choice between baseball, Bears and Bulls, baseball would be dumped by the media gatekeepers in the good ol' days. Even before the strike, baseball simply did not have many passionate advocates among the print and broadcast decision-makers. Now, Chicago's sports columnists, who only appeared in person at a handful of Cubs games each season while never missing a Bears game, began packing the press box. Many of these scribes formerly used the summer as vacation time in between the NBA and NFL seasons, or went off on jaunts to golf tournaments.

Furthermore, Sosa and baseball talk began dominating the airwaves of WSCR-AM ("The Score"), an all-sports radio station. Baseball had to fight for any kind of comprehensive coverage and discussion on The Score, which featured a cadre of program hosts who would have preferred an "all-football, all-the-time" format. Baseball talk was never vigorously encouraged and was largely pushed over to nighttime and all-night shows hosted by Mike Murphy and Les Grobstein, respectively.

But the times, they were a-changin.'

Even the *Chicago Tribune* devoted a major feature in its Sunday, September 6 "Perspective" deep-thinking issues section to Sosa's "hop of joy," showing with photo inserts his home-run pivot, his little hop off the ground as he connected, and his home-run trot. Staff writer Malcolm Moran took a serious and wistful look at the home-run hop, concluding, "It is easy to imagine a new generation, from Chicago all the way to the Dominican Republic, swinging hard, landing on their back foot, and pushing off into space. A patent is unnecessary."

Sosa might not have possessed the energy for a home-run hop on the morning of September 9. In another instance of lousy scheduling, the Cubs had to play a day game at Wrigley Field against the Pittsburgh Pirates. Although the flight from St. Louis was less than one hour, permitting the slotting of a day game in Chicago after a night game in another city, the Cubs did not arrive back at O'Hare International until 1:30 a.m.

Sosa's life was changing even as he rubbed the short night's sleep out of his eyes as he sifted through his accumulated mail before the Pirates game. Two unidentified boxes and a stuffed envelope appeared. But before he could open the mail, security swooped in and confiscated it. As was done with McGwire, Major League Baseball assigned security guards to shadow Sosa in the clubhouse, on the field, in the dugout and when he went out and about, home and road. Imported from the New York area working in three-week shifts, were off-duty police detectives of Hispanic descent, better to cater to Sosa's comfort zone. The guards were cordial and unobtrusive, but dampened down on the free and easy access that marked Sosa's career up to this point.

Also joining the Cubs' traveling party was Hall of Fame representative John Ralph, a former White Sox and Texas Rangers media-relations aide, who would tail Sosa until he hit No. 62 in order to try to collect the ball, bat, jersey and other paraphernalia connected with the feat. The bounty would be set up with McGwire's items in a special exhibit commemorating the home-run record in the front of the Hall of Fame.

Sosa's family had to adjust to the new situation, too. Wife Sonia found herself sitting down for TV interviews in the family's downtown Chicago condo. Even more besieged by reporters was Sosa's mother, Lucrecia, at her San Pedro de Macoris home in the Dominican.

"She calls me, and says she's got a house full of reporters," Sosa said. "Every day. But she doesn't mind it. And I've got my brothers there to help her."

Although Lucrecia was welcome to visit her son anytime in Chicago, she liked her own home and preferred to stay in familiar surroundings in the Dominican. The surge of events, though, would soon summon her to Wrigley Field.

Sosa continued to go homer-less in consecutive Cubs victories on September 9 and 10 against the Pirates. But he didn't care that he still lagged four homers behind McGwire.

"What I'm more into now is trying to go into the playoffs," Sosa said. "For me, Mark is at 62, but I'm not thinking about it. Everything will be done September 27. On September 27, Mark has to go home and I get to go the playoffs."

But to fulfill Sosa's dream, the Cubs were going to have to do it the hard way. Young fireballer Kerry Wood was suddenly unavailable with a sprained ligament in his elbow. A mechani-

cal flaw in his stride, causing him to throw across his body, was
the apparent cause; he had sometimes struggled with the same
problem earlier in the season. But now it had taken a physical
toll. Wood had complained of a dead arm early in August, suggested he should miss a start, and then continued in the rotation, pitching well. But going into a September 11 to 13 weekend series with the Milwaukee Brewers, Wood had not pitched
since August 31, when both he and Sosa had homered against
the Cincinnati Reds in a 5-4 Cubs' win. He was sitting on a great
13-6 record and an astounding 233 strikeouts in 166 2/3 innings.

Without Wood and his growing unhittable aura, Cubs manager Jim Riggleman called on journeyman Don Wengert to fill
in. Wengert, tried earlier to plug the hole left by Jeremi Gonzalez's
season-ending injury, was found wanting as a starter and was
better suited for middle relief. Yet Riggleman initially brushed
off suggestions to move veteran lefty Terry Mulholland, who had
10 years' big-league experience and quite a bit of success as a
starter, back into the rotation. The Cubs were really going to
scuffle for pitching down the stretch, and the shortage combined with Sosa's sense of theater would help make the Brewers series one of the most memorable in team history with 80ish
temperatures, the wind blowing out and crowds cramming
Wrigley Field to overflowing. The summer, usually banished from
Chicago by this point of the year, simply refused to quit, and the
Cubs followed suit.

Manager Phil Garner's usually scrappy Brew Crew had
sagged badly since playing the Cubs in mid-July in Milwaukee.
But without Wood to overwhelm them psychologically, the Brewers' bats came alive. After the Cubs took a 3-0 lead, they chased
Wengert in a six-run third. Reliever Terry Adams, whose season
had fallen apart just before the All-Star break, contributed three
wild pitches, a throwing error and a walk of the opposing pitcher,
all within the span of a 2/3 of an inning in the sixth. At one
point the Brewers had led 9-3.

But Sosa tried to spark a comeback with an unbelievable
bomb, good for No. 59, leading off a four-run fifth. The ball traveled all the way over the right-field bleachers onto Sheffield
Avenue. Witnesses said a homeless man, away from the usual
crowd of ballhawks massing around the corner on Waveland
Avenue, retrieved the ball and turned it over to Cubs security
personnel.

"I'm a human being," Sosa said. "I'm not going to go out every day and get a hit. But I believe in myself."

Jim Riggleman had to empty his bullpen, employing six relievers, in the eventual 13-11 loss. So starter Mike Morgan, who had not pitched well since being traded back to the Cubs from Minnesota three weeks previously, was charged with staying on the mound as long as possible on Saturday, September 12.

Morgan literally took one for the team. An error on short-stop Jose Hernandez opened up the floodgates in the third inning. Dave Nillson smacked a bases-loaded triple. Jeff Cirillo had an RBI double. Jeromy Burnitz slugged a two-run homer. Geoff Jenkins and Bobby Hughes belted back-to-back homers. Eight runs total, all off Morgan, who was finally relieved by Dave Stevens in the fourth.

Riggleman was booed lustily by the crowd for letting Morgan hang out to dry. "I hated to do that to Mike Morgan," he said. "But based on yesterday, I had to bite the bullet."

The Cubs trailed 10-2 going into the bottom of the fifth. Hernandez homered. Gary Gaetti slugged a two-run homer in the sixth to make it 10-5. The Brewers answered back with two runs in the top of the seventh. And then came the singular event that lifted the crowd and the team off the floor.

A Lance Johnson walk and a Mark Grace double with one out in the seventh brought up Sosa. No problem. On a 3-and-2 changeup from fellow Dominican Valerio De Los Santos, he crashed a long, high drive all the way over the left-field screen to close the gap to 12-8. No. 60 landed in the front yard of 1038 W. Waveland Ave., the same two-story building where Sosa had launched his famed rooftop homer against the Phillies in June. Local resident Herb Neurauter bounded up the front steps to retrieve the ball, just ahead of a horde of ballhawks who climbed the yard's fence.

Neurauter later returned the ball to Sosa. What was Sammy willing to give in return? "I forgot my check," he said, breaking up his press conference afterward. Sosa added he kept his emotions in check, even though he had just tied Babe Ruth's best year, as he rounded the bases. "I don't want to show up the other team," he said. "I've been doing that all year long. Why change?"

The Cubs were far from finished after Sosa's homer. "As down as we were, we were happy for the 60th homer and that provoked a little enthusiasm," catcher Tyler Houston said. And if it could be possible, what the Cubs would do in the next two-plus innings would overshadow their star's singular achievement of this day.

The crowd was still buzzing from Sosa's blast when Glenallen Hill slugged a solo homer in the next at-bat to make it 12-9 Brewers. The Cubs made two outs, got the Brewers out with little problem in the eighth, and pinch hitter Houston led off the bottom of the inning with a homer to right, closing the gap to 12-10.

Could anyone doubt the outcome now? Sosa went to his short game to single, leading off the ninth. Hill singled, and both runners were sacrificed to second and third. Mickey Morandini drew a walk to load the bases. Then Houston, who had come in to catch, singled to right to tie the game 12-12 and send Morandini to third.

All the Cubs needed with one out was a sacrifice fly. But pinch-hitter Orlando Merced, a onetime Cubs Killer who had just been picked up as a free agent after being released by Boston, belted a three-run homer into the right field bleachers. Cubs 15, Brewers 12, and the 39,170 fans stayed around for more than 15 minutes after the last pitch, dancing to *YMCA* in the late-summer twilight and celebrating a Wrigley Field season to make them forget most others. Balls sticking in the ivy. Balls sticking in a gutter. Sammy Sosa and Kerry Wood. Now perhaps the mother of all comebacks.

Grace, who once was on the winning end of a Cubs' comeback from a 9-0 deficit against Houston in 1989, said this monster rally was even greater.

"Without a doubt," he said. "More happened in this game. Sammy's 60th. Merced's homer."

"Unbelievable. I never could feel more happy than I feel today," Sosa said.

The Cubs were winning friends and influencing people in the media.

"The professionalism of this veteran team," wrote Ted Cox in the *Chicago Reader*, "is a quality on display from its business-like demeanor around the batting cage before a game to the easy way it unwinds—win or lose—afterward. It's a rare attitude for a team to possess, especially remarkable in the whirl-wind of Sosa's home-run chase."

"Whirlwind" was the right word. Nobody, not players or fans, had a chance to catch their breath and take a day of rest on Sunday, September 13. The Cubs jumped out with a six-run third against Brewers starter Brad Woodall. Then they built the lead to 8-3 on another piece of history.

Grace singled to lead off the fifth. Sosa promptly deposited a Bronswell Patrick pitch into the intersection of Waveland and Kenmore avenues, prompting a mad dash for the valuable souvenir. A wheelchair-bound fan was knocked over, and a fellow named John Witt of Dixon, Illinois, sitting in a van on Kenmore, snatched the ball when it rolled to him.

No. 61, making Sosa only the second man in history to ever match Roger Maris, seemed to touch off sheer lunacy in and outside the ballpark.

The Brewers then started chipping away, using solo homers in the sixth and seventh to close the gap to 8-5. Then, shockingly, the visitors took a 9-8 lead against the battered Cubs bullpen in the eighth. A Jeff Cirillo homer in the ninth made it 10-8.

Hey, nothing to fear. Sammy had one more turn at bat. Bingo. He mashed a 2-and-1 pitch from reliever Eric Plunk far over the left-field bleachers, over the street, to tie McGwire, who had gone silent in the power department since his record-breaker.

"I think Mark listened to me now," he said of his week-old admonition to the Cardinal to wait for him. "I cried inside. When I blow kisses to my mother (on TV), I cried a little bit. I can't even believe what I can do."

Sosa might not have believed what transpired outside Wrigley Field as he rounded the bases. The ball rolled past the tree that welcomed so many re-entry shots from Henry Aaron, Tony Perez, Donn Clendenon, a whole parade of sluggers over so many decades. It landed behind a utility pole on the other side of Waveland, next to a young woman tending a baby in a stroller, next to two other toddlers wearing Cubs hats in a double stroller. Somehow the crowd avoided trampling the kids amid the chaos that ensued.

The ball then began rolling northbound down an alley dividing the block between Sheffield and Kenmore avenues. All-time champion ballhawk Gary "Moe" Mullins took off in pursuit, but had too much competition from the fair-weather fans who had mobbed the street in search of souvenirs.

A crowd piled on top of Mullins in the alley, grabbing and clutching for No. 62. Somehow, a suburban interloper named Brendan Cunningham wrestled the ball away from Mullins, got up, tucked it into his shorts, and took off with the crowd in pursuit. Police hustled Cunningham into a squad car for his own protection, and drove to the nearby Town Hall police station.

Mullins later claimed the ball was stolen from his possession, and said the crowd bit and scratched him. He briefly went to court in an attempt to wrest the ball away from Cunningham. But his attempt to catch the ball was a nice tipoff to the subculture of the ballhawks who while away their summer days snagging batting practice and game homers on Waveland.

Mullins, a middle-aged delivery truck driver, is perhaps the champion ballhawk with more than 2,000 catches in four decades. His only rival for longevity is a fellow named Rich Buhrke, also with more than 2,000 baseballs to his name. Less senior ballhawks like Johnny Rosenstein and Andy Mielke have each snared many hundreds of homers.

Back in early May, during a Mark McGwire batting practice session, a reporter went out to find out how Mullins does it. He gauges the crowd reaction in the bleachers, the trajectory of the baseball, and how it bounces on Waveland—all like an outfielder getting a jump—before he makes his move. He snared a McGwire bomb, handed it to the reporter for temporary safekeeping, and then went in search of more incoming souvenirs. Mullins couldn't have possibly have kept all the baseballs, and he didn't. He used them in an over-40 men's baseball league in which he pitched.

Watching Mullins work McGwire and seeing him and the other veteran ballhawks in action over the last decade led me to believe he indeed had caught the ball—and intended to return it to Sosa without a ransom demand. A week later, fellow ballhawks drew a big "62" on the sidewalk across Waveland with Mullins' name to show their support. Of course, the hawks aren't without their own tricks. On Sosa's 60th homer into the yard at 1038 W. Waveland, Mielke said the hawks had tossed three dummy baseballs into the enclosure as a misdirection play to draw the amateurs away from the real location of the homer.

Sosa could understand the crowd mentality on the street. If he hadn't been playing, he'd have been fighting for the ball, too. But his view of the eventual possession of the ball was different.

"That ball belongs to the American people," he said. "That ball is going to go the Hall of Fame. It's not going to my house. It's not going to anyone's house."

Eventually, justice of a sort prevailed. Two weeks after the end of the season, Sosa got the ball back from Cunningham. One little ball, so much anguish and controversy, and only the lawyers benefited from the fray.

While the riot was proceeding across the street, the Cubs turned the game into mayhem. Henry Rodriguez doubled immediately after the homer. Then Gary Gaetti singled up the middle to tie it 10-10 and send the affair into extra innings.

The Cubs had nobody fresh left to pitch. With Sosa in the on-deck circle, Grace ensured that some everyday player wasn't summoned to the mound by slugging a homer into the right-field bleachers with two out in the ninth. He pumped his fist into the air as he rounded first, and was greeted by a mob of delirious teammates when he arrived at home plate. Seconds later, Houston and Servais hoisted Sosa on their shoulders and carried him off the field as he saluted the fans.

"Why not? Sammy's carried us all year," Servais said.

The crowd stuck around again, gyrating to Three Dog Night's *Joy to the World*. Inside the clubhouse, players were simply at a loss for words.

"I'm sorry I hit a homer so Sammy couldn't come up to the plate," Grace said with a grin.

Remembering all his private sessions over his first three years in which he urged Sosa to do the little things to help the Cubs win, manager Jim Riggleman also was unusually demonstrative.

"I said to Sammy, 'If you never get another hit in a Cubs uniform, I'm so proud of you,'" he said.

Sosa took calls from one of Roger Maris' sons and baseball commissioner Bud Selig during his post-game press conference. Selig's absence from the game drew media criticism. But he who is without sin should cast the first stone. Many of the columnists and writers who had followed McGwire had been diverted elsewhere after the original record of 61 homers had been shattered. Only a few New York and other journalists were in attendance on September 13.

"This is for the people of Chicago, my mother, my wife, my kids," Sosa said.

Minutes later, John Ralph and Jeff Idelson of the Hall of Fame held an impromptu press conference by Sosa's locker. They held up his No. 21 jersey and bat, which would be making a one-way trip to Cooperstown. N.Y., immediately. The baseball would be another matter.

The team couldn't hang around to savor the second miracle in a row; a charter flight to San Diego awaited. But a hero can't move easily. Sosa was the last man out of the clubhouse. After dressing in a white shirt and gray suit, Sosa had to do a last-second interview with a Dominican TV crew. With his security man, New York cop Willie Diaz, at the wheel, Sosa got into his black BMW for the trip to O'Hare. Teammate Manny Alexander followed in his gray BMW. A Chicago police car provided escort as a crowd of hundreds on Waveland Avenue and outside the players' parking lot cheered the newest 62-homer man.

Some serious business awaited Sosa 2,000 miles away. The Cubs were 84-66, one game ahead of the Mets in the wild-card chase. The New Yorkers, who had haunted the Cubs like a bad penny every time the latter team climbed into contention since the infamous 1969 season, would not go away. They had beaten the Atlanta Braves three out of four games the previous week at Shea Stadium. And they'd go into Houston at the same time the Cubs were playing four in San Diego. Road trips to the West Coast were often Death Marches for the Cubs. The pressure was on, and it was made worse when the Mets took three of four, two in last-ditch comeback style, from the powerful Astros.

The Cubs fell into a tie for the wild-card lead with a 4-3 loss to the Padres on September 14, with Sosa striking out four times for the first time in 1998. But the next night, the Cubs pulled off a near-impossible feat. They pushed across four runs against hard sinkerballer Kevin Brown in the seventh inning, all they needed in a 4-2 victory that gave them a half-game lead over the Mets. Mark Grace's two-run homer in the frame apparently shook up Brown. Back in the Midwest, however, Mark McGwire regained his composure, belting No. 63 as a pinch hitter in the ninth inning of an 8-6 St. Louis loss to Pittsburgh in the first game of a doubleheader.

Fireworks erupted in the Cubs-Padres game the next night. Sosa slashed a two-run double in the seventh to put Chicago on the board as Terry Mulholland, finally placed into the rotation by Riggleman, pitched superbly. The Padres tied it up in the bottom of the inning, but Sosa came through in the top of the eighth against reliever Brian Boehringer with the bases loaded. He launched a 434-foot upper-deck shot for No. 63 and the game-winner, prompting Padres management to set off fireworks and prompting what *Chicago Tribune* columnist Skip Bayless described as a "New Year's Eve nuts" celebration from 49,891 Qualcomm Stadium fans.

Kevin Brown was incensed at the fireworks and the pro-Sosa, apparently pro-Cubs reaction. "Screw the fans," he intoned, and his sentiments were echoed by other Padres. But that couldn't dampen Sosa's joy at coming through again at crunch time to drive in all six runs in the 6-2 victory and keep the Mets a half-game back.

"I don't think there could be a better way to do it," he said. "I said to myself, 'I've got to go up there and do it because the New York Mets keep winning every day.' The game was on the line and I wanted to go out there and come through for my team."

Sosa's power production was eminently logical. But a lot of the things that happened to the Cubs in 1998 weren't. So September 17's 4-3 victory over the Padres was a normal occurrence. The Cubs should have lost, but didn't, thanks to another lucky bounce.

Sosa went 0-for-4, but the Cubs held a 3-2 lead into the bottom of the eighth. Of course, the bullpen coughed it up, with Tony Gwynn hitting a homer off Matt Karchner to tie it up. But, a lot more shocking, ageless wonder Gary Gaetti slugged a pinch homer leading off the 10th against almost unhittable Padres stopper Trevor Hoffman. But in the bottom of the 10th, the Padres pushed the tying run to third with two out. Carlos Hernandez hit a shot up the middle that somehow ricocheted off Cubs stopper Rod Beck's leg to the right of shortstop Jose Hernandez, who grabbed the ball and fired an off-balance throw to first. Mark Grace, an expert at coming off the bag in lightning-fast fashion to persuade an umpire, snared the throw. Hernandez might have been safe by a hair, but the Cubs got the call. Game, set and match.

"It's a grand game," Beck said.

"This team makes your ulcers have a baby," Grace said.

Thoroughly happy but exhausted, the Cubs made the four-hour flight home that night facing a day game against the Reds at Wrigley Field one game ahead of the Mets and 20 games above .500 at 87-67. That represented just the fifth time since the last pennant in 1945 that the Cubs had been as many as 20 games above .500 in a season. And that also would turn out to be the season's high-water mark above break-even as the stomach-turning wrapup to the season loomed.

Somehow, neither Sosa nor the Cubs could bottle their momentum as the Reds returned to Wrigley Field, less than three weeks after their first trip to Chicago for the 1998 season. Cincinnati had played hot and cold all season. They were swept three in a row by the Cubs at the beginning of the month, but now would be different with a Chicago pitching staff that was really fraying around the edges and a team arriving back in town at 1:30 a.m. with a day game awaiting them less than 13 hours later. The Cubs had the motivation of Sammy Sosa Day on Sunday, September 20, but they had to take care of other business first.

The ballhawks, serious or not, would be thwarted as the Reds series began. Mindful of the bad public relations of the riot a week before, the Chicago Police Department blocked off Waveland Avenue to pedestrians with wooden barricades and horse-borne mounted officers. Too bad the cops couldn't have pitched. Neither starter Steve Trachsel nor the bullpen were sharp in the Cubs' 6-4 loss on September 18. Sosa was 0-for-4, a costly blanking as Mark McGwire slugged No. 64 off the Milwaukee Brewers later that night.

The Cubs looked even worse the next day in a 7-2 loss, falling back into a wild-card tie with the Mets. Sosa was starting to press, striking out three times against ex-White Sox Jason Bere, against whom he had belted No. 56 three weeks previously.

"If I was a Superman, I'd hit a home run every day," Sosa said. "I'm a human being. Not every day is going to be a good day."

At least September 20 started out as a good day, even if the final score of the Cubs' 7-3 defeat, Sosa's 0-for-5 afternoon, and a dip to one game behind the Mets with a week to go would have indicated otherwise.

The Cubs honored Sosa in pre-game ceremonies. He may have disavowed being a Superman, but the theme from the "Superman" movie played as Sosa made a grand tour of the outfield during the ceremonies, saluting his bleacher fans before coming back near third base and being embraced in a mass hug by his teammates. Sammy's family, including his mother, Lucrecia, was in attendance along with Hall of Famer Juan Marichal, now the minister of sports for the Dominican Republic. Finally, baseball commissioner Bud Selig showed up to mark his home-run feat in the pre-game festivities. Selig and Cubs general manager Ed Lynch drew a few catcalls from the crowd.

Dominican flags shared equal billing with Old Glory, while the Dominican national anthem was sung before the Star Spangled Banner. As if car aficionado Sosa needed another vehicle, the Cubs presented him with a purple Chrysler Corp. Prowler limited-production roadster, rolled out through the wagon gate in the right field corner.

"Chicago, I love you," Sosa told the crowd during the ceremonies. "The right-field bleachers, I love you. Everything I do in 1998, Chicago, you deserve it. You've been behind me 100 percent.

"God bless all of you."

Just as important as the pomp and circumstance were other folks who came to honor Sosa. Obviously giving up Sunday golf was Michael Jordan, who sat in a skybox with sidekick Scottie Pippen. In one respect, Jordan showed up to legitimize Sosa's entry into mega-stardom. On the other hand, he slyly reminded one and all who was still the reigning champion of sports.

He praised Sosa's season, even predicting he would overtake McGwire in the end. He liked what the Cubs had done, but then put a stop to comparisons of their achievement with the Bulls.

"You've got six (titles) to catch up with me," Jordan told reporters in the press box. After the game, Jordan aide George Kohler handed Sosa a cell phone at his locker. His Airness got on the horn for five minutes with the slugger.

Also endorsing Sosa were Roger Maris' six children. Four days previously, they were asked by the Cubs to sing *Take Me Out to the Ballgame* during the seventh-inning stretch. Brothers Kevin and Randy Maris donned oversized Harry Caray glasses frames as they wielded the microphone like a baton in leading the singalong.

The family wasn't thrilled that their patriarch's record of

61 homers had been blown down. "We've carried that record very proudly on our sleeves," Randy Maris said. "That was the toughest part of it going down."

But if the record had to go, they were glad Sosa and McGwire were the men to break it.

"Dad would be proud of Sammy and Mark, the way they've handled things and represented baseball, on and off the field," Kevin Maris said.

The home-run race actually was able to finish the rehabilitation of Roger Maris' reputation. He had been wrongly portrayed as a surly, standoffish man during his own chase of 61 homers in 1961. Never mind that the Yankees never gave him official help in handling the media crush, that he had to answer questions for hours after games, and even was followed into the bathroom by overzealous reporters.

"This chase has brought so much attention back to Dad," Randy Maris said. "Everyone's really gone back and looked at what he went through that year. This has really brought it to life. The younger kids who never knew who Roger Maris was now do. The greatest aspect of this season is the positive light it shed on my father."

McGwire's a kind of one-dimensional, hulking slugger-type. Sosa's always been branded a "five-tool" player, who could do everything offensively and defensively—just like Roger Maris.

"Absolutely," Randy Maris said of comparisons between Sosa and his father. "He plays hurt. That's exactly how my dad was. When he did get hurt, (Yankees manager) Ralph Houk was quoted as saying, 'I'd rather play Roger Maris at 80 percent than somebody else at 100 percent.' The Yankees told him to play at 80 percent, and pull back when he's running down the line to first base if he knew he was going to be out. But that was something they never related to the press or the fans. People would say, 'Roger Maris was dogging it.' He was getting booed."

Sosa really hit it off with the six Maris siblings after the game. He signed baseballs, hats and scorecards for them after his post-game press conference. Then he posed for photos with the Marises outside the visitors' dugout. Running off the field to the cheers of the remnants of the disappointed crowd, Sosa was glad for a day off before action resumed Tuesday night, September 22, in Milwaukee. He'd have to find a way to help right the Cubs while getting out of his own 0-for-17 slump with time quickly running out on the 1998 season.

His good humor seemed the one stable aspect as even crazier things took place. During the loss to the Reds, third-base umpire Harry Wendelstedt called a Bret Boone drive down the left-field line a homer, good for his third blast of the afternoon. TV replays showed the ball left Wrigley Field to the foul side of the foul pole, but Wendelstedt, who had hardly moved from his position behind third base to get a better look, was adamant about his call. Ninety miles north, McGwire belted No. 65—and then had No. 66 taken away in the fifth inning, changed to a ground-rule double when umpire Bob Davidson ruled a fan had reached over the wall to interfere with its flight. Witnesses said the ball actually cleared the fence and the fan could not have physically reached over. TV replays are getting more sophisticated and often lay bare umpiring mistakes, but are not going to be allowed to factor into the game's officiating anytime soon.

Later on the night of September 20, Cal Ripken, Jr. knocked the post-62 homer derby and the NFL out of top billing by pulling the plug on his eternal consecutive games streak. Ripken cleverly told Baltimore Orioles manager Ray Miller just before the game with the Yankees that he wanted his record set at 2,632 games. Thus he avoided the attending hoopla that would have accompanied any kind of advance notice of the streak's conclusion.

Normalcy was restored, if for just one night, when the Cubs upended the Brewers 5-2 on September 22 before an overflowing 52,287 at County Stadium, the majority cheering for Sosa and his teammates. When Mark Grace was hit by a pitch with two outs in the ninth, prolonging the inning, Sosa's bonus at-bat drew a wild ovation. But Terry Mulholland was the big story, hurling another crisp game on a yield of six hits and one run over eight innings. That was good enough to propel the Cubs back into a wild-card tie with the Mets, who lost 5-3 to the Montreal Expos.

Sosa was in more physical than emotional anguish afterward as his slump stretched to 0-for-21. Tagging up and sliding into home on a second-inning sacrifice fly, Sosa had been kneed in the groin by the Brewers' Bobby Hughes as he tried to reach the plate underneath the catcher. The entire ballpark fell into a hush as Sosa appeared to be injured. No, it wasn't a knee or ankle, but just as painful. "We all felt it," Jim Riggleman said.

By now Cubs staffers believed Sosa had reverted to his

old pull-or-nothing style, perhaps as he was getting caught in the dual races. "Every time he throws my pitch, I'm just missing it," Sosa said. But he was pressing. Time to go back to what got him to this point in 1998.

As Sosa began batting practice at high noon on September 23 in Milwaukee, he tried to go to right field on his first four swings in the cage. Hitting coach Jeff Pentland threw his left-handed pitches to Sosa while fellow coach Billy Williams watched from behind the cage. Williams was concerned about approach. But after Pentland finished, he walked by Williams. "He's better today," he said of Sosa.

Right field or bust it was. In the fifth inning, as 45,338 pro-Sosa fans rooted him on, Sosa sliced No. 64 off Brewers lefty Rafael Roque over an advertising sign touting the Dairyland greyhound track in right field. The ball seemed headed for a gap between the right-field grandstands and the bleachers until Cubs fan Vern Kuhlemeier of rural Dakota, Illinois leaned over the railing to make a catch with a well-worn glove. "Everything was fine with the fans. There was no fighting for the ball," Kuhlemeier said.

Sosa didn't wait to tie Mark McGwire again while keeping his newly regained good mechanics. In the sixth, he lined a 2-and-2 pitch from Brewers reliever Rod Henderson to some blocked-off old bleachers in dead center field and caromed back onto the field. The homer resembled a Dick Allen laser shot from a generation previous at old Comiskey Park. The crowd went wild again for No. 65.

Sosa had used three different "Hoosier" bats on September 22. But he singled out one on this day—"the good one," he said later. Asked why he had so much luck against Milwaukee with 12 homers for 1998, he shrugged. "This is my lucky team. Whatever has been happening with the Brewers, I can't explain," he said.

He couldn't explain what happened in the game, either. Steve Trachsel had things well under control as the Cubs amassed a 7-0 lead going into the seventh. But he suddenly lost it. The normal strategy would be to pull him. But apparently mindful of his battered bullpen, Riggleman left Trachsel in too long, allowing the Brewers four runs in the seventh and giving them hope. Milwaukee tallied another run in the eighth. Then Rod Beck pulled his usual high-wire act in the ninth, loading the bases with one out and the Cubs leading 7-5. He got Marquis Grissom to pop up for the second out. Lefty-swinging Geoff Jenkins was all that stood between the Cubs and a possible one-game wild-card lead.

Beck did his job. Jenkins sliced a fly to left field, then bathed in the late-afternoon sun. Brant Brown, brought in an inning earlier for defense, circled around and appeared to have a bead on the ball. But Brown didn't quite get squarely under it. The ball bounced off his glove as all three runners scored to give the Brewers an 8-7 victory. The ghost of Don Young's outfield muffs in 1969 was conjured up as even cynical writers stood amazed with their mouths open in the press box at the unbelievable finish, perhaps the Cubs' most crushing defeat since Games 4 and 5 of the 1984 National League Championship Series in San Diego.

In the Cubs' clubhouse, Brown at first tried to recede into his wire-mesh cubicle, as if he was trying to dig a hole for himself. But, holding back his well of emotions as best as possible, he gamely faced four waves of reporters, offering no excuses and hoping the error wouldn't cost the Cubs a playoff berth. It wouldn't, but at the time, the misplay didn't help Chicago's prospects at all.

Brown was offered support by his teammates. Center fielder Lance Johnson put his arm around Brown with whispered encouragement. One of the pitchers profanely asked approaching reporters to give Brown a few more minutes to compose himself. And Sosa endorsed his teammate, who had come through with several game-winning homers before he had separated his shoulder diving for a ball in Detroit in June.

"Everybody in the ballpark knows what happened," Sosa said. "Brownie has been with us all year long and he has been doing a great job. What happened to Brownie today can happen to anybody who plays this game. He has a lot of support from this team. We have to forget about it today and keep going."

Happy about his other-worldly homer totals, Sosa nonetheless put the Cubs first.

"What has happened to me has been great," he said. "But on the other side, I care about winning. I care about this team. Our situation right now is to win."

Once again the Cubs got lucky. The Mets lost again to the Expos, 3-0. And the San Francisco Giants, which had been left for dead in the wild-card race one week previously, suddenly were hot, creeping to within 1 1/2 games of the Cubs and Mets.

After the Brown fiasco, the Cubs needed a day off, which was spent in Houston. They tried to re-group on Friday, September 25, in one of the worst places in team history for revivals, the Houston Astrodome. Going into the three-game series to wrap up the season, the Cubs were 80-131 in the dome since it opened in 1965.

Sosa tried to defy history—and everyone who favored McGwire—with a 462-foot leadoff homer off Jose Lima in the fourth inning. For 45 minutes, Sosa led the universe, then, now and in the future, probably, with 66 homers.

But, on cue as usual, Mark McGwire responded. Forty-five minutes later, he hit No. 66 against the Expos in St. Louis.

"It's unexplainable. Let's leave it unexplainable," McGwire said.

"Mark said it would be beautiful to tie," Sosa said. "I feel great he hit his 66th. I had a good feeling about it. It would be nice if we tie."

Ties were the order of the night all around. The Cubs lost 6-2 and the Mets lost to the Braves 6-5. And, after the Giants had beaten the Pirates on Thursday, September 24, they won again, 8-6 over Colorado, to forge a three-way tie for the wild card.

Sosa's focus had to be on somehow surviving the weekend to get into the playoffs after events of Saturday, September 26, were tabulated. His chances of winning the home-run title almost disappeared when McGwire, saving his best for last, belted Nos. 67 and 68 in St. Louis. Sosa began taking stock of his place in history as the regular-season counted down to hours.

"I'd like it to last 50 years," he told reporters before the September 26 game. "It took about 37 years (for the Maris record to fall). Even if Mark finishes first and me second, the first guy (to break their record) will have to go through me to get to Mark."

What, or who, the wild-card winner had to go through was another story. After Gary Gaetti gave the Cubs the lead with another clutch hit, a two-run double in the eighth, the Cubs and Rod Beck survived yet another scary ninth inning.

Leading 3-2, Beck allowed a double to Moises Alou, who advanced to third on an infield grounder. Tony Eusebio struck out. Pinch hitter Dave Clark then hit a topper between first and the mound. Beck grabbed the ball, tried to tag Clark, apparently missed, and then threw the ball errantly off Clark in trying to nab him at first. Game tied? No! Game over! Plate ump Eric Gregg ruled Clark out for running out of the baseline.

"I still don't know what happened," Beck said, and he could have applied that to the wild-card race. The Mets were blanked by the Braves 4-0, while the Giants beat the Rockies again to remain tied with the Cubs.

For only the second time in modern Cubs history, an undecided playoff race would go down to the final day. The sheer magnitude of the Cubs flirting with the post-season after a nine-year drought eased the hurt of McGwire pulling away with two more homers in his final game to finish the season with 70.

Sosa went to his short game again, driving in the Cubs' first run with a single, his 158th RBI of the season, in the first inning against the Astros. Terry Mulholland pitched superbly for the third start in a row, and even helped his own cause with a two-run double to right center in the third. But the Astros tied it 3-3 in the eighth off Mulholland. Beck came in again, survived a bases-loaded, one-out jam in the 10th, but finally succumbed in the 11th on a Carl Everett triple and a sacrifice fly. Astros 4, Cubs 3, Sosa goes 2-for-5, Chicago finishes the season 89-73 and maybe out of the post-season with the sixth loss in the last eight games.

Maybe. The Mets eliminated themselves with their third straight loss to the Braves. But the Giants jumped out to a 7-0 lead over the Rockies. It didn't look good. Remember, though, the game was being played in Coors Field. Suddenly the Rockies cut the lead to 7-6. Then they went ahead 8-7 on Vinny Castilla's homer. The Giants tied it 8-8. And just before the Cubs walked solemnly off the field after the defeat came the news from Denver that little Neifi Perez of the Rockies led off the bottom of the ninth with a homer off Giants stopper Robb Nen to win the game 8-7.

Cubs-Giants, wild-card tiebreaker playoff at Wrigley Field, 7 p.m. Central time, Monday, September 28. The Cubs had drawn even by losing. But they had won, too. General manager Ed Lynch had made the right choice several weeks previously on a tie-breaking coin flip with the Giants to determine home-field advantage.

"We were destined to play 163 games," Mulholland said. "This is just not a normal year."

Down in Atlanta, the Mets' Lenny Harris summed it up the best: "The Cubs have nine lives."

Sosa savored the thought of the extra innings role in the spotlight.

"One chance, winner take all, and we're at home," he said.

Cubs fans, knowing nothing is ever for certain, hedged their bets long before the crazy finish became clear. Scores lined up all day near the Wrigley Field ticket windows, toting TVs and radios to pass the time. And in the minutes after the final out of the game in Houston, thousands more mimicked the Oklahoma land rush, minus the horses and wagons, in dashing toward the ticket line. The queue soon wrapped all the way around three sides of the ballpark. Scalpers quickly asked for $250 for a box seat.

Sammy Sosa had amassed a personal-achievement season nobody could have forecast. Riding his broad shoulders, the Cubs completed a season not even a crazed Hollywood scriptwriter could have forecast. Angels In The Outfield, Bad News Bears, Major League, Field of Dreams, no fantasy could compare with the reality of 1998.

When baseball ends up like this, there is no sport that can compare. A greater good was being done than just being in position to scratch the Cubs' long post-season itch.

19

A Case for the MVP

As the 1998 season ended, almost all conventional wisdom pointed to Sammy Sosa as the consensus National League Most Valuable Player.

And yet there was a minority report floating about. Mark McGwire's 70-homer season was drawing support on the basis of sheer, raw, powerful numbers and the good it did for the game.

Most Valuable Players, chosen by tenured members of the Baseball Writers Association of America, more often than not have come from the ranks of top producers on contending or winning teams—the perfect definition of Sosa's season. The reasoning went that an MVP is a player whose contributions were absolutely vital to a team's winning portfolio.

But in some years, the most outstanding offensive player was given the MVP award. Precedent could be found in the annals of Cubs history itself.

Andre Dawson's selection as National League MVP in 1987 drew some ridicule. The Hawk had a league-leading 49 homers and 137 RBI to go along with a .287 average. The Cubs finished last in the

National League East, but the cellar ending was not a traditional head-between-your-legs, 95 or 100-defeat campaign. The Cubs actually were .500 on Labor Day, 1987, and Dawson's bat and glove had kept them afloat. The team pulled off one of its patented September nosedives to finish 76-86, through no fault of Dawson's.

Back in 1958 and 1959, Ernie Banks won back-to-back MVP awards. Again, he was honored as the best offensive player in the league. Banks had 47 homers, 129 RBI and a .313 average in '58 for a Cubs team that stayed in contention through the end of July, then faded to 72-82. In '59, Banks was virtually a one-man gang for a 74-80 also-ran with 45 homers, 143 RBI and a .304 average. Thirty-nine years would pass before another Cub, Sosa, would pass up "Mr. Cub's" RBI spree.

McGwire supporters also could look at Larry Walker of the 1997 Colorado Rockies, Cal Ripken, Jr. of the 1991 Baltimore Orioles, Robin Yount of the 1989 Milwaukee Brewers, and Mike Schmidt of the 1986 Philadelphia Phillies as top offensive producers who were honored despite the fact their teams did not sniff the postseason.

But the majority of the time, the key sparkplug of a winning team is chosen, and sheer numbers sometimes be damned. Kirk Gibson won for his 25-homer, 76-RBI, .290 season for the eventual world champion Los Angeles Dodgers, and the writers' votes were in long before Gibson hit his dramatic World Series homer off Dennis Eckersley.

As the 1998 season wrapped up, many writers said Sosa was their MVP choice.

"I voted Sammy Sosa No. 1 for the Chicago Cubs and for what he's done for baseball, and I had Mark McGwire No. 5," said Hal McCoy, who covers the Cincinnati Reds beat for the *Dayton Daily News.*

"Without Sosa," continued McCoy, "the Cubs wouldn't even had had a sniff of being in the playoffs. My way of considering what an MVP is, is how important he is to his team. That's why I had Sosa No. 1. I had Moises Alou No. 2, and I had Andres Galarraga ahead of McGwire.

"I had McGwire fifth because the Cardinals didn't do anything. The only reason I put him as high as I did is because of what he has done for baseball."

Up in Suds City, Drew Olsen, Brewers beat writer for the

Milwaukee Journal Sentinel, leaned toward Sosa because of the Cubs' season.

"The thing to me, and probably what was going to be the determining factor for me, is that the Cubs, without Sammy, wouldn't have been close in the (wild-card) race. They'd have been down with the Brewers in the division. I think the Astros would have won the division even without Moises Alou, who had a spectacular year. To me, that's what the MVP is all about."

Olsen's *Journal Sentinel* colleague, columnist Mike Bauman, only had the privilege of the vote for the National League Cy Young Award. "But if I had an MVP vote, it would have gone to Sosa," Bauman said.

In the end, though, the experts on the definition of an MVP should be the players who have won the award.

Thus, the paths of wisdom must lead to Joe Morgan, who won back-to-back MVPs for the 1975-1976 Cincinnati Reds. That may be the ultimate litmus test for a player's true contribution to winning; the '75-'76 Big Red Machine is considered by some as the best baseball team of all time.

Morgan was not the leading power hitter in a muscle-bound lineup. But it did everything, and well. In addition to hitting .327 in '75 and .320 in '76, Morgan led the NL with an astounding 132 walks in '75. He stole 67 and 60 bases, respectively, each year. In '75, Morgan had 94 RBI, then upped that total to 111 RBI to go along with 27 homers the following year. He was the consummate all-around player.

"I would steal a base if we needed it," said Morgan, now a baseball analyst for ESPN. "I did this, I did that. Sammy's basically been the big guy. I was just kind of a spoke in the wheel. I had (Johnny) Bench and (Tony) Perez and all the great players behind me driving in the runs. I drove in a few runs, but I think a lot of intangible things go into being the MVP.

"You're the guy who seems to be at bat when the team needs a hit. You're the guy who seems to be there when things are going bad and you have to turn things around. I think that's kind of what I did in the years I won. I guess Sammy's in the same position. I was watching the game in San Diego when the Padres came back to tie the game, and Sammy then hits a grand slam in the eighth. Things like that are intangibles that you look back and said it meant more than one game."

So does Morgan have a narrow definition of an MVP?

"It has to do with value to your ballclub, value to base-ball," he said "It's not just about what you do on the field.

"It's hard to use my definition this year because there are so many guys who fit under that criteria. But I think Sammy Sosa is the Most Valuable Player in the league. I think he's been the guy to get the key hit for the Cubs

"But in saying that, you also have to look over at San Diego and say that without Greg Vaughn, they wouldn't have won their division. You look at Houston and without Moises Alou, they wouldn't have won the division. I just have a feeling that this guy (Sosa) has been the difference in this ballclub. I do believe, personally, that Sammy is the Most Valuable Player in the league."

A spiritual successor to Morgan as a Reds MVP is short-stop Barry Larkin. Honored with the award in 1995 for sparking Cincinnati to the divisional title, Larkin likes what he sees in Sosa.

"The MVP race came down to McGwire and Sosa, and Sammy should have gotten it," he said. "Simply because the Cubs were in the pennant race, and Sammy's out there trying to win the wild card as opposed to just going out and trying to hit home runs. He's taking his walks here and there, getting the runner over, doing the little things.

"Hitting the ball to right field is more important than just going out there trying to hit home runs. I think the MVP is the guy who's most important to his team, most valuable to his team, and I think Sammy fits the bill."

When Sosa's personable approach to the most crushing pressure an athlete can endure is taken into account, he almost was worth two MVPs.

But even in the effort to capture just one of the presti-gious awards, Sosa earned popular support he could have never conceived of in past years. When they used to call Sosa a "self-ish" player, an MVP award was the last thing anyone would have connected with him.

That's baseball. Change is constant.

20

1998's Extra Innings

Too many familiar faces greeted the more than 500 media clustered on the field on a beautiful early autumn Chicago evening on Monday, September 28, as the Cubs and Giants prepared to settle a season without end.

If an "Ex-Cub Factor" truly existed, the Giants were toast. Joe Carter, Shawon Dunston and Rey Sanchez populated their roster. The San Francisco assistant general manager, Ned Colletti, grew up as a left-field Bleacher Bum before he became a sportswriter, Cubs media relations director and player personnel chief.

"This was the craziest way to end a season," Colletti said. "We had to win seven of eight, and they had to lose six of eight for this to happen. But you have to keep going. Only a fool would stop playing."

The Cubs had some hexed baggage of their own.

"Hey, the Cubs have some ex, ex-Cubs," one Giants quipster said, pointing to Mike Morgan, Glenallen Hill and Terry Mulholland, each serving their second tour of duty at Wrigley Field.

The dignified Carter, who began with the Cubs in 1983 before being traded for Rick Sutcliffe, sensed he was coming full circle in his career. He planned to retire after the season. If the Giants lost, he would finish where he started, and the 15 years had gone quickly.

Carter looked around at the quickly-filling Wrigley Field. "This is like a World Series atmosphere, great for baseball," he said. Carter should know, having won the 1993 World Series for the Toronto Blue Jays with a dramatic ninth-inning homer off Mitch "Wild Thing" Williams. Yes, another ex-Cub.

A carnival-like atmosphere could be mixed in. A white balloon with Harry Caray's bespectacled face floated over the bleachers like some kind of ghostly apparition. A No. 67 banner, imploring Sosa to add to his amazing season one final time, was draped on a building across Waveland Avenue.

Giants manager Dusty Baker couldn't pull off the same strategy as the last time the Cubs and Giants faced off for something important. In the 1989 National League Championship Series, Baker, then a Giants coach, boldly told Cubs star Andre Dawson that they were not going to let him beat the Giants. Dawson and Ryne Sandberg were the two established veterans on a team largely made up of younger players. Dawson later admitted he was too overeager at the plate and did not take the walks that the Giants were practically giving away to him.

Baker could not pitch around Sammy Sosa in the same manner. The Cubs offered plenty of power up and down the lineup. Sosa had 66 homers, but the Cubs totaled a team record 212 homers for the season. The '89 Cubs had no such veteran help of the likes of Gary Gaetti, perhaps the best clutch hitter in baseball in September, 1998, and Hill.

Sure enough, Gaetti got the Cubs on the board with a two-run homer in the fifth against Giants starter Mark Gardner. In the meantime, Steve Trachsel, pitching at his typical deliberate pace, somehow kept the Giants at bay through wild spells. He made it into the fifth without allowing a hit. Then, into the sixth without allowing a hit. With five walks through six, though, the contest did not feel like a no-hitter in the making.

Sosa always said he was not Superman. Mere mortals ground into double plays, as he did in the first inning. Sosa also fanned in the fourth. But he trotted out his short game for when it really counted in the sixth.

With one out and Lance Johnson on first, Sosa singled to center, sending Johnson to third. Mark Grace then walked to load the bases. Lefty Rich Rodriguez replaced Gardner, and rarely-used right-handed hitter Matt Mieske was sent in to pinch hit for Henry Rodriguez. The move worked-Mieske slashed a two-run single to right to give the Cubs a 4-0 lead.

Trachsel finally allowed his first hit, a single to Brett Mayne with one out in the seventh. He then issued his sixth walk of the night. Cubs manager Jim Riggleman once again had to live with catcalls as he signaled for reliever Matt Karchner. But Karchner and Felix Heredia managed to get out of the seventh without any damage.

Then Riggleman made the moves of a manager backed into a corner by an ineffective bullpen. He summoned starter Kevin Tapani, who had pitched on September 26, three nights previously, to pitch the eighth. Tapani got out of the inning with a yield of just a triple to J.T. Snow.

In the bottom of the inning, as chants of "MVP! MVP!" cascaded down on him from the adoring crowd, Sosa blooped a single to right, advanced to third on a Grace double and scored on a wild pitch to make it 5-0. A safe lead? No, these were the 1998 Cubs.

Riggleman tried to stretch his luck by having Tapani open the ninth. But he allowed two singles. The manager summoned ...Terry Mulholland. Normally that wouldn't be a problem with the rubber-armed lefty, but Mulholland volunteered to outdo his own endurance on this night. He had thrown more than 120 pitches in his start against the Astros the previous day. I have watched baseball since the mid-1960s, and I can never remember a starter pitching as many as eight innings one day coming back in relief the very next day. If there was a Cy Young Award for courage and devotion to duty, it should go to Mulholland.

The out-of-gas gang was trying to hold the lead on fumes alone. Mulholland allowed Stan Javier's RBI single to make it 5-1, then a walk to Ellis Burks to load the bases. That brought up Barry Bonds as the tying run. Somehow, Mulholland got Bonds to keep it in the ballpark, lining hard to Sosa in right to make it 5-2. Then Beck, who would never turn down a manager's summons no matter how exhausted he was, came in to get Jeff Kent to ground into a fielder's choice to make it 5-3.

Sure enough, Joe Carter's career was now going 360 degrees. With mirrors or magic or Harry Caray's blessing from above, Beck induced Carter to pop to Grace.

All of the comeback wins, all of the team camaraderie, all of Sammy Sosa's clutch hits now counted for something. The Cubs, winners of 68 games and losers of 14 in a row in 1997, earning the disrespect of an entire industry, had won their 90th victory on overtime. Whether extra innings or tiebreakers or whatever, 90 wins was 90 wins. Nobody projected 90 wins back in February in Mesa. Only three other Cubs teams since the last pennant-winner in 1945 had won as many as 90 in a season.

Cynics and traditionalists who opposed the wild card shook their heads, but what more did they want? You could pardon the Cubs for cutting loose with joy. They mobbed each other in the infield, then retreated to the clubhouse for a champagne party. This was no insignificant celebration; this was the first time a Cubs team had clinched a post-season berth in Wrigley Field since the 1930s.

Plastic protected the lockers as champagne nailed players, significant others, team officials—including Cubs president Andy MacPhail—and media. Armed with bottles of bubbly, players ran back out on the field to share the spray with the fans. Sosa headed straight out to the right-field bleachers to give the fans not baseballs and heart-taps, but a nightcap. Others doused merrymakers in the box seats. Manny Alexander and Henry Rodriguez ran back near the clubhouse shower area to fill buckets of ice water to dump on clubhouse visitors from behind. Trying to gather notes, a reporter was nailed at least three times.

Sosa stuffed a fat cigar from his collection in his mouth, donned glasses, and practically danced around the clubhouse. "It was worth the wait," he hollered, remembering all his years wandering in the Cubs wilderness, merely packing up to go back to the Dominican at this point of the year.

Shaking a champagne bottle, Sosa saluted his fans again.

"They supported me all year long, 100 percent," he said. "This is something unbelievable. I love my country; everybody knows that. I love America, too, that gave me an opportunity to be here again."

And for the last time, he would be asked about Mark McGwire.

"I love Mark, he's my boy," Sosa said. "But tomorrow he's going to the beach and I've got to go to Atlanta."

Ah, the magic word. And the moment of truth. Atlanta. The Cubs were no General Sherman, coming down South to lay waste. The Cubs had handled the Braves six out of nine games in the regular season. But Atlanta had been on cruise control, stepping it up when necessary with 14 wins in its last 16 games.

Amid the champagne showers, the Cubs sobered up fast when the subject of the Braves came up.

"Atlanta is playing very good baseball. We have our work cut out for us," said Mickey Morandini.

Rod Beck grew somber for once. "We have a tough road ahead of us," he said. "We have to pitch well. When we won, we shut down their offense. Obviously, we'll be an underdog."

That in itself was an understatement to many. Pundits who had written off the Cubs all along virtually wrote that they didn't belong on the same field as the Braves. Maybe the Cubs themselves believed that theory, too. But there's such a thing as self-fulfilling prophecies in baseball. Players' uneasiness about upcoming opponents-in this case, the Braves' and Marlins' vaunted pitching staffs-doomed the Cubs at the start of the 1997 season, when they lost 14 in a row right off the bat. Subsequent playoff upsets in the 1998 post-season field showed that any team could come up and bite another. Beck himself had sometimes talked about negative "karma" hurting a team like the Cubs; he didn't like the idea of the white "L" flag being raised atop the scoreboard after every home defeat.

The Cubs would have to beat John Smoltz, Tom Glavine and Greg Maddux all in a row. The odds were against such a feat, yet Chicago had gone against the odds all year, winning the majority of the time. If this was a truly blessed year, wouldn't a way be found?

Braves fans disgraced themselves by not packing Turner Field for Game 1 of the National League Divisional Series on Wednesday, September 30. Some 5,000 seats went unsold as Cubs fans emerged as the most enthusiastic of the weekday crowd. The Atlanta fans were nowhere to be found prior to the Braves' emergence as a power in 1991; they didn't exactly pack the old Fulton County Stadium to cheer on Henry Aaron from 1966 to 1974. But that's baseball—the wrong towns get the best teams. Remember the early 1970s Oakland Athletics? They couldn't even crack 1 million attendance in the East Bay for the game's last dynasty.

The way to beat the Braves was by being alternately patient and aggressive. Sosa tried that in the very first inning, singling to left off Smoltz. But amid his power season, his old stolen-base prowess had diminished. Sosa tried to take the issue to the Braves by attempting a steal of second. He was thrown out. Later, in the fourth, he tried to work Smoltz deep into the count, a tactic praised by Joe Carter, making his debut as a color analyst on ESPN.

Meanwhile, Cubs starter Mark Clark, the only starter remotely possessing any semblance of rest with three days off since his last start, gamely tried to match Smoltz. He allowed only a two-run homer to Michael Tucker in the second. Riggleman even let him bat for himself down 2-0 in the sixth, mindful of the risks of bringing in the bullpen. But Clark invariably weakened, allowing another run in the sixth.

Sosa tried to stir things up by doubling to left on Smoltz's second pitch of the seventh. But Grace, showing a season-long pattern of overanxiousness with men on base, swung at the first pitch and popped up. That would turn out to be the Cubs' last gasp.

The bullpen took over in the seventh. The Braves loaded the bases. Matt Karchner dodged one bullet by retiring Andres Galarraga on a popup to first after going 3-and-0 to him. But he couldn't do it twice in a row. Ryan Klesko nailed him for a grand-slam homer on a 3-and-2 pitch after Karchner had fallen behind 2-and-0. Formalities were then exchanged, and the Braves soon had a 7-1 victory.

"Smoltz pitched good," Sosa said. "Everything was working for him, in and out and with good location. We had opportunities but didn't come through. The first couple of innings we played great, and then one mistake and after that it was history."

The only antidote was a spectacular pitching performance by a Cub. Kevin Tapani was the man for the job for Game 2 on Thursday, October 1. The right-hander had missed two chances to win his 20th game during the regular season with mediocre starts. But matched up with left-hander Tom Glavine, Tapani was up for the challenge. He strung a series of zeroes, pitching out of a one-out, man-on-third jam in the fifth. Tapani fanned Walt Weiss and got Keith Lockhart to fly out. Tapani also chipped in two perfect sacrifice bunts.

Glavine was almost as tough. He walked Sosa in the first, then worked him further and further outside in succeeding at-bats. He popped out in the fourth, then struck out in the seventh when Glavine busted him back inside with his precision control. The Cubs scratched out a run in the sixth, and that paper-thin margin was all Tapani had to nurse going into the ninth.

Riggleman elected to leave in Tapani, and why not? He was strong, not amassing a lot of pitches. When on, he and Mulholland are the most efficient and quick-working Cubs pitchers. Three decades ago, a starter going out to protect a 1-0 lead in the ninth would draw no notice; pitchers strived to finish what they started then and, deep down, still do. But bullpen maneuverings are part of the new baseball world.

But just two outs from a momentum-shifting victory, Tapani surrendered a game-tying homer to Braves catcher Javy Lopez. That meant the Cubs would have to scratch something out in the 10th. They proved positively inept.

Glenallen Hill led off with a walk, was bunted to second by Gary Gaetti, and stole third after Mickey Morandini was intentionally walked. Ex-Brave Jeff Blauser, coming off his worst season ever, was sent up to pinch hit. All season, Blauser had inexplicably taken too many pitches, including called third strikes at wrong moments. He stood with the bat on his shoulder again. Finally, as Morandini took off for second, Blauser offered a half swing, was called out on strikes, and Morandini was thrown out. The scoring chance went out the window.

The Cubs' fate was virtually sealed. The Braves pushed across a run in the 10th to win 2-1. And just about everyone prepared for the one last taste of summer at Wrigley Field for Game 3 on Saturday night, October 4.

Kerry Wood was brought out of mothballs to start for the Cubs, evoking mass media and fan concern for the condition of his sprained elbow. But he had passed all the throwing tests, including a short stint on the mound in the Arizona instructional league. He would be re-matched with Maddux, whose only career loss to the Cubs had been to Wood 2 1/2 months previously.

The hot, even humid summer weather, which had hung on much longer than usual in September, was long gone as gametime approached. Winds blew in directly off Lake Michigan at 15 to 20 mph, chilling the ballpark. The ever-cagey

Maddux, smartest pitcher in the game, surveyed the wind as he took pre-game batting practice. Maybe throw a few more fastballs that the Cubs could hit harmlessly into the gales? The battle plan was registering in Maddux's head.

One of the classiest collection of players in the game, the Braves insisted the Cubs weren't involved in a mismatch.

"Any team that improves that much, even with all the pitching injuries it has, is doing well," John Smoltz said. "The Cubs organization has been desperately trying to get to this point. They got there, and it's a pretty good level to be at."

"We respect the Cubs," Ryan Klesko said.

With 39,597 looking on, Wood earned even more respect from the Braves. In five innings, he proved his elbow held up with a yield of just three hits and one run, which scored on a passed ball in the third. Wood fanned five.

But Maddux was unyielding in the tight game. Sosa lined out hard to right in the second, struck out on a full-count pitch in the fourth, and grounded out to shortstop in the sixth. He escaped the one real threat the Cubs mounted against him in the second, when Henry Rodriguez reached third with one out, but did not break for the plate on a Tyler Houston topper to first.

Then Maddux got the insurance he needed in the eighth. The overworked Mulholland and Beck had nothing left, and the end result was an Eddie Perez grand slam off Beck to make it 6-0. The Cubs pushed across a pair of consolation runs in the eighth, and the 1998 season would now be measured in mere minutes.

Sosa fanned in his last at-bat in the eighth, and Braves reliever Kerry Ligtenberg went in to close it out. The Cubs congratulated each other, then retreated to the clubhouse. But Sosa made one more trip out to right field, saluting the fans, tossing his cap and batting glove into the bleachers.

"It was one of the great at-bats that I had," Sosa said of his final trip to the plate. "He gave me so many good pitches to hit and I missed all of them. Hey, I have to take the blame. That was the first time in the playoffs that I hit with runners on base. I have to take it like a man.

"It is real disappointing. I am not very happy about the way we played the last three games. I feel like if I could give my life to make it to the World Series, I would do that. Our destination was to make the playoffs and that's it. I am getting ready for next year."

Believe Sammy Sosa. The box score showed an ending. But under the right circumstances it could have been a beginning, too.

VINE LINE
MONTHLY NEWSPAPER OF THE CHICAGO CUBS

Subscribe today and qualify
for a special postseason offer
and FREE reader gifts.
Call (800) 248-9467 to order.

Monday, Sept. 28, 1998

1998 NL WILD-CARD RACE
(through 162 games)

Club	W-L	GB
Cubs	89-73	—
Giants	89-73	—

San Francisco

1 Armando Rios, OF
2 Chris Jones, OF
6 J.T. Snow, IF
7 Marvin Benard, OF
8 Shawon Dunston, IF-OF
9 Brent Mayne, C
10 Ron Wotus, Coach
12 Dusty Baker, MGR
13 Charlie Hayes, IF
14 Rey Sanchez, IF
15 Sonny Jackson, Coach
16 Ron Perranoski, Coach
17 Carlos Alfonso, Coach
18 Brian Johnson, C
19 Doug Mirabelli, C
20 Gene Clines, Coach
21 Jeff Kent, IF
22 Osvaldo Fernandez, RHP
23 Ellis Burks, OF
25 Barry Bonds, OF
26 Mark Gardner, RHP
28 Stan Javier, OF
29 Joe Carter, OF-IF
30 Dante Powell, OF
31 Robb Nen, RHP
32 Bill Mueller, IF
33 Rich Rodriguez, LHP
34 Ramon E. Martinez, IF
35 Rich Aurilia, IF
39 Steve Soderstrom, RHP
41 Cory Bailey, RHP
43 Mark Wohlers, RHP
46 Kirk Rueter, LHP
47 Jose Mesa, RHP
48 Russ Ortiz, RHP
49 John Johnstone, RHP
50 Julian Tavarez, RHP
51 Chris Brock, RHP
52 Alvin Morman, LHP
53 Orel Hershiser, RHP
55 Shawn Estes, LHP
59 Juan Lopez, Instructor
62 Wilson Delgado, IF

No.	Player	Pos.	1	2	3	4	5	6	7	8	9	10	AB	R	H	RBI
28	S. Javier	cf														
35	Aurilia	ss														
5	Dunston ph/7th															
25	B. Bonds	lf														
21	J. Kent	2b														
29	J. Carter	rf														
6	J.T. Snow	1b														
13	C. Hayes	3b														
47	Mesa p/7th															
18	B. Johnson	c														
26	M. Gardner	p														
23	R. Rodriguez	p/6th														
4a	Johnstone p/6th															
1	A. Rios ph/7th															
52	A. Morman p/9th															
32	Mueller ph/8th															
23	Burks ph/7th															

Pitchers	IP	H	R	ER	BB	SO	Notes
Gardner							
R. Rodriguez/6th							

CUBS

1 Lance Johnson, OF
2 Jeff Pentland, Coach
3 Dan Radison, Coach
4 Jeff Blauser, IF
5 Jim Riggleman, MGR
6 Glenallen Hill, OF
7 Tyler Houston, C-IF
8 Gary Gaetti, IF
9 Scott Servais, C
12 Mickey Morandini, IF
15 Sandy Martinez, C
17 Mark Grace, IF
18 Jose Hernandez, IF-OF
20 Matt Mieske, OF
21 Sammy Sosa, OF
24 Manny Alexander, IF
25 Orlando Merced, OF-IF
26 Billy Williams, Coach
27 Phil Regan, Coach
28 Pedro Valdes, OF
30 Jeremi Gonzalez, RHP
33 Don Wengert, RHP
34 Kerry Wood, RHP
36 Kevin Tapani, RHP
37 Brant Brown, OF-IF
38 Mike Morgan, RHP
39 Tom Gamboa, Coach
40 Henry Rodriguez, OF
43 Dave Bialas, Coach
44 Chris Haney, LHP
45 Terry Mulholland, LHP
46 Steve Trachsel, RHP
47 Rod Beck, RHP
48 Dave Stevens, RHP
49 Felix Heredia, LHP
50 Jason Maxwell, IF
51 Terry Adams, RHP
52 Matt Karchner, RHP
53 Kurt Miller, RHP
54 Mark Clark, RHP
59 Rodney Myers, RHP
63 Rick Kranitz, Instructor

No.	Player	Pos.	1	2	3	4	5	6	7	8	9	10	AB	R	H	RBI
1	L. Johnson	cf														
12	Morandini	2b														
21	Sosa	rf														
17	Grace	1b														
40	H. Rodriguez	lf														
20	Mieske ph/6th-lf															
8	Gaetti	3b														
7	Houston	c														
18	J. Hernandez	ss														
46	Trachsel	p														
25	Merced lf/7th															
52	Karchner p/7th															
49	Heredia p/7th															
45	Mulholland p/8th															

Pitchers	IP	H	R	ER	BB	SO	Notes
Trachsel	6⅔	1	0	0	6	6	A-39,556
Karchner/7th							
Heredia/7th							
Tapani/8th	1	3	2	2	0	0	

Track Sammy Sosa's Home Runs

67	68	69	70

Mulholland/9th
Beck/9th

9/28/98

Epilogue

After the final pitch was thrown and Sammy Sosa's season could be viewed in hindsight, the only accurate feeling of his contemporaries was awe.

"He had some scary numbers, way beyond what anybody could have thought for him and anyone else," said old friend Frank Thomas of the White Sox.

"Without a doubt, I don't think anybody else has ever had this. This is the best year in the history of baseball," said teammate Mark Grace. "It's obvious it's better than Babe Ruth. He hit more home runs. Better than Ruth, better than anybody. There's a lot of history to this game."

Well, maybe Grace exaggerated a bit. But he has a point. Sosa was a more productive run-producer than Mark McGwire, despite the later hitting four more homers. The RBI count is where Grace really gets his fodder. With a major-leagues leading 158 RBI, one more than old minor-league teammate Juan Gonzalez, Sosa drove in more runs than any other player in the last 49 years. He came within two RBI of ranking as the National League's third-best season RBI producer ever.

Sosa also came within four hits of 200, another benchmark for top hitters. His season was so awesome that his still-prodigious strikeout total of 171 attracted little attention or criticism.

Combined with his affable personality, Sosa's celebrity portfolio was almost complete. Along with Mark McGwire, he made his first national McDonald's commercial. And then he went Hollywood.

Sosa made his *Tonight Show* debut with Jay Leno on October 8, 1998, displaying an easy good humor in front of the cameras that can only come from a natural ham. "I told Michael Jordan, no breaking pitches," he said of His Airness throwing out the ceremonial first pitch before the Cubs-Giants wild-card tiebreaker on September 28, 1998. "He threw 100 mph over my head. I can't jump like Michael."

Leno asked him if the media demands tired him out. "No, because I'm only 29," Sosa said with a laugh. And he was asked about being a role model and not chewing tobacco like so many other players. "I don't do anything to hurt people," he said.

He also received a hero's welcome from the Chicago City Council. Poor Major Richard M. Daley. A lifelong White Sox fan, Daley had to honor a man his favorite team pulled a quick hook on, trading him to the Cubs in 1992.

"I want to say that I was a Chicago White Sox fan, too," Sosa said as Daley paused in putting on a Cubs hat.

Aldermen clamored for Sosa's autograph. Several representing South Side wards, in the supposed heart of White Sox country, came out of the closet to admit they were Cubs fans.

But Sosa used the forum to rally support for his efforts to aid Dominicans left homeless and hungry by Hurricane Georges.

"Everything I'm doing now is not for me," he said. "I've got to go down to my country and take care of all the people there. They don't have no houses. They don't have nothing to eat. They don't have anything."

"But they do have Sammy Sosa."

Daley and the City Council presented a check for $8,500 to Sosa for his foundation's work in shipping relief goods to Santo Domingo. At that point, the foundation had sent 80,000 pounds of supplies. He had also enlisted the support of the Rev. Jesse Jackson and Operation PUSH.

Sosa was truly doing it the Michael Jordan way. When asked why few resented him for his immense wealth, Jordan replied that he didn't throw his money in people's faces. Sosa is building a $14 million mansion in the Dominican. He possesses a fleet of luxury cars. But after taking care of his own material desires, Sosa adheres to the basic tenet of Dominican culture: He shares.

That kind of caring personality can only boost Sosa's popularity in the long run if he continues having the productive career he has already established.

"Ernie Banks will always be Mr. Cub," said John McDonough, the Cubs' vice president of marketing and broadcasting. "I don't think that designation will ever leave him. Sammy will have a great career, possibly a Hall of Fame career. He could be one of the most popular players in baseball history, one of the greatest Cubs of all time.

"But because he's playing in an era where accomplishments are featured nightly on global TV, he could go down as the most popular Cub of all time."

Sosa could further cement his status as an icon if he could make it to the Fall Classic and perform his heroics in front of potentially hundreds of millions of TV viewers.

"This is not enough for me," he said. "I want to make it to the World Series."

But Sosa's ability to reach the Classic, though, is out of his hands. Sosa said himself over the years he couldn't do it alone. His present teammates can't do it as presently constituted. Their fates rest with the executives on the 24th floor of Tribune Tower in Chicago.

So maybe the Cubs wouldn't make a big profit, if any, in the first year if the payroll was increased to New York Yankees or Baltimore Orioles levels. But if you build it, the Cubs fans will come. Assured of a powerhouse team, they'd sell out Wrigley Field wire to wire in the same manner as the Cleveland Indians at Jacobs Field. There would be more ticket revenue, more skybox revenue, more concessions revenue, higher ratings on WGN-TV and radio, and the resulting higher advertising rates. The Cubs' brief post-season fling in 1998 was a viewership bonanza for the various broadcast carriers.

The Tribune Co. stockholders would approve, they surely would. They are the big dogs whose appetites must be sated before anyone else's. But, remember, the stock market rises and falls largely on emotion. What would be more uplifting than the

Cubs playing—and winning—a World Series? The lovable losers, after nearly a century wandering in the wilderness, reaching the Promised Land. That would boost prices—and keep those
healthy double-digit quarterly profits coming.

There's hope. At least some Cubs officials are starting to
recognize the potential of a Sosa-led Cubs winner.

"Look at all the national attention we received by being
barely a wild card team," John McDonough said. "It was almost
like a Bulls NBA Finals situation. We had more subplots with
Sammy, Kerry Wood, the wild-card race, everything. It was more
exciting than (divisional titles) 1984 and 1989.

"Winning the World Series would be the biggest (sports)
event in our lifetime. If we ever went to the prom..."

Long before that happens, however, Sosa must bottle the
controlled aggression that he practiced in 1998. He cannot afford to lapse into his old hitting style of all-or-nothing. He's going to have to continue the improvement he displayed after
working with hitting coach Jeff Pentland starting late in 1997.
And he's going to have to set realistic goals. This may be a new
age of sluggers and power hitting, but 66 homers just isn't going to happen every year.

Business advisor Bill Chase always sits down with Sosa
before each season to set goals. Before the 1998 season, Chase
suggested 30 homers. Sosa reached for the moon and stated 50
homers. Realistically, he ought to not exceed that number when
projecting for 1999. Stay under control, go to right field, and
wait for a little help from your friends in the lineup and, hopefully, the suits in the Tower.

Home runs aren't a given, to Sosa, McGwire, Ken Griffey
Jr. or anyone. You have to be in the right frame of mind and
connect on the sweet spot of the bat. But the little things in the
game are always there to be executed. As Sosa himself said, you
don't have to hit a homer to win a game.

He should repeat that in the last year of an unbelievable
century. Everybody has witnessed a personal miracle, the rise
from Parque Duarte and the shoeshine kit to a permanent exhibit in the Hall of Fame. Now for the second miracle, the one
that everybody—the fans in the bleachers, the shut-ins at home,
the numbers-crunchers in the TV networks—dearly desire.

Sammy Sosa has made all but one dream come true. The
last one will be the toughest, but also the sweetest. We can hardly
wait.

Appendices

SAMMY SOSA'S CAREER
YEAR-BY-YEAR

Born: November 12, 1968 in San Pedro de Macoris,
Dominican Republic
Bats: Right Throws: Right
Signed as non-drafted free agent by Texas Rangers, July 30, 1985
in the Dominican Republic (signing scouts: Omar Minaya and
Amado Dinzey)

Year	Club	Avg.	Games	AB	H	RBI	SB
1986	Gulf Coast (rookie)	.275	61	229	4	28	11
1987	Gastonia (A)	.279	129	519	11	59	22
1988	Port Charlotte (A)	.229	131	507	9	51	42
1989	Tulsa (AA)	.297	66	273	7	31	16
	Texas	.238	25	84	1	3	0
	Oklahoma City (AAA)	.103	10	39	4	0	0
	Vancouver (AAA)	.367	13	49	1	5	3
	White Sox	.273	33	99	3	10	7
1990	White Sox	.233	153	532	15	70	32
1991	White Sox	.203	116	316	10	33	13
	Vancouver (AAA)	.267	32	116	3	19	9
1992	Cubs	.260	67	262	8	25	15
	Iowa	.316	5	19	0	1	5
1993	Cubs	.261	159	598	33	93	36
1994	Cubs	.300	105	426	25	70	22
1995	Cubs	.268	144	564	36	119	34
1996	Cubs	.273	124	498	40	100	18
1997	Cubs	.251	162	642	36	119	22
1998	Cubs	.308	158	643	66	158	18

SAMMY SOSA'S
CAREER HIGHLIGHTS 1989-1997

— Slugged first homer off Boston Red Sox's Roger Clemens on June 21, 1989 at Fenway Park as a Texas Ranger

— Belted a homer in a 3-for-3 night in White Sox debut on August 22, 1989 against Minnesota Twins at Metrodome

— Only American League player to rank in double figures in doubles (26), triples (10) and homers (15) in 1990

— Hit first Cubs homer May 7, 1992 against the Houston Astros' Ryan Bowen

— Went 6-for-6, completing a nine straight hit performance, on July 2, 1993 against Colorado Rockies at Mile High Stadium in Denver on July 2, 1993

— Became first Cub ever to hit 30 homers and steal 30 bases with theft of second in sixth inning against San Francisco Giants at 3Com Park on September 15, 1993

— Had career-high 17 outfield assists in 1993, ranking second in National League and most by a Cub since Lou Brock in 1963

— Named to the National League All-Star team for the first time in 1995, going 0-for-1 in Midsummer Classic at Ballpark at Arlington

— Slugged 10 homers in a 13-game span from August 17 to August 29, 1995

— After finishing tied for second in homers (36) and second in RBI (119) in NL, named to league's postseason Sporting News all-star team

— Became first player to belt two homers in one inning on May 16, 1996 against Houston Astros, leading off the seventh with a solo shot off Jeff Tabaka and adding a two-run blast off Jim Dougherty later in the inning.

— Recorded his first career three-homer game on June 5, 1996 against the Philadelphia Phillies at Wrigley Field

— Selected as NL Player of the Month for July, 1996 after a 10-homer, 29-RBI, .358 performance.

— Was leading NL with 40 homers on August 20, 1996 when pitch by the Florida Marlins' Mark Hutton broke his right hand in game at Wrigley Field

— Set a career single-game high with six RBI with a homer and triple on May 16, 1997 against the San Diego Padres

— Slashed first inside-the-park homer in career on May 26, 1997 in the sixth inning off the Pirates' Francisco Cordova at Three Rivers Stadium

— Led major leagues in RBI with 158 in 1998. That total is the fourth highest single-season total in National League history

— Passed up both Roger Maris' old season big-league record of 61 homers and Ted Kluszewski's National League record of 34 homers hit at home in the ninth inning on September 13 against the Brewers' Eric Plunk at Wrigley Field.

— Passed up Hack Wilson's Cubs season of 56 homers in the first inning on September 4 against the Pirates' Jason Schmidt at Three Rivers Stadium in Pittsburgh.

— Passed up Rudy York's one-month record of 18 homers in the seventh inning on June 25 against the Tigers' Seth Greisinger at Tiger Stadium in Detroit.

— Passed up Hack Wilson's one-season Cubs record of 33 homers at Wrigley Field in the fifth inning on September 13 against the Brewers' Bronswell Patrick at Wrigley Field.

— Passed up one-season Cubs record of 23 homers on the road, co-held by Ernie Banks, Hack Wilson and Dave Kingman, in the first inning on August 28 against the Rockies' John Thompson at Coors Field in Denver.

— Passed up top home-run seasons of Cubs Hall of Famers Ernie Banks (47) and Billy Williams (42), along with other great Cubs such as Andre Dawson (49), Hank Sauer (41), Gabby Hartnett (37), Andy Pafko (36) Ron Santo (33), and Bill Nicholson (33).

— Passed up top RBI seasons of Banks (143), Williams (129), Dawson (137), Santo (129), and Sauer (121).

— With three bases-loaded homers, became first Cub to hit three grand slams in one season since Ernie Banks with five in 1955.

— Became first Cub to hit grand slams in back-to-back games on July 27 and July 28 at BankOne Ballpark in Phoenix.

— 241 homers in seven seasons ranks as fifth highest total in Cubs history.

SAMMY'S HOME-RUN LIST

Following is a list of Sammy Sosa's home-run totals for 1998:

HR	Date	Game	Opponent	Pitcher	Inning	Runners on	Direction
1	April 4	5	Montreal	Marc Valdes	3	solo	RF
2	April 11	11	At Montreal	Anthony Telford	7	solo	RF
3	April 15	14	At New York	Dennis Cook	8	solo	LF
4	April 23	21	San Diego	Dan Miceli	9	solo	CF
5	April 24	22	At Los Angeles	Ismael Valdes	1	solo	CF
6	April 27	25	At San Diego	Joey Hamilton	1	two-run	CF
7	May 3	30	St Louis	Cliff Politte	1	solo	LF
8	May 16	42	At Cincinnati	Scott Sullivan	3	three-run	CF
9	May 22	47	At Atlanta	Greg Maddux	1	solo	CF
10	May 25	50	At Atlanta	Kevin Millwood	4	solo	RF
11	May 25	50	At Atlanta	Mike Cather	8	solo	CF
12	May 27	51	Philadelphia	Darrin Winston	8	solo	LF
13	May 27	51	Philadelphia	Wayne Gomes	9	two-run	LF
14	June 1	56	Florida	Ryan Dempster	1	two-run	LF
15	June 1	56	Florida	Oscar Henriquez	8	three-run	CF
16	June 3	58	Florida	Livan Hernandez	5	two-run	LF
17	June 5	59	White Sox	Jim Parque	5	two-run	RF
18	June 6	60	White Sox	Carlos Castillo	7	solo	CF
19	June 7	61	White Sox	James Baldwin	5	three-run	CF
20	June 8	62	At Minnesota	LaTroy Hawkins	3	solo	RF
21	June 13	66	At Philadelphia	Mark Portugal	6	two-run	RF
22	June 15	68	Milwaukee	Cal Eldred	1	solo	RF
23	June 15	68	Milwaukee	Cal Eldred	3	solo	LF
24	June 15	68	Milwaukee	Cal Eldred	7	solo	CF
25	June 17	70	Milwaukee	Bronswell Patrick	4	solo	LF
26	June 19	72	Philadelphia	Carlton Loewer	1	solo	LF
27	June 19	72	Philadelphia	Carlton Loewer	1	solo	LF
28	June 20	73	Philadelphia	Matt Beach	3	two-run	LF
29	June 20	73	Philadelphia	Toby Borland	6	three-run	LF
30	June 21	74	Philadelphia	Tyler Green	4	solo	RF
31	June 24	77	At Detroit	Seth Greisinger	1	solo	LF
32	June 25	78	At Detroit	Brian Moehler	7	solo	RF
33	June 30	82	Arizona	Alan Embree	8	solo	RF
34	July 9	88	At Milwaukee	Jeff Juden	2	two-run	CF
35	July 10	89	At Milwaukee	Scott Karl	2	solo	LF
36	July 17	95	At Florida	Kirt Ojala	6	two-run	CF
37	July 22	100	Montreal	Miguel Batista	8	three-run	RF
38	July 26	105	New York	Rick Reed	6	two-run	CF
39	July 27	106	At Arizona	Willie Blair	6	two-run	RF
40	July 27	106	At Arizona	Alan Embree	8	grand slam	CF
41	July 28	107	At Arizona	Bob Wolcott	5	grand slam	LF

42	July 31	110	Colorado	Jamey Wright	1	solo	RF
43	August 5	115	Arizona	Andy Benes	3	two-run	LF
44	August 8	117	At St. Louis	Rick Croushore	9	two-run	LF
45	August 10	119	At San Francisco	Russ Ortiz	5	solo	LF
46	August 10	119	At San Francisco	Chris Brock	7	solo	CF
47	August 16	124	At Houston	Sean Bergman	4	solo	RF
48	August 19	126	St. Louis	Kent Bottenfield	5	two-run	LF
49	August 21	128	San Francisco	Orel Hershiser	5	two-run	CF
50	August 23	130	Houston	Jose Lima	5	solo	LF
51	August 23	130	Houston	Jose Lima	8	solo	LF
52	August 26	133	At Cincinnati	Brett Tomko	3	solo	LF
53	August 28	135	At Colorado	John Thompson	1	solo	RF
54	August 30	137	At Colorado	Darryl Kile	1	two-run	LF
55	August 31	138	Cincinnati	Brett Tomko	3	two-run	LF
56	September 2	140	Cincinnati	Jason Bere	6	solo	RF
57	September 4	141	At Pittsburgh	Jason Schmidt	1	solo	RF
58	September 5	142	At Pittsburgh	Sean Lawrence	6	solo	RF
59	September 11	148	Milwaukee	Bill Pulsipher	5	solo	RF
60	September 12	149	Milwaukee	Valerio De Los Santos	7	three-run	LF
61	September 13	150	Milwaukee	Bronswell Patrick	5	two-run	LF
62	September 13	150	Milwaukee	Eric Plunk	9	solo	LF
63	September 16	153	At San Diego	Brian Boehringer	8	grand slam	LF
64	September 23	158	At Milwaukee	Rafael Roque	5	solo	RF
65	September 23	158	At Milwaukee	Rod Henderson	6	solo	CF
66	September 25	159	At Houston	Jose Lima	4	solo	LF

SAMMY IN THE CLUTCH, 1995-98

More so than pure, raw power, Sammy Sosa became a true clutch hitter in 1998. He improved his performance with men on base across the board—especially with the bases loaded.

STATS, Inc. has broken down Sosa's performance over a four-year period from 1995 to 1998. Different categories show his batting average, homers and RBI. He made a huge leap in efficiency in driving in runs.

1998 (through games of September 15)

Category	Average	At-bats	Hits	Homers	RBI
None on	.321	302	97	34	34
Runners on	.301	296	89	28	114
None on/out	.275	120	33	9	9
Scoring position	.321	137	44	12	74
Scoring position/					
two out	.255	55		5	23
Close and late	.300	100	30	10	21
Bases loaded	.308	13	4	2	11
Inning 1-6	.319	407	130	44	107
Inning 7 and later	.293	191	56	18	41

1997

Category	Average	At-bats	Hits	Homers	RBI
None on	.243	317	77	19	19
Runners on	.258	325	84	17	100
None on/out	.229	144	33	10	10
Scoring position	.246	183	45	9	78
Scoring position/					
two out	.278	79	22	5	33
Close and late	.240	96	23	7	20
Bases loaded	.188	16	3	0	13
Inning 1-6	.244	442	108	21	76
Inning 7 and later	.265	200	53	15	43

Category	Average	1996 At-bats	Hits	Homers	RBI
None on	.255	231	59	16	16
Runners on	.288	267	77	24	84
None on/out	.302	106	32	9	9
Scoring position	.246	142	35	13	60
Scoring position/ two out	.269	78	21	8	33
Close and late	.304	92	28	7	24
Bases loaded	.111	9	1	0	2
Inning 1-6	.259	340	88	27	61
Inning 7 and later	.304	158	48	13	39

Category	Average	1995 At-bats	Hits	Homers	RBI
None on	.216	283	61	15	15
Runners on	.320	281	90	21	104
None on/out	.244	119	29	6	6
Scoring position	.341	164	56	14	84
Scoring position/ two out	.338	65	22	7	34
Close and late	.226	84	19	3	11
Bases loaded	.143	7	1	0	2
Inning 1-6	.270	389	105	19	77
Inning 7 and later	.263	138	46	17	42